THE SALEM CLIQUE

The Salem Clique

OREGON'S FOUNDING BROTHERS

Barbara S. Mahoney

Oregon State University Press   Corvallis

Library of Congress Cataloging-in-Publication Data

Names: Mahoney, Barbara S., author.
Title: The Salem clique : Oregon's founding brothers / Barbara S. Mahoney.
Description: Corvallis : Oregon State University Press, 2017. | Includes biblio-
    graphical references and index.
Identifiers: LCCN 2017006330 | ISBN 9780870718915 (paperback : alkaline paper)
Subjects: LCSH: Oregon Territory—Politics and government. | Salem (Or.)—Poli-
    tics and government—19th century. | Bush, Asahel, 1824-1913. | Politicians—
    Oregon Territory—Biography. | Young men—Oregon Territory—Biography.
    | Small groups—Political aspects—Oregon Territory—History. | Political
    culture—Oregon Territory—History. | Democratic Party (Or.) —History—19th
    century. | Oregon Territory—Biography. | BISAC: HISTORY / United States /
    State & Local / Pacific Northwest (OR, WA). | HISTORY / United States / 19th
    Century. | POLITICAL SCIENCE / Government / State & Provincial.
Classification: LCC F880 .M27 2017 | DDC 979.5/03—dc23
LC record available at https://lccn.loc.gov/2017006330

♾This paper meets the requirements of ANSI/NISO Z39.48-1992
(Permanence of Paper).

Oregon State University Press
121 The Valley Library
Corvallis OR 97331-4501
541-737-3166 • fax 541-737-3170
www.osupress.oregonstate.edu

Contents

Acknowledgments

That a focused study of the Salem Clique and its role in the days of the Oregon Territory has never before been attempted reflects the fact that the required research was very extensive. I turned to many sources and found the requisite assistance. Geoff Wexler and Scott Daniels of the Oregon Historical Society Research Library devoted considerable time and energy to the project. I cannot exaggerate their contribution. Others who aided my research include Mary McRobinson, the Willamette University archivist; Ross Sutherland, the director of the Asahel Bush House Museum; Kylie Pine, the curator at the Willamette Heritage Center; and David Hegeman of the Oregon State Library.

Micki Reaman, Marty Brown, and Mary Braun of the Oregon State University Press guided me through the publication process with patience and humor. Jennifer Manley Rogers was a tireless copy editor.

As important as those who aided my research and the book's publication are those who offered encouragement and counsel. Oregon historians William Robbins, Carl Abbott, and Richard Etulain argued for the need for a book about the Salem Clique and promoted me as the prospective author. Marianne Keddington-Lang and Bill Lang took an early interest in the project and provided valuable guidance as did Eliza Canty-Jones, the editor of the *Oregon Historical Quarterly*. The late John McMillan, the publisher of the *Salem Statesman Journal*, was both an advocate and a resource.

Finally, essential to this undertaking was the support afforded me by my children, Michael, Brian, Ellen and Colin, and most especially by my husband, Tim.

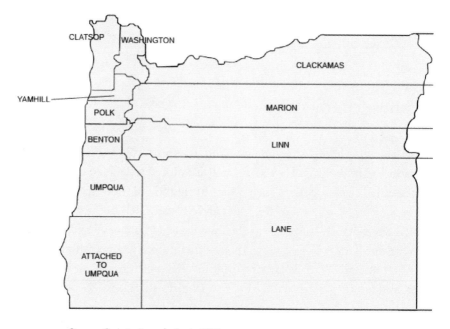

Oregon County Boundaries in 1851.

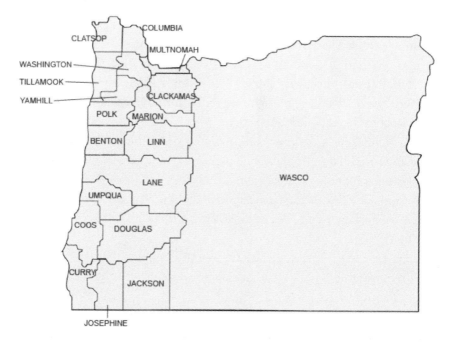

Oregon County Boundaries in 1856.

Introduction

Writing in 1913, Oregon scholar Walter Carleton Woodward observed: "A complete story of the capricious, arrogant rule in Oregon under the regime of the Salem Clique would form one of the most picturesque chapters in the political history of the West." The Salem Clique was a group of young men who came to the Oregon Territory late in the 1840s or early 1850s. Their names are familiar to students of Oregon history: Matthew Deady, James Nesmith, Lafayette Grover, Asahel Bush, and others. Some had been recruited by the Territory's delegate to Congress, Samuel Thurston; others had come of their own initiative, attracted by the promise of the Oregon country. Most were lawyers by training. Once in Oregon, several took up farming with land grants from the government. A few entered the business sector, one establishing a newspaper, another a flour mill, and yet another a woolen mill. But, whatever their other pursuits, Oregon politics was their focus through the decade of the 1850s.

At Thurston's invitation, Asahel Bush, generally seen as the leader of the Clique, founded the *Oregon Statesman* newspaper, which became the organ of the Clique. As editor of the *Statesman*, Bush proved to be both an excellent writer and an able manager. His often scathing editorials addressed the significant issues of the day with vigor and a generous measure of sarcasm. The *Statesman* was without equal in the Territory, not least because of the network of Clique members that provided information and support. Through the newspaper and through their individual efforts, the Clique shaped public opinion and with it the actions of elected and appointed officials.

Under Bush's direction, the men of the Clique organized the Democratic Party and made it the Territory's most effective political instrument for nearly a decade. They set its agenda and backed like-minded candidates for public office. Their adherents triumphed in legislative elections and, once in office, elected Clique members to the leadership positions. Opponents were attacked while supporters enjoyed the benefits of patronage and presidential appointments to executive and judicial positions.

Intertwined with the story of the Clique is the account of its relationship with Oregon's most prominent and powerful political figure of the 1850s, Joseph Lane. Serving as delegate to Congress and then as US senator, Lane represented the Oregon Territory and, for a short time, the state and its interests in Washington, DC. His association with the Clique was symbiotic. Lane depended on the Clique and its command of the Democratic Party for the votes necessary to keep him in office. The Clique depended on him for the patronage of the federal government and the substantial benefits the government provided, benefits that were vital to its dominance. But, as the decade progressed, the Clique was divided by its members' often conflicting opinions of Lane and his actions. The Clique and its alliance with Lane deteriorated.

The Clique initiated the Oregon Territory's campaign to become a state. The process was long and challenging because of opposition both within the Territory and in Washington DC. Once the Territory's voters were ready to support statehood, the Clique called for a constitutional convention that met in August of 1857. Its members were chosen to preside over the convention and to chair six of the eleven standing committees. Despite their occasionally competing viewpoints on important issues, they managed the deliberations of the convention and shaped its product. In the face of vigorous resistance from some quarters, they were able to convince the electorate to ratify it.

Nevertheless, during the last years of the decade, the challenges to the Clique's supremacy by the so-called "Softs" within the Democratic Party intensified. Joseph Lane's role, both real and conjectured, in the erosion of its power ended his partnership with the Clique. Further, the major issue of the day, slavery, divided the state and the Clique itself. Its dominance of Oregon politics ended.

The primary sources for this study were found in the Oregon Historical Society Research Library, the Bush House archives in Salem, the Willamette University archives, and the State Library. Of particular importance is the voluminous correspondence among the members that has been preserved. Also key to an understanding of the players and of the times are the contemporary newspapers, their stands on issues, and their support for or hostility toward particular politicians and parties.

Thomas Dryer, the editor of the rival newspaper, the *Portland Orego-nian*, first named the "Clique." In editorial after editorial, he accused its members of deception, corruption, and dictatorship. Other contempo-raries were of a different opinion. In his 1902 address to the Oregon Pio-neer Association, the early settler John McBride, although a Republican, remembered the Democratic control of Oregon politics as beneficial "for the masses of the people. Taxes were low, economy was practiced in public expenditure and no reproach of corruption ever tainted its administration. . . . [The Clique] demanded unhesitating service to itself but it allowed no lapse from equally faithful duty to the people."

Whatever their view of the Clique, neither contemporary nor later observers have questioned its power. Despite the prominence accorded the Clique in so many works of Oregon history, no detailed study of the Clique, its members, and their pursuits has been undertaken until now.

The Oregon City building where the legislature of the provisional government met. (Courtesy Oregon Historical Society, ba014130)

CHAPTER ONE

"Bring all your guns to bear and reach Oregon."

—Samuel Thurston

During the nineteenth and early twentieth centuries, the "machine" with its "boss" figured prominently in American political life. Usually urban, the machine promoted the interests of a particular party through an organization that extended down to the neighborhood level. The machine cultivated the local citizenry by providing social services unavailable in a time of limited and inefficient government. It paid particular attention to recent immigrants, assisting them and thus ensuring their loyalty. It demanded kickbacks from local businesses for the favors it was able to bestow. Through its control of public offices, the machine awarded thousands of government jobs and lucrative contracts in exchange for votes at the ballot box, enough votes to guarantee its continued dominance. The boss exerted absolute control. The New York City machine of William Tweed, known as Tammany Hall, managed to elect its supporters to public offices ranging from precinct committeemen to mayors and even a state governor. Others who have been identified as bosses include Thomas Pendergast of Kansas City, James Curley of Boston, Thomas Crump of Memphis, Frank Hague of Jersey City, and Anton Cermak of Chicago. Regardless of the setting, graft and corruption were common features. While rewards to followers were substantial, party discipline was strictly enforced and a price was paid for any deviation from the prescribed course.

That a political machine could exist in the isolated and rural Oregon Territory in the 1850s seems improbable. Yet, over years of study, many historians have identified the so-called Salem Clique as just such an entity, one that used its command of the Democratic Party and of the patronage provided by the federal government to rule the Territory. They have described the Clique as a "disciplined little band of freebooters"[1] who "gave to Oregon an arrogant and narrowly partisan rule. Rebellion in the ranks was not tolerated, and erring members were ruthlessly read out of the party."[2] But, just as some historians have seen positive aspects of the eastern political machine, Oregon observers have not always been critical of the Clique. In the judgment of one witness writing in 1908, the Salem Clique "though much reviled in those days has passed unscathed by time, and no allegation was ever made that the 'clique' was composed of any other than honest and honorable men, either as private citizens or partisans."[3]

While the existence of the Clique machine in so remote a setting may seem an anomaly, in fact, scholars have identified other such "machines" in the territorial histories of Minnesota, Washington, and Wyoming. Each championed the interests of its supporters and secured federal largesse to ensure its dominance. The nature of territorial government enhanced the power of the machines. The status of "Territory" was granted by the national government to new lands it had acquired through war, treaty, or purchase. In the judgment of one writer, the various territories of the United States were essentially colonies.[4] Like the thirteen English colonies in what is now the United States, their executive and judicial office-holders were appointed by the national government. The inhabitants of the original colonies elected the members of a legislative body, the Virginia House of Burgesses or the Massachusetts Legislature, for example. Likewise, the residents of the territories chose the members of their legislatures. In time, just as the inhabitants of the original colonies sought independence from the British Empire, the settlers in the territories claimed their rights to self-government.

The history of the "Oregon country" reflects the experience of other territories of the United States and their progression toward self-government and statehood. Oregon was unknown to the rest of the world when the Spanish explorer Bruno Heceta reached the mouth of the Columbia River in 1775. While the Spanish government kept the discovery secret to protect its own interests, the British government too intended to explore the potential of the region. In 1778, James Cook sailed along the Pacific Northwest shore in search of the elusive Northwest Passage and concluded that it did not exist. The competition between the Spanish and the British was resolved when the Spanish government surrendered its claims through the Nootka Convention, a settlement reached in Madrid in 1790.

The agreement led the British naval captain George Vancouver to explore the Northwest coast in 1792, with special attention to the coast north of the Columbia River. Meanwhile, the American captain Robert Gray undertook a similar mission on behalf of his government. In the course of his travels, Gray ventured a short distance into the Columbia River. Although he was soon turned back by the river's challenges, the name he gave it, that of his ship, has endured.

The explorers' accounts of the abundance of fur-bearing animals immediately caught the attention of the Montreal-based Northwest Company and the London-based Hudson's Bay Company. The former sponsored the overland journey of Alexander Mackenzie who in 1793 became the first white man to cross the continent. The American acquisition of the Louisiana Territory in 1803 and his concerns about British intentions in the Pacific Northwest led President Thomas Jefferson to commission the Lewis and Clark expedition to assess the region and its potential. The explorers traveled via the Missouri and Columbia Rivers to reach the Pacific Ocean in 1805. They returned to Washington with exuberant reports of the resources and the promise of the Pacific Northwest along with dire warnings about British endeavors in the region. Soon, John Jacob Astor of New York founded the American Fur Company and sent sea and land expeditions to the mouth of the Columbia River where they established Fort Astoria. But Astor's claim to the area was short-lived. The War of 1812 led him to sell his interest to the Northwest Company, which would be absorbed by the Hudson's Bay Company in 1821.

Despite the acquisitive aspirations of each country, the United States and British governments agreed in 1818 to enter upon a joint occupation of the area between 42° N and 54° 40 N latitudes, bounded on the east by the Rocky Mountains and on the west by the Pacific Ocean, the lands that today make up British Columbia, Oregon, Washington, and parts of Idaho, Montana, and Wyoming. Seeking to reinforce the American claim, the Virginia congressman John Floyd promoted "the expediency of occupying the Columbian River." His fellows in the House of Representatives rejected the idea; Oregon was simply too far away.[5]

In contrast to the reluctance of the Americans, the British took immediate action. Motivated by the promise of the fur trade, they sent Dr. John McLoughlin of the Hudson's Bay Company to Fort Astoria. Before long, the hazards at the Columbia River bar led McLoughlin to abandon Fort

Astoria and establish Fort Vancouver at the junction of the Columbia and Willamette rivers in 1825.[6] From there, he supervised and supplied the French Canadian fur trappers sent to the region by the company.

In the Willamette Valley, McLoughlin found another potential for profit. To clear the ground for the cultivation of camas, a plant basic to their diet, the Native Americans of the valley had regularly burned trees and other native vegetation. The result was land ready for European-style cultivation. Impressed by his reports of the Willamette Valley's agricultural promise and anxious to protect the fur trade in other parts of the territory, the Hudson's Bay Company sponsored migrants, for the most part French Canadians, to settle in the valley. Their numbers included fur trappers who had left the company, taken Native American wives, and turned to farming. Along with the French Canadians came Catholic priests to provide for the spiritual needs of the settlers and to convert the Native Americans to their religion.[7]

In the United States, opinions about the potential of the Pacific Northwest varied. Horace Greeley, the editor of the *New York Tribune* and generally an enthusiastic supporter of western expansion, was skeptical about the Oregon country, not sure it was worth the efforts and sacrifices of transcontinental migration and settlement. He concluded that it was too distant ever to be part of the Union and urged the United States and Britain to give up their claims to the region. In his judgment, the best solution was for settlers to establish an independent republic.[8]

Others were of a very different viewpoint. In 1828, Hall J. Kelley founded the American Society for Encouraging the Settlement of the Oregon Territory and convinced the Massachusetts legislature to charter it. In a speech to Congress, he shared his vision of Oregon's potential: "Science and the Arts, the invaluable privileges of free and liberal government, and the refinements and ordinances of Christianity, diffusing each its blessing, would harmoniously unite in meliorating the moral condition of the Indians, in promoting the comfort and happiness of the settlers, and in augmenting the wealth and power of the Republic."[9]

Kelley's efforts to settle in the Oregon country proved unsuccessful. After a challenging trip from Boston he landed on the east side of the Willamette River near Swan Island. But he did not find the prosperity he had expected and left Oregon five months later.[10] Still, others were inspired by the Society. His fellow Massachusetts native Nathaniel Wyeth ventured west in 1832. He established Fort Hall on the Snake River as a way-station along what became known as the Oregon Trail. When he reached Oregon, Wyeth found McLoughlin to be gracious and accommodating: "Dr. McLoughlin, the Governor of the place, is a man distinguished as much for his kindness and humanity as his good sense and information; and to whom I am so much indebted as that he will never be forgotten."[11]

The initial coterie of American immigrants were the so-called "Mountain Men," adventurers attracted by the fur trade. Their numbers were small and their aspirations limited. Before long, other Americans came to farm. McLoughlin was welcoming, even loaning cattle to newcomers.[12] As time passed, he exercised sufficient authority to create an atmosphere of law and order unusual in frontier society, even to the point of settling arguments among American settlers. While the fact that settlers were dependent on the Hudson's Bay Company for their provisions facilitated that accomplishment, McLoughlin's leadership skills played a considerable role.[13]

The Methodist missionary, Jason Lee, came to Oregon in 1834 to bring Christianity to the Native Americans. Finding the native population decimated by disease, Lee turned to encouraging new American settlers to come to the region. In 1838, he traveled to Washington, DC, to promote the occupation of the Oregon country by the United States. He found an ally in the ardent proponent of American expansion and of the settlement of the Oregon country, Senator Lewis Linn of Missouri. Linn introduced a bill in the Senate that called for a greater American presence through the stationing of troops, construction of a fort, and creation of a port of entry. His bill did not become law but laid the groundwork for an expanding role for the federal government in the region.

In Lee's mind, John McLoughlin was the major obstacle to his efforts. McLoughlin had retired from the Hudson's Bay Company and settled on a landholding in Oregon City, the town that he had founded at the Falls of the Willamette River. Lee's hostility toward him was heightened when he became a Catholic. Lee also launched bitter attacks on the Catholic French Canadian farmers who had settled in the Willamette Valley. His crusade created such problems that the Mission Board of the Methodist Church recalled him in 1843 and ordered the sale of the mission's properties. Methodist settlers bought up the land, mills, and stores that had belonged to the mission and came to exercise considerable political and economic influence in the territory. Known as the "Mission Party," they reflected Lee's animosity toward other factions.[14] Viewing control of Oregon City as key to domination of the Territory, the Methodist Mission launched a campaign to seize McLoughlin's property. McLoughlin wrote the governor of the Hudson's Bay Company, astounded that "persons calling themselves Ministers of the Gospel would do what their countrymen in the most humble station in life having the least regard for right, would condemn."[15]

As the number of American settlers in the Willamette Valley grew, the question of some sort of government emerged. The Pioneer Lyceum and Literary Club, formed in 1842 by a group of Oregon City leaders, passed a declaration that "it is expedient for the settlers on this coast to establish an independent government."[16] The immediate incentive was the death in 1841 of the pioneer Ewing Young who left his very substantial estate to "the government." Since no government existed, a group of settlers met at Champoeg in May of 1842 to explore the matter. The meeting's sometimes fractious proceedings reflected the tensions between two factions. On the one hand, the American settlers, including the Mission Party and the Mountain Men, favored organizing a government that they expected to dominate. On the other, the English, French Canadians, and Catholics were opposed, fearing that such a government would inevitably lead to American control.

After extensive and very heated deliberation, the Americans prevailed. A legislative committee was created and charged with formulating the laws that would govern the region. Its product reflected the language of the Ordinance of 1787, the foundational laws of the Northwest Territory that comprised the future states of Ohio, Indiana, Illinois, Michigan, and Wisconsin. Their work completed, the committee called for another mass meeting to ratify the Organic Act, which the settlers did on July 5, 1843. To enforce the act, they selected a three-member executive committee, a secretary and a treasurer, as well as a ten-member legislative committee whose immediate assignment was the codification of the provisions of the act. Predictably, Americans were chosen for each of these positions.

The Organic Act afforded the customary protections of individual rights and mandated, ineffectively, that "the utmost good faith shall always be observed towards the Indians." It banned slavery throughout the territory, a measure that was soon supplemented by the legislative committee with an amendment "requiring all persons who had brought slaves into the country to remove them within three years, and providing that free negroes should leave within two years, under penalty of being flogged by the constable."[17] The provision reflected the dominant settler view that the presence of African Americans jeopardized social and economic stability. Oregon was not alone in its attempt to exclude African Americans. At the time, the states of Indiana and Illinois and the Territory that became the state of Iowa had similar laws. While word of the exclusion law undoubtedly discouraged African Americans from coming to Oregon, the law was hardly enforced. In the only court case on record, a white resident of Oregon City filed a complaint against Jacob Vanderpool, a black sailor who had come to Oregon City in 1850. Judge Thomas Nelson ordered Vanderpool to leave Oregon within thirty days.[18] Other cases were brought but were dropped because white settlers signed petitions for exemptions. Census records for 1850 indicate that there were fifty-eight blacks in the Oregon Territory. In 1860 there were 154, mainly in Benton, Lane, Polk, and Yamhill counties. While some were independent, most lived with white families and, although identified as servants, were for all practical purposes slaves.

The most significant impact of the Organic Act resulted from its provision giving 320 acres of land to any white man in the territory and 640 acres to married couples. The concept was not a new one. In 1839, while still an independent republic, Texas had passed a Homestead Act granting free land to new settlers. Senator Linn had long advocated a program of grants of a thousand acres to attract Americans to other newly acquired lands. In fact, the Senate passed his bill to that effect on February 3, 1843, but the House took no action on it.

As word of the Organic Act spread, the prospect of acquiring farmland brought thousands of settlers to Oregon. For the most part, they came from the Middle West, particularly from the southern counties of Ohio, Indiana, and Illinois. They traveled overland on the Oregon Trail, most of the way on wagon trains, then on foot or horseback until the final miles of the trail were improved. When they reached the Oregon country, they often used rafts to come down the Columbia River. Jesse Applegate was one of the leaders of the "Great Migration" in 1843. It ended in the Willamette Valley after the loss of several members, including Applegate's son, during the expedition's passage on the Columbia River. Sometime later, the tragedy led Applegate to survey an alternate land route that came to be known as the Applegate Trail. Between 1840 and 1848, 11,512 people came by the overland routes alone.[19] After the United States acquired California in 1848, many potential settlers avoided the hardships of the land route by sailing from the East Coast to Panama, crossing the Isthmus by mule, sailing to San Francisco and thence to Oregon. Another alternative was the longer route, sailing around Cape Horn to San Francisco. For everyone who undertook it, the journey to the Oregon country by any route was an enormous challenge.

Before long, American settlers had claimed nearly all the land suitable for agriculture in the Willamette Valley, while other Americans came to Oregon to establish the stores and other businesses needed to supply and support the farmers. Not surprisingly, the American influx raised questions about the future of the Joint Occupation. The Democrat James K. Polk chose as the slogan for his 1844 presidential campaign "54° 40 or fight" claiming for the United States all the land up to the southern tip of Alaska, at the time a Russian possession. When Polk took office, he proposed to the Senate an ultimatum to Britain. He faced resistance precisely because of the danger of war, especially since war with Mexico already seemed imminent. John C. Calhoun, the senator from South Carolina and former secretary of state, convinced the Senate to favor negotiations.[20] The American side was represented by James Buchanan, the secretary of state, and the British by their ambassador to the United States, Richard Pakenham. After considerable dispute both in Washington and in London, Polk, backing off from his campaign pledge, authorized Buchanan to offer a boundary at 49° N. Pakenham objected, but the Foreign Secretary George Gordon, Earl of Aberdeen convinced members of Parliament of the need for closure and directed him to reach a settlement. Aberdeen considered the ratification of a treaty possible given the current composition of the US Senate and feared that the approaching elections might alter that prospect. The 1846 Buchanan-Pakenham Treaty set the boundary between the American and British holdings at 49°N, today's border between the United States and Canada, with the Americans agreeing to a concession giving all of Vancouver Island to the British. Even with the support of the Polk administration, Congress ratified the treaty only after considerable debate.[21]

While the treaty negotiations proceeded, American settlers agreed on the Second Organic Act, which substituted an elected governor for the three-man executive committee established by the original act. They chose George Abernethy, who had come to Oregon in 1840 as a member of the Methodist mission, over several opponents including A. L. Lovejoy, a Democrat and one of the founders of the city of Portland. The Mission Party, with its emphasis on American settlement, its opposition to the Catholic Church and to the French Canadian settlers who supported it, and its dedication to temperance, ruled the day.

In February 1846, the Oregon Territory reached another important milestone when members of the Oregon City Pioneer Lyceum and Literary Club formed the Oregon Printing Association in order to found the *Oregon Spectator*. The first newspaper west of the Missouri River, preceding the first in California by seven months, was published in four pages twice a month. Its editors made their intentions clear: "It will be our object to give foreign as well as internal news. Our means of obtaining news at present are limited. But as the country improves, facilities for obtaining news will improve. Our columns will be open for the reception of literary productions, and all scientific gentlemen are invited to contribute to enable us to give as much general information as possible."[22] The caveat about the difficulty of obtaining news of distant events reflected the isolation of the Oregon country, which through the 1850s had neither direct cross-country telegraph nor rail connections. That isolation made many, both in Oregon and in the East, continue to question whether it could ever be a real part of the United States.

Few "scientific gentleman" responded to the *Spectator*'s invitation. The newspaper consisted largely of commentary and advertising. It championed economic development and the construction of roads and railroads. Its first editor was W. G. T'Vault, a lawyer and an officer of the Oregon Printing Association. While the association had early disavowed the newspaper's use "by any party for the purpose of propagating sectarian principles or doctrines, nor for the discussion of exclusive party politics," T'Vault printed his own political opinions and was soon dismissed. Two other men, H. A. G. Lee and James Fleming, took charge for a few months until the editor's post passed to George Curry. Originally from Philadelphia and only twenty-six years old, Curry had just arrived in Oregon after a short time as editor of a newspaper in Saint Louis. He took the *Spectator* position with a disclaimer about his lack of experience along with an expression of his pride in being the editor of the only paper in the Oregon country. Curry pledged that the paper would have a "consistent *American* tone" and would promote "temperance, morality, science and intelligence." But less than two years later, he too was dismissed, an outcome he attributed to his resistance to Governor Abernethy's demand that the paper serve his own partisan interests.[23]

Abernethy's concerns about his political future were certainly heightened by Curry's role in efforts to get Congress to pass legislation formally establishing the Oregon Territory. If Oregon became an official Territory, its governor would be appointed by the president of the United States rather than elected by the people. Abernethy was well aware that it was highly unlikely that the president would appoint him to the office. Despite his opposition, an organized campaign gained strength within the Oregon country. But its supporters found winning congressional support for territorial status for Oregon a challenging process. The Organic Act's provision against slavery provoked the opposition of southerners who feared that it would set a precedent for other Territories including the recently acquired Texas. After considerable argument, the House of Representatives passed the Oregon bill on January 16, 1847, by a 133–35 majority, only to have it tabled in the Senate. When word of the standstill reached the territory, the pressure from Oregon heightened. George Curry was one of three signers of a Petition to Congress formulated by a convention of delegates from throughout the Territory and dated October 2, 1847. Proclaiming the desperate need for an effective government, it appealed to Congress for "magnanimity and justice." The petitioners lamented the reality that "we, a *small, distant,* and *poor community* of few citizens in Oregon, shall be the *sole, solitary* victims of our country's neglect and injustice—it was *this* that pierced our heart. . . . Our forefathers complained that they were oppressed by the mother country, and they had a just right to complain. We do not complain of oppression, but of *neglect*. Even the tyrant has his moments of relaxation and kindness, but neglect never wears a smile."[24]

Before the petition could arrive in Washington, the House sent a second bill to the Senate. Senator Calhoun led the opposition, convinced that if Congress outlawed slavery in Oregon it was declaring slavery wrong, and claiming the right to address that wrong anywhere in the country.[25] In his argument, he rejected the cardinal premise of the Declaration of Independence, that all men are created equal, and instead asserted that "All men are not created. Only two, a man and a woman, were created, and one of these was pronounced subordinate to the other. . . . Instead of liberty and equality being born with men, and instead of all men and classes being entitled to them, they are high prizes to be won—rewards bestowed on moral and mental development."[26]

Senator Thomas Hart Benton of Missouri, who had also vigorously supported the Buchanan-Pakenham Treaty, parted company with Calhoun on the Territory issue. Such was his advocacy that Jesse Applegate acclaimed him as "the one who had more influence in the matter of securing this country to the US than all other men put together."[27] An enthusiastic expansionist, Benton was knowledgeable about the Oregon country and concerned about the wellbeing of the settlers in light of Native American hostility. In his view, a territorial government afforded the best defense. Although he represented a slave state, he dismissed that issue in the case of Oregon which he thought poorly suited to slavery.[28]

On August 13, 1848, after months of argument and legislative maneuvers, the Senate finally passed the bill by a narrow margin and sent it to President Polk who signed it despite Calhoun's pleas for a veto. The law directed that a territorial government be formed with members of the executive and judicial branches chosen by the president of the United States. The territorial legislature, elected by white, male, adult settlers, was made up of a nine-member council with three-year terms and an eighteen-member assembly serving one-year terms. The legislature was to hold annual sessions. Also to be elected by the people was the delegate to Congress who would represent the Territory in Congress although he would not have the right to vote on measures before that body.

The organization of the Territory's government had hardly gotten underway when word arrived of the discovery of gold in California. As many as two-thirds of the able-bodied men left Oregon for the mines. The absence of so many men frightened the remaining settlers who saw themselves as more vulnerable to Native American attacks. They also feared that "reckless, vicious and abandoned men" would come to Oregon and that their presence would constitute yet another threat to the Territory's peace and stability. The solution to both hazards, proposed in the columns of the *Oregon Spectator*, was that "the importation into, and manufacture and sale of intoxicating drinks in Oregon, should be prohibited by law, and that such a law would contribute more to the rapid, permanent and healthful settlement of the country than any other conceivable statute."[29] No such law was passed, but sentiment in favor of the temperance movement remained strong throughout the territorial period and beyond.

Contrary to the prevailing trepidations, the California gold rush turned into a bonanza for Oregon by creating a tremendous market for its products. Wages rose. New towns were founded. Flour mills and lumber mills flourished. Ships plied the rivers ready to sail to California with cargos in demand there. And the gold earned from the commerce, as well as that brought back by returning miners, provided a vital medium of exchange. As the call for more farmers and workers spread, more settlers came.

Along with the impact of the gold rush, the people of the Oregon Territory faced the implications of territorial government. The prospect of legislative elections in the new Territory raised the question of organized political parties. Oregon pioneers brought their party loyalties, either Democrat or Whig, with them. The national Democratic Party traced its origins to Thomas Jefferson but had evolved in a more populist direction under the leadership of President Andrew Jackson. Its members tended to be farmers and other rural dwellers. The national Whig Party developed in reaction to the Democratic Party and generally represented a more urban, entrepreneurial constituency.

Oregonians embraced the leaders of the national parties and followed events of a political nature, even though news of those events generally did not arrive in Oregon until at least a month after they had occurred. Although there were certainly exceptions, Whigs lived in the emerging towns, especially Oregon City and Portland, where they established stores and mills and other commercial and manufacturing operations. Democrats were, for the most part, farmers settled in the Willamette Valley to take advantage of its rich agricultural resources. In these early years, there was little in the way of party organization on the part of either the Democrats or the Whigs in the Oregon Territory. Legislative candidates espoused the policies of their parties but no party hierarchy existed to select nominees for office or to enforce party discipline.

The Whig candidates William Henry Harrison and Zachary Taylor won the presidency in 1840 and 1848. The Democrat James Polk held the office from 1844 to 1848. While President Polk and the Democrats strongly advocated for national expansion as the country's "Manifest Destiny," the Whigs were focused on strengthening the existing states and the substantial lands that had already been acquired. When Polk declined to run for a second term in 1848, Taylor was elected. Based on their conversation during the ride back to the White House after Taylor's inauguration, Polk recorded Taylor's opinion that the remoteness of California and Oregon precluded their *ever* being part of the Union.[30]

Before his departure from the presidency, Polk appointed the first governor of the newly recognized Territory, the Democrat Joseph Lane, who came to play a significant role throughout the 1850s. Lane was born in North Carolina, grew up in Kentucky, and then moved to Indiana where he farmed. Asked in a questionnaire years later where he had gone to college, Lane responded that he "had not the pleasure of seeing a college until long after manhood."[31] In 1822, at the age of twenty-one, he was elected to the Indiana state legislature where he served intermittently until 1846. He then fought in the Mexican-American War and rose to the rank of major general. He was seriously wounded while commanding the American forces in the Battle of Vera Cruz. No doubt it was Lane's valiant leadership in the war, his acquaintance with the West, and his legislative experience in Indiana that attracted the attention of President Polk. Lane arrived in Oregon in March, 1849.

While there was already widespread resentment of the president's imposing his appointments on the Territory, Lane quickly ingratiated himself by what one historian has described as "a capacity for dramatic action as well as a knack for well-placed flattery."[32] In a later reminiscence, Lane praised the provisional government he encountered on his arrival: "Peace and plenty blessed the hills and vales, under the benign influence of that government, reigned supreme throughout her borders." He was reluctant to impose his authority, but the people of the Territory welcomed him and the closer ties to the United States that he represented.[33] Lane's first address to the members of the council and the assembly began with a statement of the need for good relations with the Native Americans: "The well-being of the inhabitants of Oregon, no less than the cause of humanity, requires that we should always encourage relations of a most friendly character, with our red brethren." The new governor then announced the expected arrival of a military regiment whose first assignment was the capture and execution of the Cayuse Native Americans held responsible for the 1847 massacre of the missionary Marcus Whitman, his family, and other members of his party. Based on his own meetings with representatives of various tribes and their perceived willingness to sell their lands, Lane advocated the purchase of the tribal properties and the relocation of the natives before "civilization, by destroying the resources of the Indians, dooms them to poverty, want, and crime."[34]

Lane presented his assessment of the tremendous potential of the Oregon Territory with its rich lands for farming and raising cattle, its "inexhaustible forests of the finest fir and cedar in the world," its "never-failing streams," and its still-to-be-determined mineral wealth. While he anticipated the return of the miners from California with "upwards of two million dollars, in gold dust," he reminded his listeners that "the wealth of a country does not consist so much in dollars and cents, as in the numbers, virtue, intelligence and patriotism of her population, in cultivated fields, flocks and herds, and those facilities, natural and artificial, which afford an easy and certain market for its surplus productions." Lane pointed to the need for good roads and harbors, a reliable revenue source, and the codification of the laws while promising greater support from the federal government. He strongly advocated for a system of public schools financed by the sale of portions of the lands granted by the federal government. With such an educational structure in place, he maintained that "the rising generations of Oregon will proudly vie, in respect to useful knowledge and moral culture, with that of the older, settled portions of our common country."[35]

Lane certainly expected that he would be the governor to lead Oregon to the achievement of these goals, but after the 1848 election, the new Whig president Zachary Taylor removed him and appointed John Gaines to be governor. While the Gaines appointment was clearly partisan, other considerations might have influenced Taylor. Lane had served under General Zachary Taylor in the Mexican-American War and perhaps had not impressed him—or perhaps had intimidated him with his ability and popularity. The great majority of the American settlers regretted Lane's dismissal. A. L. Lovejoy, then speaker of the assembly, wrote Lane and enclosed the assembly's declaration:

> Resolved that they regret sincerely that the President of the United States has deprived the Territory of Oregon of the future services of one so eminently useful, and whose usefulness was enhanced by the unbounded confidence of the people over whom he was placed. Resolved that the conduct of General Lane in his private life has been such as to secure the warmest friendship of the people. And the purity of his private relations has not been less than his energy has been great in the discharge of his official duties.[36]

With Lane removed, attention shifted to other issues. Because the members of new Territory's executive and judicial branches were appointed by the president, the delegate to Congress was the most significant official actually chosen by the Territory's electorate. The fractious campaign for the office began immediately. The principal candidate was Samuel Thurston. Born in Maine in 1816, Thurston attended Dartmouth College and graduated from Bowdoin College in 1843. He moved first to Iowa where he briefly edited the *Burlington Gazette* and then to Oregon in 1847. As Thurston was a Methodist, his settling in Oregon may well have been inspired by Jason Lee. He quickly involved himself in the Democratic Party, was elected to the provisional legislature, and then set his sights on the office of delegate. Thurston fashioned his campaign to appeal to the Methodist faction: he espoused temperance, rejected the Catholics, and attacked John McLoughlin. His campaign slogan proclaimed his opposition to "Alcohol, Romanism, and McLoughlin."

Lafayette Grover, a member of the Salem Clique who became a significant figure in Oregon politics through the 1880s, noted in his memoir that Thurston

> introduced into Oregon the vituperative and invective style of debate, and mingled with it a species of coarse blackguardism such as no Kentucky ox-driver or Missouri flat-boatman might hope to excel. Were it more effective, he could be simply eloquent and impressive; where the fire-eating style seemed likely to win, he could hurl epithets and denunciations until his adversaries withered before them, . . . yet I am bound to say that what this scurrilous and unprincipled demagogue promised, as a rule he performed.[37]

Among the candidates opposing Thurston in the June 6, 1849, election was another future member of the Salem Clique. James Nesmith had come to the Oregon Territory with the Applegate party in 1843. Once there, he studied law and was chosen as a judge under the provisional government. Nesmith had attracted the attention of the populace in a controversy over the comparative safety and ease of travel over two different trails, the "Oregon Trail" and the "Southern Route" that prospective settlers took to get to the Oregon country. An article in the *Oregon Spectator* signed by

Nesmith's father-in-law David Goff recounted the problems of the Southern Route and attacked its proponent J. Quinn Thornton. The article was
widely thought to have actually been written by Nesmith and resulted in
acrimonious exchanges between Nesmith and Thornton. When Nesmith
challenged him to a duel, Thornton refused. In response, Nesmith posted a
broadside in Oregon City:

> To the World!!
> J. Quinn Thornton,
> Having resorted to low, cowardly and dishonorable means,
> for the purpose of injuring my character and standing, and
> having refused honorable satisfaction, which I have demanded;
> I avail myself of this opportunity of publishing him to the world
> as a reclaim less liar, an infamous scoundrel, a black hearted
> villain, an arrant coward, a worthless vagabond and an imported
> miscreant, a disgrace to the profession and a dishonor to his
> country.
>
>   James W. Nesmith[38]

The delegate campaign was heated. Grover remembered an encounter
between Thurston and Nesmith noting that Nesmith was expected to prevail, because he was "accustomed to browbeat every man that came about
him, and drive him off either by ridicule or fear. . . . But discussion proved
that Thurston was a full match for any man in the practices in which his
antagonist was distinguished and the result was that Thurston carried the
election by a large majority."[39] Nesmith's defeat did not end his political
ambitions, ambitions that he later realized.

Because of his frontier background, most eastern observers underesti-
mated Thurston, but he rose to the challenge as the *New York Sun* reported
on March 26, 1850: "Coming from the extreme west where, it is taken for
granted, the people are in a more primitive condition than elsewhere under
this government, and looking, as Mr. Thurston does, like a fair specimen
of the frontier man, little was expected of him in an oratorical way. But
he has proved to be one of the most effective speakers in the hall, which
has created no little surprise."[40] Aside from his speaking ability, Thurston
was an able writer and regularly submitted articles to eastern newspapers.
He tirelessly promoted the Oregon Territory as a land of unparalleled

opportunity, urging his countrymen to "bring all your guns to bear and reach Oregon for if you land there without staff or scrip, and having but one coat, or *none at all*, you have nothing to fear. Money is plenty, the highest wages are paid for men's and women's labour, and we have a generous and free people who know how to sympathize with another's woes, toils and hardships."[41]

Having won the election, Thurston assumed his duties as delegate. Although the delegate to Congress was an elected official, his role might be compared to that of a lobbyist today. The delegate worked to inform members of Congress and build support for measures in Oregon's interest. While without voting privileges, the delegate could introduce bills. Thurston's immediate objective was getting Congress to address the uncertainties around the Organic Act's land grant provision. His proposed legislation would give clarity and federal sanction to Oregon's land grant program while limiting its beneficiaries to US citizens and those intending to become citizens, a clear swipe at McLoughlin. Indeed, McLoughlin had become something of an obsession for Thurston. He accused McLoughlin of having earned $200,000 from the sale of his land claim property. McLoughlin adamantly protested Thurston's allegation, pointing to his gifts of land to Methodists, Catholics, Presbyterians, Congregationalists, and Baptists: "In short, in one way and another I have donated to the county, to schools, to churches, and private individuals, more than three hundred town lots, and I never realized in cash $20,000 from all the original sales I have made."[42]

As Thurston worked to get the Land Law through Congress, word came from Oregon of the development of a Whig opposition and its plan to launch a newspaper in Portland. While Portland was as yet hardly worthy to be called a town, it was competing with Oregon City and Milwaukie to become the dominant trading center on the Willamette and Columbia Rivers. Its leaders saw the importance of a newspaper to advance its fortunes. Oregon City already had the *Spectator,* and Milwaukie's leading citizen, Lot Whitcomb, was in the process of founding the *Western Star.* In the summer of 1850, Portland promoters William Chapman and Stephen Coffin traveled to San Francisco to purchase a printing press and other necessary materials. There they encountered Thomas J. Dryer, a forty-two-year-old man with a journalism background who was looking for a job. Born in New York, Dryer had lived and worked in Ohio, Indiana, and Michigan before coming to California in the gold rush. He was briefly the city editor of the *San Francisco Courier*. At least as important to Chapman and Coffin, he was an outspoken Whig. He readily accepted their invitation to come to Portland and found a newspaper.

The prospect of a Whig newspaper convinced Thurston of the need for a paper to further the interests of the Democratic Party as well as his own political career. Early in 1850, he began looking for the appropriate person to establish and run his newspaper. His diary recounts his efforts to convince several different men with editorial experience to undertake the task. After ordering a printing press and recruiting Wilson Blain, A. W. Stockwell, and Henry Russell, Thurston found the man he was looking for when he encountered the twenty-six-year-old Asahel Bush during a visit with his wife's family in Chicopee, Massachusetts. Born in Westfield, Massachusetts, Bush had become a printer after his father's death in 1839. He worked for newspapers in Cleveland, Ohio, and Saratoga, New York, before returning to Westfield in 1849 to edit the *Standard*, a Democratic newspaper. Along the way, he had studied law and passed the bar. His appointment as town clerk reflected the support he enjoyed among the Democrats of the small town. Thurston judged him "a gentleman of high integrity and of the first order of ability" as well as a committed Democrat. He proposed that Bush go to Oregon and establish a Democratic newspaper there.[43]

While Bush was considering his response, he traveled to Washington where he witnessed a debate on the Land Law in the House of Representatives that left no doubt as to Thurston's attitude toward the most contentious issue confronting the country. An Ohio congressman proposed adding an amendment admitting free African Americans into the Oregon Territory. Bush paraphrased Thurston's response in his report to the *Westfield Standard*: "The people of Oregon were not pro-slavery men, nor were they pro-negro men; there were but few negroes in the territory and he hoped there never would be more; the people themselves had excluded them and he trusted that Congress would not introduce them in violation of their wishes."[44]

Following a series of negotiations, Bush agreed to go to Oregon and launch the *Oregon Statesman,* a name chosen by Thurston, perhaps with himself in mind. Already Thurston's allies in Oregon were working to get subscribers, and he expected the paper to be "triumphantly supported." Still Bush would face a "political war" with the Whigs, one that Thurston expected him to win but not without effort. He directed Bush to treat his opponents "with dignity and courtesy, but with decision, ability and firmness." While Thurston would provide the initial funding for the paper, he expected to be repaid, with Bush gradually assuming ownership. Bush was to travel to Oregon as quickly as possible and once there "let no one get up earlier, work later or steal a march on you."[45]

Traveling via the Isthmus of Panama, Bush reached Oregon City on September 30, 1850, after being seasick "nearly all the way on both oceans."[46] When Bush arrived, Oregon City had a population of only seven hundred people. Despite its small number of inhabitants, a letter to the editor of the Milwaukie *Western Star* bragged that Oregon City had two flouring mills, five sawmills, three hotels, three dozen stores, bakeries, manufactories, a tailor, a saddler, two barbers, six doctors, a dentist, "a score or more lawyers," and Methodist, Baptist, Congregational and Catholic meeting houses.[47] As the center of government of the Territory, Oregon City would be Bush's base for the time being. The inauguration of the *Oregon Statesman* awaited the arrival of the printing press Thurston had purchased.

While Bush was traveling to Oregon, Thurston continued his legislative endeavors. Thanks in part to Lane's efforts while governor, Congress had established a process whereby federal commissioners would negotiate treaties with the Native Americans to accomplish the "extinguishment of their claims to lands lying west of the Cascade Mountains" and "leave the whole of the most desireable portion open to white settlers."[48] On September 27, 1850, Thurston's efforts were rewarded with the passage of the Donation Land Law recognizing existing land claims in the Territory and offering grants to new American settlers. After this success, Thurston returned to his battle with John McLoughlin and the Hudson's Bay Company, which he saw as an ongoing threat to American control over the Territory. He promoted a plan to seize and then sell McLoughlin's land claim in Oregon City which, in his mind, belonged to the Territory. The proceeds would go to the founding of a public university: "Let the watchword be—*the education of the youth of Oregon* against the British Hudson's Bay Company, and ring it upon the tree tops and in the valleys." Bush was to see that the legislature accepted the funds and approved the plans, "I must be sustained and the Hudson's Bay Company's influence must be put down."[49]

Although the newspaper did not yet exist, Thurston wrote an anonymous letter intended for publication in the *Oregon Statesman* with an unflattering portrayal of members of Congress: "To walk on the Pennsylvania Avenue at this hour of the day, when Congress is in session, is certainly profitable to a man who reflects. Here you will see poor fallen human nature exhibited in its true light—and while you lament the depth to which it has fallen, you feel a contempt for the creatures in which it appears, as they start or mince along, to all appearance believing that to be one of God's noblemen, it is only necessary to procure a decorated exterior." He went on to decry the failure of the Millard Fillmore administration to defend the Monroe Doctrine against British ambitions in Central America, which he saw as a threat to the United States' status as the "leading nation of this continent." He condemned the establishment of cross-country mail service to San Francisco rather than directly to Oregon, warning that California was plotting to make Oregon subservient to her and urging resistance: "Destiny has decreed Oregon a standing that California can never have."[50]

While Thurston had written many Oregon acquaintances recommending Bush and asking them to help him, he made sure that Bush understood that his role in founding and partially financing the paper was to be kept confidential. He further instructed: "In your first issue, in a dignified manner, state that I have no control or influence whatever over the paper and that I will be no further respected nor supported than any other good Democrat." "Most of all," he wrote, "have the good of Oregon in view, and let all other things, party included, be secondary."[51] Bush assured him that the *Statesman* would be a Democratic newspaper independent of Thurston's influence, but he warned that "it has been noised all about here that the *Statesman* was not to be a democratic paper but merely your organ (the last *Spectator* reiterated the story) and many good democrats are half suspicious that such is the case."[52]

At the beginning of December, Thurston's fears were realized: the *Oregonian* began publication as a four-page weekly. In its first issue, the publishers vowed to support the Fillmore administration and the Whig party "so long as they tend to produce results beneficial to the interest of the country at large" and "to foster and protect the agricultural and commercial interests of Oregon." The masthead read "Equal Rights, Equal Laws, Equal Justice to All Men." Dryer, optimistically or disingenuously, promised that "under no circumstances will we be drawn into individual controversies on local or rival interests."[53]

Above left: Joseph Lane
(Courtesy Oregon Historical Society,
bb009960)

Above right: Jesse Applegate
(Courtesy Oregon Historical Society,
bb007055)

Right: John McLoughlin
(Courtesy Oregon Historical Society,
bb005722)

Samuel Thurston
(Courtesy Oregon Historical Society,
bb015398)

Thomas Dryer, the editor of the
Portland *Oregonian*
(Courtesy Oregon Historical Society,
bb005654)

George Curry
(Courtesy Oregon Historical Society,
bb004593)

Asahel Bush
(Courtesy Bush House Museum)

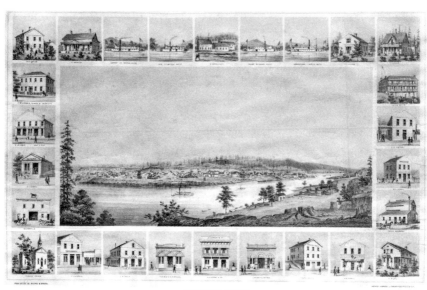

An 1858 lithograph of Oregon City. (Courtesy Oregon Historical Society, bb008615)

CHAPTER TWO

"No favor sways us; no fear shall awe."

—*Oregon Statesman*

Despite Thurston's assertion that as long as he was delegate he would not "engage as a partizan but consult solely the best interests of Oregon," from the beginning of their negotiations he had made Bush's mission plain. Along with the newspaper, he was charged with the organization of the Democratic Party in the Territory. As to the structure of the Democratic organization, Thurston wrote: "You are on the spot—I am not, hence you can tell better than I, what is, and what should be, but I am of the opinion, that it is best perhaps for the party, to organize in their several counties, but not to have any Territorial Convention next year."[1] If the organization process moved forward as he anticipated, Thurston foresaw a territorial convention in 1853 when he expected that a Democratic president would replace the Whig Millard Fillmore. He added, "And I would not be surprised if we moved to become a state at that time." Bush was not to commit Thurston to anything but to let him alone to "quietly attend to the wants of the Territory." He would announce his candidacy for reelection in February or March.[2]

Thurston urged Bush to acquaint himself with the Democratic members of the territorial legislature and to get himself elected clerk of the assembly, which Bush very quickly managed to do. During the assembly session, Thurston instructed Bush to "watch the maneuvers, conversations, and inclinations of *men* and *cliques* and *parties*" and to send him a weekly report. In all cases, Thurston insisted his letters be kept "strictly confidential, unless I order otherwise." Bush's term as clerk was limited to the second regular session of the legislature, which met from December 2, 1850, until February 8, 1851. He wrote to his family in Massachusetts that he had been chosen over his competitor by a five-to-one majority, that his pay was $5.00 a day, and that his duties included "calling the roll, reading bills, papers, etc., keeping a journal of the proceedings, etc., etc. Some days I have scarcely anything to do and others I have about as much writing as I can well do, just in proportion to the business the House transacts."[3]

His assignment clear, Bush soon began to gather the group of men that would prove to be essential to the Territory-wide organization and to the success of the Democratic Party. Most of his recruits held land grants in one or another of Oregon's ten counties. Their wives and children lived on their farms while the men divided their time between their farms and Oregon City, the center of the territorial government. The small community of Oregon City was hospitable to newcomers; its very isolation encouraged camaraderie. Each of Bush's new friends had grown up back in the United States and had neither parents nor siblings nearby. While a few had been able to attend prestigious colleges, others had struggled in a variety of jobs to support themselves. Like Bush, some had newspaper experience. Nearly all had studied the law. Most important, they were like-minded in their political preferences. Together, they formed the fraternity that came to be known as the Salem Clique.

In his effort to become clerk of the assembly, Bush found an advocate in Matthew Deady. Deady was born in Maryland in 1824, the eldest child of an Irish immigrant school teacher. For reasons that are not clear, the family moved around a great deal during Deady's childhood, living in Virginia, Ohio, Missouri, and Kentucky. He attended the schools where his father taught and worked on the family farms. After his mother's death and a falling-out with his father, perhaps because he was unwilling to become a priest, Deady left his family. He apprenticed as a blacksmith then studied to become a teacher. While teaching to make a living, he read law and passed the Ohio Bar in 1847. Dissatisfied with his law practice in Ohio, he journeyed to Oregon in 1849 and settled in Yamhill County, where he lived until 1853, when he moved south to Douglas County. He quickly involved himself in politics with such success that he was elected to the assembly in 1850. As a member of the judiciary committee, Deady drafted many of the early laws of the young Territory and, after the session ended, was recruited to organize and codify those laws. He and Bush soon became friends and allies, even rooming together at the local hotel while both worked in the legislature.

Like Deady, Benjamin Harding was elected to the assembly within a few months of his arrival in Oregon and served during the 1850–1851 legislative session after a short stint as US Attorney. He was born in Pennsylvania in 1823, studied law, and practiced briefly in Illinois before coming to Oregon. He settled in Salem where his farm and his law practice took second place to his political endeavors. He did not run for office in 1851 but was chosen chief clerk of the assembly for the 1851–1852 session. The voters of Marion County returned him to the assembly for the special session that lasted three days in July, 1852, and then for the regular session in December. His fellow legislators elected him Speaker for both sessions.

James Nesmith was already known in the Territory as Thurston's challenger in the 1849 delegate to Congress election. Born in Washington County, Maine, in 1820, the infant Nesmith was raised by relatives and friends after his mother's death and a fire that destroyed his father's fortune. In middle age, he noted that he had gone to school "only a few years in my life. But I have a habit of reading and informing myself, and I believe I have now the best library in the State."[4] As he grew up, he moved west to Ohio and Missouri and then to Kansas where he joined the Applegate migration and came to Oregon in 1843. The party happened to include a number of lawyers who passed the time as they crossed the plains by arguing imaginary legal cases. Nesmith listened and then participated with an aptitude that led his companions to encourage his study of the law when he got to Oregon City. Two years later, he was selected to be a judge under the provisional government. He was among the members of the Pioneer Lyceum and Literary Club, which founded the first newspaper in the Territory, the *Oregon Spectator*, in Oregon City.

When word came of the discovery of gold in California, Nesmith went south. His considerable success in the mines provided him with substantial resources. He returned to his wife and children in Polk County where he farmed and established a flour mill. He was generous in providing financial assistance to other members of the Clique, even to the point of becoming a part-owner of the *Oregon Statesman*. Nesmith's fellow Clique member and later rival, Lafayette Grover, commented on his retentive memory and his writing skills while observing that he had "the Scotch characteristics in regard to his enemies."⁵ After years of contention, a far more passionate rival described him as "a man of keen and ready wit, without much cultivation or refinement. He had a wonderful faculty of seeing the ridiculous side of things, and this faculty sometimes worked to his personal disadvantage."⁶

Bush's association with Reuben Boise had begun in Massachusetts where he read law with Boise's uncle. Boise was born in Blandford, Massachusetts, in 1818, to a family that had farmed there for four generations. While he was growing up, his father held several elective offices, no doubt inspiring the young man's interest in politics. Boise graduated from Williams College in 1843 and taught school in Missouri for two years before returning to Massachusetts to study law with his uncle. Like Bush, Boise was attracted to Oregon by Samuel Thurston's enthusiastic descriptions of the place. Bush was "much pleased" to have his "old friend" in the Territory and was sure he would be very successful.⁷ Despite Bush's efforts to keep him in Oregon City, Boise initially settled in Portland and opened a law practice that he advertised in the *Oregonian*: "Law Notice: Reuben P. Boise, Attorney-at-Law. Address: Rear of the Printing Office, on the corner of Front and Morrison Streets, Portland."⁸ For whatever reason, his stay in Portland was short. He moved to Polk County in 1852 to take up farming while also opening a law office in Salem.

Another federal appointment, this time by President Polk, brought the young Orville Pratt to Oregon in 1849 as a justice of the Territory's Supreme and District Courts. In many ways the most problematic Clique associate, Pratt had attended West Point but left after two years to pursue legal studies. After passing the Ohio Bar, he set up practice there and soon attracted the attention of local politicians who brought him to President Polk's attention. Aside from his career in the judiciary, Pratt was a successful businessman, a talent foreshadowed when he brought with him to Oregon a number of $10 cooking stoves that he sold for $150, stoves being a rare convenience in the Territory at the time. Pratt handed the editor of the *Oregonian,* Thomas Dryer, one of his most-used epithets when he bought cattle from a man named John Durham then sold them falsely as blooded Durham stock, an especially valuable breed. Dryer took to calling the Democrats, particularly the Salem wing, the "Durhamites."

While Bush served as clerk of the territorial assembly, he came to know George Curry who was clerk of the council, the upper house. After being dismissed from his post as editor of the *Oregon Spectator* in 1848, Curry had started his own newspaper in Oregon City, the *Oregon Free Press*. The paper lasted only a few months, perhaps a victim of the depopulation of the Territory that was caused by the California gold rush. A Democrat, Curry was elected to serve in the fourth and final session of the provisional legislature, which met from December, 1848, until February, 1849. It was in that role that he was a signer of the petition to Congress for the creation of a territorial government. When Joseph Lane came to the Oregon Territory as its governor, Curry served as the Territory's public printer, promoting Lane and his plans and aspirations for Oregon and for himself.[9]

Lafayette Grover, a native of Maine, graduated from Bowdoin College and was admitted to the Pennsylvania Bar. Like Bush, he was recruited by Thurston and came to Oregon in 1851 after a trip around Cape Horn and a short stay in San Francisco. Grover accepted the invitation of the chief justice of the Territory's Supreme Court, Thomas Nelson, to be a clerk of the US District Court in southern Oregon. Later he settled in Salem where he briefly joined Benjamin Harding's law practice but soon left it to become prosecuting attorney and deputy US district attorney. Grover was one of the Clique's most successful politicians through the 1850s and beyond. A promoter of Oregon's economy and an able businessman, he was instrumental in the founding of the Willamette Woolen Manufacturing Company and later an owner of the Salem Flouring Mills, two of the Territory's earliest corporations.

Fred Waymire, who had been a farmer and a millwright in Ohio, took up a land claim in Polk County in 1846. He participated in the creation of the provisional government before Oregon officially became a US territory and then served in the territorial council. In 1873, his obituary in the *Oregonian* described him as "a pioneer by habit as well as by situation," and "in the rude society of the early days of the Territory he was always a conspicuous figure." While he possessed "neither learning nor eloquence," he had "vigorous common sense and was honest and frank."[10]

Although he did not arrive in Oregon until 1852, Delazon Smith quickly allied himself with Bush and his compatriots. Born in New York, he attended Oberlin College but left before graduation because of his opposition to the antislavery movement at the school. After legal studies, he passed the New York Bar and then edited newspapers in Rochester, New York, and Dayton, Ohio. His efforts on behalf of John Tyler during the 1840 presidential campaign earned him an appointment as special commissioner of the United States to Ecuador, a post he held from 1842 until 1845. When he returned to the United States, he became a minister in the Methodist Episcopal Church in Iowa. Once in Oregon, he started a law practice in Linn County, turned to politics, and embraced the Clique. Admirers called him the "Lion of Linn." Much later, a contemporary described him as "a man of generous impulses and many intellectual gifts" including noteworthy speaking skills. But he "lacked stability and strength of character. He was better fitted to follow than to lead men."[11]

The Clique's membership extended to the less-populous southern part of Oregon. Stephen F. Chadwick came to Oregon from New York where he had been admitted to the Bar. At first, he settled in Scottsburg where he practiced law and was the town's first postmaster, then in Roseburg where he served as a judge and a deputy district attorney. After his appointment as associate justice of the Oregon Territory's Supreme Court, which involved holding court at different locations around the Territory, Matthew Deady took up a land claim in what became Douglas County. The far southern counties were represented by J. W. Drew from Umpqua County and William Tichenor from what is now Coos County. Drew later moved north and became a valuable source of information on relevant happenings and their participants in Portland. Other men have also been identified by one historian or another as members of the Clique. All came together initially in Oregon City and later in Salem.

Thomas Dryer of the *Oregonian* first coined the name "Salem Clique," and its use soon became customary among the opposition.[12] While some have seen Pratt as the "boss" of the Clique, others Deady, Bush was in fact its leader, although not as completely dominant as many scholars have supposed. Nor were the members as single-minded or subservient as they are often pictured. They frequently disagreed on the important issues of the day. Their correspondence, with its sarcasm and cynicism, reveals the occasional competition and contention among them. In an 1852 letter to Bush from Scottsburg, for example, Chadwick wrote of a meeting that Joseph Drew called in Umpqua City. "He has declared himself a 'whig'" and is "playing a game of policy and will until the Whigs become strong." Chadwick added that Drew had become an ally of the Whig Jesse Applegate."[13] No indication of Drew's supposed disloyalty appears in any further correspondence.

Along with being an emergent political power, the Clique in its early days was predictably a collection of young men with the usual preoccupations of young men. That they paid little attention to the tenets of the temperance movement is demonstrated in a letter from Deady to Bush: "I have snored long and soundly. Got up without the headache, the fumes of the 'burning water' have silently evaporated during the night, leaving me a sadder, and a sober-er man."[14] Bush echoed the theme, writing Deady, "I am going down to Astoria on the [steamer] *Willamette* next Wednesday to meet the mail. If you will go along I will pay your liquor bills." In a letter written the following day, he added, "If you are 'short' I will pay your fare."[15] On a later occasion, Deady wrote Nesmith that Boise had bought a farm near Nesmith's properties: "Now, whatever you do, don't let him drink too much whiskey. I am afraid he has made a bad location in that respect for a man of his national tendencies."[16] Boise did not hesitate to taunt Bush: "What the devil were you all doing at Salem this winter that made everybody sick—I think the liquor must have been bad."[17]

Both bachelors, Deady and Bush were on the lookout for attractive women, as when Deady described to Bush a camp meeting he had attended: "There were some damned pretty women present, which as you may easily imagine stirred up in my bosom the feelings of other days, and well nigh reasoned me to the conclusion of Mr. Paul, 'better marry than burn,' but then we moderns in the advance of arts and sciences have discovered a way of avoiding either form of so disagreeable a dilemma."[18] Despite his assertion that there must be an alternative to the "marry or burn" dilemma, Deady married later in 1852. Bush followed in 1854.

After Salem became the capital of the Territory, Bush, Deady, Nesmith, Smith, Harding, and Curry stayed at the Bennett Hotel on High Street during legislative sessions. Nesmith once paid the night watchman to awaken Bush at 4:00 a.m. for a specious errand to The Dalles. Bush then paid the same watchman to awaken Nesmith with the message that Bush was being sent to the hospital after an accident. Nesmith hurried to the lobby only to find Bush there laughing at him. Nesmith claimed he had only come down because Bush had borrowed his watch and "I felt that I must get it before they took you to the hospital, because the executor of your estate might claim it if your injuries proved fatal."[19]

The sarcasm constant in exchanges between and among the Clique can be seen in a letter Bush wrote to Deady in 1856: "Nesmith was here yesterday. Says he has a boy, but I suspect it is minus a *pecker*."[20] Even their cautions to one another were laced with humor as when Deady reproved Bush: "Leave out your vulgarity when you address decent folk. Think how your memory will suffer, when a future Biographer will give your memoirs to the world, with your blackguard letters to myself interspersed through the dog-eared volume." On the other hand, the closeness of their relationship surfaces in the final sentence of the same letter: "Write often as it is damned lonely."[21]

Early in 1851, Deady's advocacy and Bush's acquaintance with the members of the assembly led to his appointment to the position of public printer, a lucrative contract coveted by every newspaper in the Territory and particularly problematic since Bush did not yet even have a printing press. When the editors of existing newspapers responded by attacking the legislature, Deady questioned their motives, writing Nesmith: "For the first time in the annals of Oregon, each journal comes out with a long spun leader on the imbecility of the late legislature, but unfortunately for the effect intended to be produced by these laudable efforts of the gentlemen of the quill; the secret of their righteous indignation and apparently disinterested labors, will discover itself in the fact that none of them has been *elected public printer*."[22]

With the approaching delegate election in mind, Bush was concerned that the *Statesman* would be viewed as Thurston's organ, an eventuality opposed by even the most committed Democrats. He wrote Thurston that the *Statesman* would not endorse anyone until the party had made its decision.[23] Through January and February of 1851, while Bush awaited the arrival of the printing press, Thurston continued to keep him apprised of happenings in Washington that, in his mind, threatened Oregon's wellbeing and his own political career. In these controversies, Bush was expected to support and defend him. Further Thurston made it clear that Bush would have editorial control of the paper, expressly limiting the influence of Blain, Russell, and Stockwell, each of whom soon left the enterprise. When the press finally arrived and the first issue was imminent, Thurston instructed Bush to "be extremely careful to have your paper dignified with chaste and gentlemanly language," an admonition that Bush soon violated.[24]

On March 28, 1851, the *Oregon Statesman* at last made its debut with an editorial stating its mission. Bush declared that the paper would be devoted to the interests of all of Oregon and to those of the Democratic Party while maintaining "a courteous and respectful demeanor towards those who may chance to differ with us, awarding to all the same freedom of opinion that we claim for ourself." The *Statesman* would refuse "on all occasions, to lend our columns to further the purposes of factions, cliques or individuals." In religion, it would "know no sect or creed, but will favor that universal toleration which secures to every man the unrestricted enjoyment of his opinions and the privilege of worshipping God after his own manner." And in morals, it would advocate "Truth, Temperance, Sobriety, Industry and all those virtues and graces which adorn the human character." The motto on its masthead proclaimed: "No favor sways us; no fear shall awe."[25]

Bush's compatriots were firm in their support of the enterprise. Deady dismissed the *Statesman*'s rivals, the *Oregonian* and the *Spectator*, the latter as the tool of "some corrupt and contemptible clique."[26] After the second issue of the paper was published, Bush wrote Deady complaining that the "tender footed, toady Democrats" in Yamhill County were denouncing the *Statesman* as too violent and vowing to kill it. He asked that, if it would not harm their chances of victory, the Democratic candidates at their county meeting pass a resolution in support of the newspaper and its management.[27] Deady reported that potential subscribers were enthusiastic: "I think you will be well patronized. All are loud in praise of the paper, except a few whigs who are looking forward and know that the weight of its popularity must fall upon the democrat side." With his customary humor, Deady ended his letter: "Excuse my hasty scrawls as I have to write when I can, between drams."[28]

When word reached Portland that the publication of the *Statesman* was imminent, Boise warned Bush that Thomas Dryer had reacted with a threat to "go to you with a revolver in his jacket. . . . I don't think he will trouble you but it is well enough to be on your guard." Boise assured Bush that the paper would sell well in Portland, despite the presence of the *Oregonian*. In fact, Dryer was already protesting that he was "persecuted." Boise added a cautionary postscript: "Say nothing about this, but to those you can trust."[29] Dryer's ongoing attack on Bush's appointment as public printer triggered Bush's response in the second issue of the *Statesman*: "Complaints of this kind come with a special grace from a paper devoted from its first to its last number almost exclusively to the grossest personal abuse, the most foulmouthed slander, grovelling scurrility, falsehood and ribald blackguardism." He went on to suggest that Dryer study the Quaker adage: "Be not affronted at a jest. If one throw salt at thee thou wilt receive no harm, unless thou hast sore places."[30]

The *Oregonian* editor immediately became the favored victim of the Clique's derision. In another letter, Boise described a Portland public meeting in which Dryer said that if "he could be king of this country he would have better regulations about this town. But no one was heard to exclaim *God save King Dryer* so I suppose he has but faint hope of being crowned." Boise also forwarded local rumors that Dryer intended to run for the legislature. Those rumors proved to be mistaken; Dryer did not do so until 1856.[31]

Bush's exchange with Dryer over the public printing matter marked the beginning of the infamous "Oregon Style" of journalism. That style was described by one early twentieth-century historian as "a species of storm-and-stress composition, strong chiefly in invective, and—in a community where everyone's private affairs and personal name were known to every inhabitant—to coin amusing and even offensive titles for opponents."[32] Editors regularly indulged in sardonic derision of one another and the stands each took on the issues of the day. Mockery and sarcasm were a feature of most contemporary American newspapers but one observer later pronounced the Oregon Style to be "as much superior to the personal gratings which may be seen in almost any number of the present day *New York Tribune*, as the wit of an Irishman is to the raw slang of an English butcher." He added that "the pioneer editors of Oregon were men of imagination and could put wings on their scorpions."[33]

The *Statesman* in no small part owed its success to the Clique. Members sold papers and kept an eye on the competition.[34] When the various attacks on Bush and the *Statesman* in the *Oregonian* and elsewhere appeared to be taking their toll, Bush's friends stood behind him. Nesmith wrote Deady: "I predict that Bush will be triumphant in this malicious prosecution, but if he is to suffer pecuniary losses, to satisfy their envy and malevolence, this will be the time for his friends to lend him a helping hand. He must and shall be sustained." Deady responded with the same commitment to Bush although he was far less able to provide "pecuniary" support than was Nesmith.[35]

Even more important to the *Oregon Statesman* and to Bush than his fellows' encouragement and support was the intelligence network they represented from their bases around the Territory. Throughout the 1850s, the members of the Clique kept one another, and especially Bush, informed of happenings significant and trivial. They let him know which individuals to cultivate, which to oppose, and which to ignore. Those who could be trusted were often rewarded with important appointments. In return for their information, Clique members could rely on supportive coverage in the newspaper.

Besides the public printing question, the second edition of the *Statesman* featured another controversy. Given his obligation to Thurston, it was hardly surprising that Bush rejected some letters John McLoughlin sent for publication. After McLoughlin complained in a letter to the *Spectator*, Bush explained his decision: "A few words as to the reasonableness of our refusal to publish the letters except as an advertisement, and we close the matter. The letters we deemed to be of little interest to anyone except Dr. McLoughlin, and probably not twenty out of our hundreds of patrons would have read them. . . . If the Doctor was anxious to have the letters published by us, ordinary generosity would have prompted him to pay for such publication; but if penuriousness dictated otherwise, manliness should have prompted him to say nothing about the matter, or give the reasons of our refusal."[36] Since this was only its second issue, Bush was certainly premature in alluding to the *Statesman*'s "hundreds of patrons," but the newspaper soon attracted a significant audience as attested by the Whig leader Jesse Applegate, who wrote Bush about a territorial matter in November on the grounds that "your paper has the largest circulation and your party is the ruling one."[37]

The *Statesman* had hardly begun publication when Joseph Lane returned to the Territory. After President Zachary Taylor replaced him as the governor of the Territory, Lane had gone to California in a failed search for gold. He returned to Oregon with his sons Nat, John, and Lafayette and launched a gristmill and sawmill operation in Douglas County. Lane remained very popular in Oregon at a time when many were becoming disenchanted with Thurston, in part because of his fixation on McLoughlin.[38] Even before Lane's arrival, Matthew Deady wrote Nesmith deriding the *Spectator* for its "wanton calumnies against the reputation of Gen. Lane, whilst in the discharge of his official duties among us." In another letter to his trusted colleague, he even went so far as to declare that "I wish to God Gen. Lane was here and would consent to run. . . . I should like to see a man elected whom I had some respect for." Bush too defended Lane against the *Spectator*'s attacks.[39]

Few doubted Lane's talents, as Delazon Smith described them in an 1853 letter to Bush: "As an orator, though he is not *brilliant*, he is pleasing, argumentative and agreeable . . . He has a very happy and apparently perfectly natural faculty of going 'from grave to gay, from lively to severe.' All he says is said earnestly and candidly, but courteously and good naturedly. His auditors are either convulsed with laughter or silently nodding assent to either his statement of facts or the conclusions drawn from them."[40] Much later, Lafayette Grover noted that "as a statesman he had a strong and positive voice on every leading question, and intelligence enough to comprehend the whole subject." In 1901, George Williams, whose own experience in public office included territorial Supreme Court Justice, US senator, and US attorney general, remembered that Lane had "all the essential qualifications of a successful politician."[41]

The prospect of Lane's candidacy for delegate, which had Lane's full if somewhat discreet approval, created an obvious dilemma for Bush because of his obligation to Thurston. When a group of Democrats in Yamhill County, led by the respected pioneer and founder of the town of Dayton, Joel Palmer, nominated Lane for the delegateship, Bush wrote Deady: "You are aware of and can appreciate the embarrassments by which I am surrounded, or under which anyone publishing a Democratic paper would labor during the Delegate to Congress elections. . . . I shall pursue an independent course and I shall endeavor to pursue a judicious one. I think I can do it. I intend to go for the party and its principles rather than its individual members." Perceiving Bush's dilemma, Dryer in the *Oregonian* came out in support of Lane over Thurston.[42] Bush's "embarrassments" were resolved when he got word that Thurston had died at sea on April 9 while en route from Washington, DC, to Oregon. By the time of his death, Thurston's reputation in the Territory had suffered to the extent that few settlers grieved. Still, other newspapers made a show of sorrow, leading Deady to remark, "It reminds me of paid mourners in a funeral procession or the tears of a young spendthrift upon the death of a rich relative."[43]

Thurston's death was announced in the *Statesman* on May 2. The *Statesman*'s endorsement of Lane for delegate appeared in the next edition of the paper, on May 9. Bush had become, and would remain for some time, Lane's most enthusiastic advocate. But not all of the Clique shared Bush's enthusiasm for Lane or his optimism about Lane's prospects. From his base in Portland, Reuben Boise wrote criticizing Lane for not committing himself in opposition to the Hudson's Bay Company and for "trying to sham every question that is asked." He reported that "Lane made a very lame speech here Saturday, and seems to be under the entire direction of Dryer and his friends." Boise told Bush to be "very cautious about supporting him" and added that many Portland voters were doubtful about Lane and opposed to his election. Despite his earlier letter favoring Lane, Deady too was concerned about any connection he might have with the Whigs. He warned that such an association would discredit Lane with Democrats who would then withdraw their support. Benjamin Harding, on the other hand, reported that Lane had made a "good impression" at a speech in Salem and that "many who were opposed to him before are in favour of him now." Harding reiterated his own commitment to Lane but supported Deady's contention that Dryer's endorsement would injure him.[44]

Another matter bothering Bush and his allies was the perception that Lane had intended to challenge Thurston for the delegate office before Thurston's death. Harding worried that it would compromise Lane's efforts in Polk and Linn Counties where Thurston had been particularly popular. Deady was more vehement: "I see that d——d fool of the *Oregonian* has come out and said that Lane intended to run any how." He urged Lane to confront Dryer on the issue. Deady's concern was that the allegation would alienate Thurston loyalists whose support was crucial to a Lane victory.[45] In the end, the *Oregonian* reiterated its endorsement of Lane's candidacy. The *Spectator* and the *Milwaukie Western Star* also supported him.

Lane's challenger for delegate was William H. Willson, also a Democrat but more significantly the candidate of the Mission Party. Having come to Oregon as part of Jason Lee's "Great Reinforcement" in 1837, he settled in what was then called Chemeketa and is credited with changing its name to Salem. When the provisional government was formed in 1843, Willson was named its treasurer. In his challenge to Lane, however, the Methodist connection did not serve Willson as well as might have been expected, a clear indication of the rapidly declining power of the Mission faction. After campaigning aggressively and making many promises to the electorate, Lane defeated Willson by a vote of 2375 to 543.[46] The 1851 delegate election was the last time the Mission Party presented its own candidate for government office.

While the Lane connection sometimes strained his relations with his fellows, Bush was careful to encourage their political aspirations as well.

As a candidate for the council from Yamhill County in the June, 1851, legislative elections, Deady wrote Bush: "I tell people publicly that I have no fears of my election, but between ourselves I think it somewhat doubtful." Still he was determined to prevent the office from falling into the hands of the Whigs. Deady's opponent was David Logan, a Whig who had come to Oregon from Illinois where his father was a prominent politician and a law partner of Abraham Lincoln. Deady wrote to a friend that, while he would not admit it, Logan was in the hands of Dryer and the *Oregonian*, even to the point of selling the newspaper in the county. Deady added that the election of Whigs would inevitably result in the party gaining traction and eventually becoming the majority party in the council.[47]

Bush assured Deady of his support while pressing him to unleash a much more aggressive campaign: "I am fearful from what I hear from various sources from your county that you are going to be beaten. I would work like the Devil from now till the day of election and press all my friends into service, if I were you. Don't let a feeling of security cause you to relax your efforts." By June, he was more optimistic. Before the vote count was in, he wrote Deady that he would "be willing to take a small bet on you."[48] Deady won a seat in the council, a victory his foes attributed to his success in getting Logan drunk, thereby impairing his performance on the campaign trail. After his defeat, Logan moved from Yamhill County to Portland where he was elected to the assembly in 1854. During that campaign, Deady wrote an anonymous letter to a Portland newspaper accusing Logan of raping a Native American girl on the street in Jacksonville. Logan rejected the charge and, when he learned of Deady's role, threatened his life. The letter had no discernible effect on the outcome of the election. Logan won and collaborated with Dryer to organize the only Whig Party convention in the Oregon Territory in December of 1854.[49]

The 1851 legislative elections demonstrated the *Statesman*'s emerging influence and its commitment to the Democratic Party. The newspaper as a blatant political tool was not uncommon for the times. In 1850, 95 percent of America's English language newspapers and periodicals declared a party affiliation. The dean of the graduate school of journalism at Columbia University has described the nineteenth century as the era in which journalism was a "branch of politics." Another journalism scholar states the case even more strongly: "The newspaper press was the political system's central institution, not simply a forum or atmosphere in which politics took place. Instead, newspapers and their editors were purposeful actors in the political process, linking parties, voters, and the government together, and pursuing specific political goals."[50] Through the territorial period and into statehood, Oregon demonstrated precisely that reality. Editors identified the issues, set the agenda, and dominated the players.

The newspaper represented only the first step in Bush's efforts to build the Democratic Party infrastructure in the Oregon Territory. He made his intentions clear in the first edition: "Whenever the Democracy shall organize, the Statesman will be the uncompromising advocate of regular nominations, fairly made; by which system only can a party give efficiency to its action and success to its principles." Pointing to recent events in the United States where the issue of slavery was dividing the Democratic Party, Bush called for respect for one another's opinions, asserting that the "benign principles and measures of Democracy can never triumph while the established usages of the party are wantonly disregarded." Only a robust party structure committed to democratic standards and processes in its choice of leaders and candidates could guarantee success. The *Oregon Statesman* would uphold those principles whenever they were "menaced or assailed" no matter who the attackers might be.[51]

In keeping with Thurston's counsel, Bush focused first on organization at the county level. He sought his comrades' cooperation in his efforts, urging them to write supportive letters for publication in the *Statesman* from their bases around the Territory and to promote Democratic goals in their counties.[52] Bush encouraged a Democratic convention for Marion County and called for others: "We are pleased to witness this movement and hope that before another election shall take place, it will have extended to every county in the Territory, ensuring an undisputable victory, and ranking young Oregon with the party of the People, of Progress and Popular rights." He maintained that no intelligent man could not have a preference as to party. Oregon settlers were "as firmly wedded" to party principles as they had been in the states.[53]

Since the president, Millard Fillmore, was a Whig, Democrats were able to take advantage of the widespread resentment of the president's power to appoint members of the executive and the judiciary in the Territory. As Bush reported in the *Statesman*, a resolution passed at a Democratic meeting in Portland demanded from Congress an amendment to the Organic Act to give settlers the right to elect their own leaders. The

Declaration of Principles issued by the party's June convention reiterated that stand while also calling for free trade "consistent with a necessary revenue," voting rights, and government support for infrastructure. It rejected the establishment of both national and local banks.[54]

Contemporary observers and later scholars have attributed the organization of the Democratic Party and its subsequent control over Oregon's politics and government to Asahel Bush. Whether they characterized that dominance as a "dictatorship" or as "benevolent despotism," they considered Bush essential to its creation. They credited his personality and his management skills as well as his ability as a writer.[55] Theodore Geer, the Republican governor of Oregon from 1899 to 1903, observed in 1912: "Having the *Statesman* at his command, as well as the English language, his meat and drink were found in lampooning and lambasting his political enemies and the last five years of the territorial regime were luminous with the lavish display of his wonderful power as a writer and political dictator."[56]

There was no question as to the opposition that the Democrats faced: the Whig party championed by Dryer and the *Oregonian*. To Bush, the differences between the Democratic and the Whig Parties were evident to any observer, even to recent European immigrants. The Democratic Party, as well as the legislative bodies it controlled, was committed to the interests of the common man. On the other hand, "the continual object of Whig principles and measures, when that party is in power, is simply to benefit *property*, enable favored classes to accumulate it, and in fact, make *man its mere incident*." The Whigs sought to "fertilize the rich man's soil with the sweat of the poor man's brow."[57]

Although Dryer was a Whig and the *Oregonian* had been founded as a Whig newspaper, the burgeoning success of the Democratic Party caused him to distance himself and the *Oregonian* from the Whigs. He repeatedly rejected the introduction of political parties into the local environment, arguing that the national issues the parties pursued were irrelevant to the Territory because of its isolation. He distrusted the motives behind the organization of the Democratic Party: "If the object is to secure the election of such men as have already disgraced the Territory by the party votes and regard for local interests, the people are not to be benefited thereby. If it is to support the rickety and sinking prospects of the *Statesman* press, or to endorse and justify the deplorable course pursued by the Chicopee stripling who conducts it, who has undertaken to teach the people their duty to his party, the country will surely not be benefited by it." Bush's response came quickly: "Prominent among the many reasons that can be urged in favor of organization is the interest it begets among all classes in the affairs of Government; the desire it creates in the minds of all to examine and understand the nature and practical working of our institutions, and the political history of our country. The absence of party organization and the attendant political discussion is soon followed by a lamentable indifference respecting governmental matters and the conduct of public servants."[58]

An issue that immediately took on a highly partisan character was the controversy over the location of the capital of the newly recognized Oregon Territory. Under the provisional government, Oregon City had been the capital, and Joseph Lane, as the first governor of the Territory, upheld that designation. But, late in 1850, in private discussions with his fellow Democratic legislators, Matthew Deady introduced the idea of moving the capital to Salem, then a small Willamette River town of merchants and craftsmen well-equipped to meet the needs of the farming families that lived nearby. Deady's argument for Salem was a sound one. More than half of the Territory's population and most of the land under cultivation were concentrated in Marion, Polk, Linn, Benton, and Lane counties. The Willamette Valley, with its fertile soil and its readily accessible water resources, provided a substantial return on the efforts of its settlers who came, for the most part, from the northern Mississippi, Ohio, and Missouri River Valleys. They were almost all Democrats and shared a distrust of the business class.[59]

Still Deady's proposal was largely a reaction to the fact that Oregon City was dominated by Whigs, especially since the arrival of the Whig governor and Fillmore appointee John Gaines. At its January 1851, session, the assembly passed a bill locating the capital in Salem, the penitentiary in Portland, and the university in Corvallis. On the advice of Amory Holbrook, the Territory's US attorney and another Whig appointee, Gaines immediately rejected the bill as containing more than one object in defiance of legislative rules. Despite his support for the Salem site, Deady himself was uneasy about the legislation from a legal standpoint.

Boise wrote Bush suggesting that Gaines's real motivation was maintaining the value of his Oregon City properties. Bush, however, preferred to characterize the battle as a contest between the Democrats who defended the rights of the people, and the Whig appointees who denied those rights.

Bush called Gaines's action "uncalled for, indelicate and impertinent" and insisted that the Organic Law gave neither the governor nor any other federal appointee veto power over legislative measures. He encouraged the legislature to issue a statement accusing Gaines of seeking "by indirect and extra official acts to usurp the powers placed in the hands of the representatives of the people alone, and the consequence has been that confusion and discord have, like the cloud that precedes the storm, overshadowed our public affairs."[60]

Although, as he wrote Deady, "no one knows better than you that I have no sort of interest in this matter and no preference of localities," Bush pursued the matter so aggressively that it has been identified as "the crucible in which Oregon's Democracy was created."[61] When the issue was referred to the territorial Supreme Court, Bush pressured his fellow Clique member, Judge Orville Pratt, for a decision in favor of Salem. With a measure of sarcasm, Deady reported Pratt's initial response: "Judge Pratt requests me to say to you that he received your communication this evening, and is absorbed in his official duties as to be unable to attend to it at this time." When the decision came, the court split along party lines with the two Whig appointees supporting Gaines and Pratt upholding the legislature's bill. That Pratt's district included Washington, Yamhill, Polk, and Benton Counties may have affected his decision, but he informed a friend that he only went for Salem "from the stern dictates of duty and from no other consideration—It is a turning point with us, and I feel the necessity of facing the responsibility boldly."[62]

In December 1851, the Democratic majority, eighteen of the twenty-two members of the assembly and eight of nine members of the council, met in Salem, while in Oregon City the Whigs met each day for two weeks but then had to adjourn each day, because they were unable to assemble a quorum. With the support of his fellow legislators, Deady wrote a memorial to the Democrat-controlled Congress asking for a decision on the capital matter and rejecting the right of the appointee governor to override the elected legislature. The memorial's criticism of Governor Gaines, President Fillmore, Amory Holbrook, and the Whig party heightened tensions in the Territory. Deady warned Lane against any association with Holbrook: "Between ourselves beware of him. You have seen enough of him to know that he is unscrupulous; you and he can have nothing in common in a political point of view. He did not leave here in very good odor, but with these trashy rumors I shall not trouble you." Holbrook was building a case against Pratt, Deady maintained, because of his desire to replace Pratt as judge.[63]

Deady's memorial defended Pratt for his dissenting vote on the court decision, prompting a reaction from James McBride of Lafayette who wrote Lane of Pratt's unpopularity in his district: "I pray you not to ask for Pratt's reappointment. And I equally pray and entreat you to not be deceived by Deady's *personal, undignified, calumniating* & superlatively lying and slanderous memorial!!" Pratt appealed for support, reminding Lane of his devotion: "You *know* I did not fail *you* in your hour of need. I *am* your friend; I *was* your friend; I can never fail at all times and places to be your *friend*; and, if you fail *me* & those for whom & with whom I act at this juncture, *God only can tell in what [?] & bitterness of spirit I must and will be plunged!*"[64]

For Dryer of the *Oregonian*, the location question and Pratt's decision were evidence of a rising political force determined to draw party lines in the Territory. He decried the attempt to override the court decision and attributed it to the group of men he identified as the "nullifying clique," with Pratt as its leader and Bush as its spokesman. Dryer raised the question: "Is it not time that these party and political hacks and BAR-ROOM BRAWLERS—who have disgraced themselves, the territory, and the people by their miserable policy—should be consigned to a political death, and that good men, and true lovers of the country should hereafter be sent to the legislature?"[65]

While most saw the issue as a matter of Whigs versus Democrats, Gaines presented Lane with a different view: "If you think this is a controversy between whig and democrat please dismiss that thought—It is a fight between two wings of the Democracy—One headed by Pratt, Bush, Parker, King, Waymire, etc., the other by Lancaster, Wait, Ford, McBride, Kinney etc." Pratt too wrote Lane of dissension in the ranks. While the Whigs were united in their opposition to the Democratic Party, they were "backed up & sustained by a very considerable number of (so styled) democrats, who seem determined to rend the Democratic party into a thousand fragments, if necessary, to achieve a nominal triumph and thus prove to the world that it is impossible for them to be mistaken!"[66]

Both the Gaines letter and the Pratt letter suggest that the Clique's control of the Democratic Party was not, at least at the time, as absolute as contemporaries and scholars have assumed. In fact, rebellious Democrats who resented the Clique's command of the party represented a challenge throughout the decade, a challenge that the Clique and its followers could not always overcome. The dissenters were, for the most part, concentrated in the north, particularly in Portland where Democrats such as A. L. Love-joy resisted the control of the Clique.

In April, after Lane's persistent lobbying, the House of Representatives passed a unanimous resolution declaring Salem the capital and providing funding for the construction of a capitol building. For Clique Democrats and their followers, the prospect of serving in Salem was an attractive one both because of their dominance in the area and because of its potential. The region's appeal went beyond the economic. In a speech he made years later, Reuben Boise remembered his March 1852 trip to Salem, then a three-day horseback ride from Portland: "Most of the way was over open prairie, or along dim paths between scattered settlements. . . . The Willamette River flowed clear and beautiful as now, between banks covered with cotton wood, alder, maple, ash and towering fir, undisturbed by crafts of commerce, except the bateau and the Indian canoes. Indians then camped in numbers along the banks of both North and South Mill-creeks."

Through the decade, Salem thrived. In an 1860 letter to his parents, Boise wrote of the town's progress: "Seven fine brick stores were built here last summer. . . . We are by no means out of the world here, mails come regularly twice a week. Steamers are continually plying on the river and there is as much life here as in Hartford or Springfield. There are 4 churches in this place which are very well attended. The town is rapidly building up and all has the air of thrift and progress."[67]

With the capital question apparently resolved, the next step was to move the *Oregon Statesman* to Salem. Benjamin Harding, from his base there, had earlier assured Bush that such a move would prevent the establishment of a Whig paper in the community, and that Salem would "spare nothing to keep you alive." In June 1852, the *Oregon Statesman* was first published in Salem. Writing Deady a few months later, Harding attached the greatest importance to the move as a means to reinforce the Democratic Party's standing in the Territory. Since so much of the party's support came from the farmers and merchants in the Willamette Valley, an additional benefit was easier distribution of the paper: "As the Statesman is the organ of the Democratic party it is important to every Democrat that its influence shall not be lessened."[68] Time would demonstrate that, along with the talents of its members, the Clique and Bush enjoyed a significant advantage because of his base in Salem.

A more amicably settled matter than the capital controversy was the creation of the Washington Territory. The 1850 census indicated that only 1,049 whites lived north of the Columbia River. In August of 1851, a gathering of settlers met at Cowlitz to explore a division of the Territory on the premise that the area north of the Columbia River was too distant to be governed effectively from Oregon City. In November 1852, after the move to Salem, the territorial legislature agreed that "distant government was equally burdensome to both the governors and the governed." Lane was able to speed a bill to establish a new Territory through Congress and it was signed by President Fillmore in March of 1853.[69]

Matthew Deady
(Courtesy Oregon Historical Society,
bb004255)

Lafayette Grover
(Courtesy Oregon Historical Society,
bb004261)

James Nesmith
(Courtesy Oregon Historical Society,
bb008854)

Reuben Boise
(Courtesy Oregon Historical Society,
bb015003)

Fred Waymire
(Courtesy Oregon Historical
Society, bb015396)

Stephen Chadwick
(Courtesy Oregon Historical
Society, bb015009)

Benjamin Harding
(Courtesy Oregon Historical
Society, bb015007)

Delazon Smith
(Courtesy Oregon Historical
Society, bb004595)

William Tichenor
(Courtesy Oregon Historical
Society, bb015006)

Orville Pratt
(Courtesy Oregon Historical
Society, bb015552)

CHAPTER THREE

"I love Oregon as much as a newly married woman loves her husband."

—Joseph Lane

With an eye toward future elections, Lane encouraged Bush's ongoing endeavor to organize the Democratic Party: "I am glad to witness your efforts to get a democratic organization. Lose no time in urging democrats to organize and unite. All local and sectional issues should be dropped. WITH THE ORGANIZATION AND UNION OF DEMOCRACY ALL WILL BE WELL IN OREGON." As Lane no doubt expected, Bush was quick to print an extract from the letter in the *Statesman*.[1] During the first year that the *Statesman* was published, the Whigs stagnated while the Democrats progressed. Democrats dominated both the assembly and the council during the December 1851 to February 1852 legislative session. Clique members Joseph Drew and George Curry were elected to the assembly while Benjamin Harding was chosen chief clerk. Fred Waymire and Matthew Deady served in the council. Throughout the session the Democrats caucused regularly. In January, they met to organize a Territory-wide party with a central committee. James Nesmith was chosen its chairman, despite his own misgivings. He wrote Deady that he had neither the education, the ability, nor the experience to qualify for the position. He suggested that either Deady or Pratt would be better choices.[2] Deady dismissed his doubts. Time would tell that Nesmith was more than up to the job.

In their efforts toward organization, the Democrats enjoyed a considerable advantage over the Whigs. A large majority of the settlers had come to the Territory to farm and settled in the Willamette Valley on land they received through the Oregon Donation Land Act. They brought with them the values of the Democratic Party with its emphasis on rural life and its suspicions of those who chose to pursue urban endeavors. Their views were in part a reflection of the fact that many were natives of the Democratic states of Kentucky, Tennessee, and Missouri and the southern parts of Indiana, Ohio, and Illinois.[3] The pro-Democratic sentiment would be reinforced by the infrastructure the Clique managed to put in place in the various counties. On the other hand, the Whig opposition lacked any discernible Territory-wide identity let alone any sort of party structure.

The *Oregon Statesman* played an essential role in the development of the Democratic Party. Before the launch of the *Statesman,* the Territory had seen four other newspapers: the *Oregon Spectator* founded in 1846; the short-lived *Free Press* in 1848; the *Milwaukie Western Star,* later to become the *Portland Weekly Times,* in 1850; and the *Oregonian* in 1850. At its founding, the *Spectator* had appeared twice a month but it soon came out each week as did the others. Advertising was the main source of revenue and filled a good portion of each paper's four pages. Like newspapers around the country, the Oregon press was exempt from taxation by the federal government, which also subsidized postal rates, significant components of the newspapers' budgets. The Territory's newspapers were less purveyors of news than of opinion and marketing. Settlers had little free time and little interest in national events since the month it took to get news from the East to Oregon meant that reports lacked immediacy. With no staff of reporters, territorial newspapers devoted scant attention even to local news. Articles on science and the arts lifted from eastern papers attracted readers living with a shortage of other reading material. Submissions of commentary from the public were encouraged.

The *Oregon Statesman* quickly became the leading newspaper in the Territory, an achievement that must be attributed to its editor. Bush's intelligence, skill as a writer, energetic pursuit of significant issues, and often sarcastic humor attracted a substantial readership, even among those who disagreed with his politics. As the organ of the Democratic Party, the *Statesman* promoted the party's principles, its candidates, and their careers. Bush's capacity for leadership and for invective led one contemporary historian to conclude that "he was the most influential and feared of any man in the Territory."[4]

Before long, the paper outpaced the competition in circulation and advertising revenue while its principal rival, the *Oregonian*, was handicapped by the fact that Thomas Dryer was a poor businessman whose management of his paper was haphazard at best. The *Statesman*'s financial wellbeing was heightened by the benefits derived from Bush's position as the Oregon Territory's public printer responsible for the printing of legislation and other government documents. That the *Statesman* and its printing press were located in the capital city, whether Oregon City, Salem, or, briefly, Corvallis, made Bush's appointment appropriate and he would hold the office until 1862 despite occasional challenges.

Although it provided some coverage of the Territory's business and commercial enterprises, from its inception the *Statesman* focused more on politics than did the other newspapers.[5] No Whig was safe from Bush's pen, least of all President Millard Fillmore who sent an "interminably long and tediously uninteresting" message for publication. Bush was "unwilling to incur the displeasure of our readers by giving place to it."[6]

The symbiotic relationship between the *Statesman* and the Democratic Party was not lost on the opposition, nor was the role of the Clique in both. Early in 1852 the *Oregonian* introduced a five-part satirical drama aimed at the Clique: "The plot is laid in Oregon, and of recent date. The characters will readily be recognized by those who are 'posted up' on recent events." Judgment as to the relevance of the "poem" was left to its readers.[7] The author was William Lysander Adams who had come to the Oregon Territory in 1848. Adams had attended Knox College in his home state of Illinois but then became closely involved with the Disciples of Christ Church and moved to Virginia to enroll in the church's new Bethany College, perhaps intending to become a minister. In Oregon, he taught school briefly, then went to California during the gold rush. After some measure of success in the mines, he returned to Oregon and took up farming in Yamhill County. While his farm was the main source of his income, he began writing articles and opinion pieces for the *Oregonian* in 1851.

The title of Adams's satire, "Treason, Stratagems and Spoils," came from a line in act 5 of *The Merchant of Venice*, and the pen name he assumed, "Breakspear," was an obvious play on Shakespeare's name. "Treason . . ." appeared in the *Oregonian* as a series on February 7, 14, and 21 and on March 6 and 13, 1852. It was reprinted as a pamphlet in April 1852 and enjoyed wide readership. Its characters were thinly disguised political figures, including Bush, Deady, Nesmith, Pratt, and Waymire. While very humorous, "Treason . . ." was also an astute examination of the political scene.

Particularly insightful was its portrayal of Orville Pratt and his ambitions. Throughout the capital controversy, Bush in the *Statesman* was
effusive in praise of Pratt. But Dryer perceived a change of heart and wrote
in the *Oregonian* on March 27: "A few weeks ago the *Durham democratic
organ* was filled with songs of praise for its great chief, O. C. Pratt. . . . But
now, alas, no word of praise is chanted to the great sanctifier of Prattocracy.
Why is this?"[8] Dryer's appraisal was correct. Already some members of the
Clique had their misgivings as when Deady wrote Nesmith of his uneasi-
ness about Pratt and his limitations but cautioned, "I have spoken very
frankly to you about Pratt in this letter. Of course it will remain between
ourselves." Bush on the other hand continued for some time to support
Pratt on party grounds and in light of his assistance during the capital controversy: "Whatever else may be said of Pratt, he is a sound Democrat and
will do what he can consistently to aid the party."[9]

Among its various aspersions, the satire portrayed a conspiracy
between the "Judge" [Pratt] and the Mormon leader Brigham Young to
transform the Oregon Territory into a polygamous Mormon republic. The
Church of Jesus Christ of Latter-Day Saints had been a controversial presence in Illinois during Adams's youth. In Oregon, widespread suspicions
about the intentions of the Church and its adherents made the allegation
a sensitive one. When the opposition tried to make a connection between
Democrats, specifically the *Statesman,* and the Mormons, Bush wrote
Deady that he grasped the dangerous potential of such an accusation and
assured him, "When Dryer alludes to it again, I'll show him up on the
subject."[10] He soon had the opportunity. Dryer wrote that "the *Statesman*
has a long header this week (probably written by Judge Pratt) which savors
strongly of Mormonism." Bush defended the *Statesman* article: "It savors of
religious toleration simply. If that is Mormonism, then it 'savors' of Mormonism. If not, not." Dryer did not surrender but instead advised Bush "to
take something warm and go to bed" so that he could devise "some new
plan for drawing party lines in Oregon, and to the end that the Statesman
may linger a little longer, and continue its labors in paving the way for the
final ushering in of Brigham Young rule—independent Mormonism."[11]

Although "Treason . . . " attracted a good deal of attention, the Clique
took it in stride. Adams had adopted Dryer's "Chicopee" as Bush's pseudonym, a nickname that came to be widely used among Bush's friends as
well as his enemies. The satire marked a highpoint of the "Oregon Style" of

journalism and the ridicule and derision between editors that was its defining characteristic. Later, when Adams founded the *Oregon Argus,* Bush took to referring to him as "Parson Billy of the Airgoose." Adams countered by regularly suggesting that Bush took his pay in product for the *Statesman* advertisements of Dr. Czapky's tonic for the restoration of lost manhood. Nor was Dryer immune from Bush's sarcasm. After he wrote in support of the Maine Law temperance movement, despite his well-known proclivity for alcohol, Bush gave him the name "Toddy Jep." Deady, too, did not miss an opportunity to deride the editor of the *Oregonian.* When he heard that Dryer was complaining about the rising price of whisky, Deady wrote Bush, "I hope the change in the market has not found him with short rations. If so, that accounts for his chagrin. The damned old sot! Where I have drank a pint he has drank his gallons."[12]

The immediate challenge for the Clique was the Summer 1852 legislative election. In a letter in which he modestly took credit for the organization of the Democratic Party, Curry assured Lane that the Democrats were "backed by at least three fourths of the popular vote, on the other side are the hungry, haughty and dishonored batch of Whig federal officers."[13] Deady was also optimistic, as he wrote Boise, "I don't think the whigs are manifesting so much zeal as formerly. I believe they are confident of success and have grown indolent."[14] Bush, however, was not so sanguine. He wrote Deady that the Democrats would lose Washington County "for want of proper candidates." Five days later, he described a Clackamas County meeting where both Democrats and Whigs voted unanimously against "drawing party lines."[15] Bush's concerns proved to be well-founded; when the election came, men in Clackamas and Washington Counties voted in favor of Whigs and the rebellious Democrats the Clique labeled the Softs. Despite those victories, the Whigs lost a substantial number of seats in the other counties. Their defeat in the 1852 election inspired them to organize their party. But the effort was half-hearted and did not, in the end, result in Whig victories in subsequent elections.

On the other hand, the election indicated that the dominance of the Clique over the Democratic Party was by no means secure. For the most part, the renegades came from the northern part of the Territory and included such prominent Portlanders as James Kelly, William Farrar, and A. L. Lovejoy. The Softs resisted the leadership of the Clique and therefore were the focus of ongoing condemnation by Bush and his fellows. Aaron

Wait, an anti-Clique Democrat based in Oregon City, wrote Lane, "Our election is over and you would suppose from the statements of the Statesman that a Democratic organization was complete throughout the Territory, and that the Democratic party had swept the whole southern county. Pratt, Bush, & Co. know how to raise a storm, but they seem as incapable of governing it as the merest children."[16]

In his own report to Lane, however, George Curry dismissed Wait and his ally Lot Whitcomb: "Perdition take *such democrats* as Wait and Whitcomb! The latter inflated individual (and isn't he the greatest specimen of a walking gasometer that you ever saw?), thanks to the sensible yeomanry of the upper Molalla, got but five votes at the precinct, out of a poll of fifty."[17] Although he made a poor showing in that particular precinct, Whitcomb nevertheless won a seat in the legislature. But, despite Whitcomb's election and that of other dissenters, the Clique dominated the legislative session. Members of the council elected Deady as their president and the members of the assembly chose Harding as Speaker when the legislature met.

The resentment widely felt toward Governor Gaines was a significant factor in the Democratic victory. Around the Territory, Whigs had recognized that anger and were reluctant to declare for the party. Before the election, Chadwick had reported to Bush that Applegate, who "was, is and will die a whig," nevertheless distanced himself from the Whig administration and its appointments "to save the Whig party."[18] After the election, Bush used the *Statesman* to mount ongoing attacks against Gaines as well as other Fillmore appointees. In a letter to Lane, Lovejoy described Gaines's response:

> The old Governor the other day got so mad at Bush that he could
> not stand it any longer so he availed himself of an opportunity to
> kick up a row in the streets with Bush and cane him but as Bush
> says he only done as he did once before on a more public occasion,
> surrendered or in other words backed out and only made himself
> appear the more ridiculous which is entirely unnecessary for
> God knows he is low enough in the estimation of the community
> without any additional foolishness.[19]

Nesmith wrote Lane of another incident that occurred when Gaines was outraged by some anonymous *Statesman* articles that Nesmith had in fact written. "His Excellency took exception to some cool facts contained in my productions and swore that he would cowhide the author and accordingly called upon Bush for his name. Bush as a matter of course refused to give it, whereupon the Gov. accused him of writing the articles and swore that he should take the cowhiding, and drew a cowhide from under his coat."

Bush drew his revolver and Gaines backed off. Not wanting to create more difficulty for Bush, Nesmith told him to tell Gaines that he was the author. The matter was dropped and Nesmith observed, "I suppose that His Excellency came to the conclusion that I was too obscure an individual for him to waste his valuable time in cowhiding."[20]

When the assembly convened, Democrats quickly took advantage of the growing bitterness toward Gaines. Gaines sent a pro forma message to which the legislative majority responded by passing a resolution condemning his presumption that he had any right to address the body in any manner. From Portland, Dryer denounced this and nearly all other actions of the session as the maneuvers of the Clique to exert its control. Despite his earlier observation that the Clique was separating itself from Pratt, he charged that "Democracy" meant nothing more than "Prattocracy."[21]

An immediate task of the territorial legislature was the formation of a commission to draft a new code of law. Wanting the Clique to have a voice in the process, Bush encouraged Boise to seek an appointment to the commission. Boise, however, required some reassurance. Although he was confident that he would be supported in the council, he was concerned about the assembly. He expected opposition, particularly from the Portland representative Benjamin Stark, and feared that he would not get any votes at all. He sought Bush's counsel.[22] In the end, Bush was able to convince Boise to allow his nomination. Despite his fears, the legislature approved his appointment to the three-member commission. His fellow commissioners were Daniel Bigelow from Olympia, a significant figure in the soon-to-be Washington Territory, and James K. Kelly, a Portland "Soft" and ally of A. L. Lovejoy. The commission completed its work within a few days and the new code was quickly approved by the legislature.

While attention had been focused on the assembly election, speculation regarding the approaching delegate election was rampant even though the election was more than a year away. Lane's ambitions, never modest, were raised during an 1851 visit with his family in Indiana where his wife and eight of his children had lived without him for three years. Lane's fame as a military leader and his years of service in the Indiana legislature made the trip a great success. Local politicians even talked of nominating him for the presidency at the approaching Democratic convention. Lane humbly replied that he was not a candidate but, if chosen by the convention, he would of course do his best. He wrote Bush of the warmth of his reception but added the reassurance he thought necessary: "The people, though as clever as any in the world, don't look healthy as they do in Oregon; nor is the country like Oregon. I long to be there. I would not give up my claim in Oregon for twenty miles on the banks of the Ohio, and be compelled to remain in this country. Oregon is my country—my home." Bush printed the key portions of his letter in the *Statesman*.[23]

Lane's major contribution during the 1852 congressional session was the passage of the House resolution locating the capital in Salem and the bill extending the Donation Land Law. His other efforts on behalf of the Territory and its settlers included filing objections to the actions of federal officers, seeking compensation for the expenses of the American Indian Wars, and building support for the improvement of navigation on the Willamette River along with other infrastructure projects. He urged Deady to "bear in mind that I succeeded in geting more bills through the House for Oregon than has been got through for any Territory at any one session. Many of them did not pass the Senate for want of time but will pass the coming session." When Congress reconvened he would "be at my post, promptly and faithfully doing my duty, nothing shall be left undone that I can do for the promotion of the interest of Oregon."[24]

In the meantime, Lane had taken to sending mixed messages about his own plans. In an earlier letter to Deady, he urged that the party focus on the next delegate election but added that "I shall not be a candidate for reelection for the reason first that I don't want the office and second because I shall at the close of this Congress take my family overland to Oregon, there to spend the balance of my days in peace and quiet, except holding myself ready to defend our frontiers against Indian depredations." Only a month later, he responded to Bush's report that some were predicting that he would not be reelected delegate in the 1853 election: "I have no fears, if you will only give me a chance to see the people, at all events I am a candidate for nomination, and it is the only occasion that perhaps may occur in my life when I shall be anxious for Election, and hope that democrats will not abandon me at the coming nomination. . . . One more time and I am if my friends wish it out of the way." Perhaps because he was being mentioned as an alternative to Lane for delegate, Deady wrote to encourage him to even higher aspirations. Having read a laudatory biography of Lane that was circulating, he urged him to send more copies to the Territory and added, "I believe you will be President yet!"[25]

In his interest or their own, some cautioned Lane not to depend on the Clique. T'Vault warned him that his other Democratic correspondents, including Deady, Pratt, and Bush, shaped their reports to benefit themselves. T'Vault complained that the Democrats' Central Committee had abandoned party principles and failed to recruit appropriate candidates for the coming legislative elections. He warned that "it is the intention of your professed Democratic friends to bring about your political defeat in Oregon." Such allegations only made Lane work harder to ensure the loyalty of the Clique. When Gaines confronted Nesmith about his article in the *Statesman*, Lane declared that Nesmith's quarrel was *his* quarrel.

Lane's son Nat was not enthusiastic about his candidacy but reported the Democrats' belief that he was the only one who could beat "the whigs, softs and no party tickets." Nat concluded that "if nothing else will do you will have to run" and urged Lane to get back to Oregon as quickly as possible. While he was not critical of the Clique specifically, Nat warned that "the Oregon democrats are the weakest brethren I ever knew. The greater portion are only democrats when that party is in power."[26]

Lane continued to portray himself as a reluctant candidate, writing Bush in October: "You are aware that I do not wish it, but am willing and always will be to promptly comply with the wishes of the Democratic party, and obey their orders or requisitions." And to Deady the next day: "Many friends have written me relative to the next delegateship. I have said to them all that I do not wish it, but if the people wish it, let it be so, in that event I will be in Oregon in April next. There must be no split in our ranks. I am for any democrat who may be selected by the democratic party. "[27]

Whether because of Lane's professed lack of enthusiasm or their own competing aspirations, others began to explore the possibility of running for delegate. Certainly they did not want to surrender the office to the Whigs. Nesmith and Harding encouraged Deady to consider a campaign.[28] Curry reported to Lane that Deady wanted the office but would not, in his opinion, be a good candidate. As to the Whig opposition, Curry was reassuring: "I suppose you know by this time that the few whigs among us most cordially hate you, and are doing whatever they can to cast blemish on your name. No doubt they will be united to a man at the June election and have their best man out—to be whipped like thunder I hope."[29] Another prospective candidate was Orville Pratt. Although President Franklin Pierce had appointed him chief justice of the Territory's Supreme Court, the Senate did not confirm him due to the efforts of Illinois senator Stephen A. Douglas. Previously Pratt's supporter, Douglas had changed his mind after accusations that Pratt had allied himself with the British Hudson's Bay Company. Humiliated by his rejection, Pratt saw being elected delegate as the way to redeem himself.[30]

With the election approaching, Lane again faced charges that he was befriending Dryer. He assured Deady that Dryer "was deceived in me, and I was not in him, he was weak enough to believe that by making a show and noise in my favor that he and his whig friends could use me. . . . The first time I seen him I could read him like a book." Using very similar language, he also denied the charge to Bush, adding "I love Oregon as much as a new married woman loves her husband." But he cautioned, "This letter is not for publication."[31]

The election to the presidency of the Democrat Franklin Pierce, whom Lane referred to as "my old friend Frank," raised the possibility in some minds that Lane would be named governor of the Territory. Curry urged him to accept the anticipated appointment and "come as quick as kind heaven will let you by the shortest route, that we may be relieved of our odious rulers as soon as possible. If you will not be our moral Hercules and haste to the clearing of the Augean stables, in God's name, who will?" Bush added his encouragement: "Your own appointment will give entire satisfaction to the Democracy of the Territory and no one would be more pleased than your humble servant."[32] Two days later, Bush wrote Lane that the Portland Democrat A. L. Lovejoy, had requested his endorsement for the governor's office. Bush enclosed a copy of his "purposely ambiguous" letter of recommendation. While he, at least at the time, had a cordial relationship with Lovejoy and would "cheerfully recommend him for any place he was competent to fill," his appointment as governor would weaken the Democratic Party. "The opposition would laugh at and ridicule him and you are aware that he is open to that species of attack." Bush expected Lane to intervene with the president and prevent the selection of Lovejoy for the post.[33]

To a letter from Lane concerned about his chances in the delegate election, Bush answered that the perception that he was not interested in running again had raised the names of other possible candidates including Matthew Deady. "Don't misunderstand me, that anybody would object to you but many have got their minds fixed on others, and some are pledged to go for the nominations of particular persons." Bush added that it was imperative that he come to Oregon to campaign as soon as possible. Deady himself wrote Lane that friends were encouraging him to enter the race "but with me the great question is unanimity and success." While he could not offend his friends by supporting Lane's nomination at the Democratic convention, if Lane were nominated by the convention, he would support him.[34] Still Lane was coy about his plans and wrote Nesmith that, while he did not wish another term as delegate, he would run if it proved necessary for the wellbeing of the party and the Territory. Nesmith quoted Lane's remark in a letter to Deady to their mutual amusement.[35]

Writing Lane about the challenges of the current session of the territorial legislature, an observer explained, "The whole upshot of the matter consists in the fact that about two thirds of the members want to run for Delegate to Congress at the next election, and every man is trying to beat his neighbor." Still, "Pratt, Deady, Lovejoy, Parker & all will have to stand back if Old Joe wants to come in."[36] Deady did not give up easily, reporting to Bush that many young Whigs "say publicly that they will vote for me for delegate against any other man." While Bush assured Deady that he would do his best for him, he implored him not to run: "I believe your defeat in the convention is certain, and to run against Lane and be beaten would injure you."[37] Accepting Bush's assessment of his chances, Deady did little further to procure the nomination, although he did not prevent his friends from putting his name forward.

Pratt, on the other hand, continued to campaign. Lane was concerned about Pratt's candidacy but reassured by the strong endorsement Bush printed in the *Statesman*. While some of the Clique remained conflicted, Delazon Smith applauded Bush's statement: "Knowing that you have ever battled manfully for the right—ever faithfully maintained the integrity of the noble motto at the head of your paper—'No favor sways us; no fear shall awe' I could not think that your sense of justice towards your absent friend Lane . . . would allow you to remain silent. Thank God I have not been disappointed!!"[38]

As anticipated, President Pierce removed Gaines from the governorship, a decision many attributed to the efforts of Asahel Bush and the
Clique. Also as expected, President Pierce did appoint Lane governor,
which no doubt gave him a good deal of satisfaction since he had been
forced out of the position by President Fillmore in 1850. He returned to
Oregon but resigned after three days in office to enter the delegate race. It
has been suggested that he felt that his chances for the presidential nomination would be better if he were in Washington as delegate rather than in
Oregon as governor.[39] To no one's surprise, except perhaps that of Orville
Pratt, the Democratic convention named Lane its candidate for delegate by
an overwhelming vote.

Alonso Skinner, the first judge of the circuit court established by
the provisional government in 1846, was Lane's opponent in the 1853
general election. When Congress recognized the Oregon Territory in
1848, Pratt had been selected to replace him in the court. Skinner subsequently served as prosecutor in a case of Native Americans accused
of killing some settlers. More recently he had represented the territorial government in a series of negotiations with different tribes. Skinner
was a Whig but distanced himself from the party which, given its lack
of organization, could be of little help to him. The fact that a Democrat,
rather than a Whig, was president of the United States made Skinner's
campaign against Lane that much more difficult. Thanks to President
Pierce, all the significant government positions in the Territory were held
by Democrats, a fact that most Oregonians attributed to Lane's influence.
The Clique, in particular, benefited from those appointments and from
other patronage opportunities. Once Lane was nominated by the Democratic convention, the Clique made every effort to secure his victory in
the general election.

Lane was not without his detractors. From his base in Linn County,
Delazon Smith reported that he was hearing Lane denounced as "immoral,
destitute of talents, as no orator, as being coarse, vulgar and dissipated,
etc., etc." But Lane was as effective as ever on the campaign trail. At an
Albany debate with Skinner, Lane pointed to his influence in Congress
and the White House and the benefits reaped by Oregon as a result of that
influence. According to Smith, by the time the meeting ended "there was
little more of Skinner left than his rosy cheek and venerable beard! The six
feet and well proportioned old general was unscathed."[40]

So confident was Bush that he wrote Deady that he would bet five hundred dollars that Lane would beat Skinner by a thousand votes. Lane's margin of victory was even more comfortable than Bush had anticipated, 4516 votes to Skinner's 2951.[41] The Democratic Party triumphed in other races around the country much to Lane's satisfaction as he wrote to Nesmith from Washington: "Now my Dear friend, democratic principles are the true principles of our Governt and cannot be compromised, nor should local questions and strifes be permitted to interfere. . . . Our principles are as well worth maintaining and contending for in Oregon as in the States."[42] In the *Statesman*, Bush reported that no less an authority than Horace Greeley had concluded that the Whig party was dead in the States, "But like all animals of the reptile order, it dies in the extremities last; and him of the Sewer [Dryer] is the last agonizing knot in the tail."[43]

Before long, however, a new controversy surfaced in one of the stranger episodes of the territorial period. The actual document appointing Deady to the Territory's Supreme Court named "Mordecai Deady" rather than "Matthew Deady," which made the appointment invalid. The appointment of Obadiah McFadden followed. Deady's friends were outraged and attributed the mistake to the machinations of the federal officers with whom Deady had clashed over the years. Several suspected the Whig United States Attorney Amory Holbrook of being responsible for the error. Many questioned how such a thing could have happened under the Democratic president Pierce. In the *Statesman* Bush wrote: "We do not suppose these vile assaults annoy Judge Deady; and we are aware that they cannot injure him where he is known, and where the character and motives of his assailants are known. He can well afford to condemn and despise the whole yelping batch, who honor him with their impotent hatred and spleen."[44]

When McFadden arrived in Oregon to take over the judicial position, Nesmith reassured Deady that he did not have to repay Nesmith's loan that had enabled him to buy his land claim near Winchester. If it would help, he would lend him more. Nesmith wrote Lane that "no time or pains should be spared to repair the wrong."[45] Harding too protested to Lane: "Nothing of a political nature has ever given me so much pain. I have always regarded Deady as a man of much more than ordinary talent and integrity. And since he has been upon the bench I have formed the most favorable opinion of his legal learning. . . . I am certain that the President has been deceived by the grossest falsehood." When Dryer attacked him in the *Oregonian*,

Deady responded with an angry letter for publication in the *Statesman*. But Nesmith was a voice of caution and convinced Bush not to print the letter, explaining to Deady that "I didn't believe it good policy or taste to let Toddy know that he gave you the least annoyance."[46]

Bush unleashed a torrent of attacks on McFadden in the *Statesman* that triggered an angry response from John Waterman, the editor of the *Portland Weekly Times*, a Democrat but not Clique-controlled newspaper. While he supported Deady, he wrote Lane that he opposed blaming McFadden for the blunder. He condemned Bush for his assault on McFadden, maintaining that "Bush is bound to ruin the Democratic Party of Oregon or rule it."[47] The vehemence of Bush's backing sometimes embarrassed Deady. He told Nesmith of the laudatory resolution Bush introduced on Deady's behalf when the Democratic convention met. "And what was worse after it had passed took me to one side and read it to me. I have no distinct recollection of the phraseology or the sentiment of the resolution (as I tried to shut my ears) but my impression is that you'll find it a piece of sublime balderdash."[48]

Deady had support outside the Clique. Cyrus Olney, already a justice on the territorial Supreme Court, weighed in, telling Lane confidentially: "Judge McFadden cannot sustain himself. He has not the clearness of intellect, nor the legal knowledge, nor the habits of studious application, necessary to sustain a judge on this coast." McFadden, in Olney's opinion, fell "immeasurably below Judge Deady." The newly appointed governor, John W. Davis, urged Lane to settle the issue "for as matters now stand the democratic party is greatly at loggerheads and unless harmony can be restored defeat is inevitable in the Territory."[49]

To some extent, the controversy over the "Mordecai" incident reflected the tensions within the Democratic Party and the challenges to Clique dominance. His own disappointment notwithstanding, Deady perceived a positive outcome for the party: "It will be the means sooner or later of breaking up this cursed coalition that the party formed last spring with a set of Softs and nondescripts who whatever they may be in name and profession are by nature and habit opposed to the principles, practices and usages of the Dem. Party."[50] While his colleagues were pressuring Lane to get him reinstated, Deady was skeptical of Lane and his supposed outrage over the name error and the McFadden appointment. He became convinced that Lane had in fact been instrumental in the Mordecai/Matthew error: "Lane has been cognizant of the treatment that I have received at the hands of the administration from the blunder in the name to the removal that he has procured it to be done, or purposely assented to it." Deady had come to the conclusion that Lane's victory in the delegate election was "a misfortune to the party from which it will not soon recover." From the end of his campaign until he returned to Washington, Lane in Deady's judgment had "done more to strengthen the hands of the Softs and Whigs than anything that has happened since they have had a name."[51] The Mordecai affair reinforced Deady's aversion to Lane, an opinion that put him at odds with Bush and other Clique members.

To Nesmith, Lane denied charges that he was doing nothing to secure Deady's restoration: "I am and have been from the first greatly pained at the removal of Deady and if it had been possible would have had him put right before now, it shall be done." Thus far, however, he had not been able to determine the circumstances that led to the error or where to place the blame. Once he had the full picture, he would meet with the appropriate officials including President Pierce to address the situation.[52] Whether or not it was because of Lane's efforts, Deady was reappointed to the court while McFadden was reassigned to the Washington Territory court. Nesmith, somewhat disingenuously, assured Lane that Deady had never doubted his sincerity and that since Deady's reappointment, "I think that you never stood fairer with the people of Oregon than at the present moment." Deady himself wrote Lane assuring him that he had never questioned his commitment: "Your efforts to have me restored to the position from which I was removed have been properly appreciated by me, and if any one at any time was disposed to doubt their sincerity I think the result has satisfied them."[53]

The relationship between the Clique and Lane became increasingly complex. Notwithstanding his frequently sarcastic exchanges about Lane with Deady, Nesmith often lent Lane money although he also complained about Nat Lane's failure to pay a debt owed him.[54] At Lane's request, Nesmith looked after his sons John and Lafayette who remained in the Territory and attended the Oregon Institute in Salem. Lane sent money to cover expenses and asked that Nesmith "encourage John & Lafayette to give their whole attention to hard and faithful study, that without education they must be miserable and with it they may be happy & useful."[55] Despite, or perhaps because of, his difficulties with other members of the

Clique, Lane was particularly solicitous of Bush. Some misunderstanding between the two led Lane to write that he had not "at any time or under any circumstances felt aggrieved or in the slightest displeased" with Bush. Pointing to Bush's "able and manly support of Democratic principles," he assured him that his confidence in Bush "as a gentleman, friend, and editor remains unshaken and I have not the slightest reason to believe I shall ever have good reason to regret the friendship and confidence I entertain in and for you."[56] In 1854, Bush made an extended trip to the United States, leaving the *Statesman* in the hands of Lafayette Grover. While in the East, he spent some time in Washington, DC. Through his own observations and his encounters with other officials, Bush came away impressed with Lane and the job he was doing there. When Bush returned to Salem and resumed his management of the paper, Lane wrote from Washington, "I am sure that your return will be hailed with joy by the entire democracy of Oregon, and your paper read with renewed interest."[57]

CHAPTER FOUR

"The poorest hacknied rotten hearted set of office seeking sons of bitches."

—Nathaniel Lane

With a Democratic president in office, the fortunes of the Clique advanced. Having some level of influence over federal appointments of whatever rank was a significant factor of its power. Aside from the problematic Deady appointment, Lane's "old friend Frank" in 1853 also named Benjamin Harding US district attorney, George Curry secretary of the Territory, and James Nesmith US marshal. While the Clique welcomed those appointments, the Pierce presidency raised expectations that Lane was not always able to satisfy. The Clique's Fred Waymire accused Lane of ignoring his letters while answering others. He allowed that "every man has a right to make pets of whomsoever he pleases." Some who opposed Lane's nomination had received posts or public favors, but Waymire had not, even though "I put you in nomination before the Territorial convention, and through my management you was elected on the first ballot. If this is the *sin* for which I am to be discarded by you!!! *I ask pardon!*"[1]

Lane must have particularly dreaded the frequent letters from Orville Pratt. He often aroused Pratt's ire by failing to respond. Noting that some of his letters were written as a friend and others as a constituent, Pratt wrote angrily, "The *former*, I am of course compelled, in the absence of all replies, to cease writing, but the *latter* will be continued whether the suggestions in them are heeded or not." Hearing from Lane that he saw no way that the Senate's refusal to confirm him as chief justice of the territorial Supreme Court could be reversed, Pratt described himself as left "without a hope for the future and almost broken hearted." A month later he added: "I cannot ask you to say or do more on my account. It is out of your power to aid me without injuring yourself. Leave me, therefore, alone."[2]

When Lane attempted to placate him with a long and highly complimentary letter, Pratt answered to the effect that all of Lane's compliments were certainly true and expressed his gratitude. On the other hand, he added: "My own view of your worth, services there and elsewhere to the country and to the Democratic party, I have already, and a long time ago, given you ample proof in unmistakable ways to a discerning man like yourself, and hence need no repetition at this time or place."[3]

Predictably, Democrats outside the Clique often resented whatever advantage the Clique may have had and sought to undermine its influence to their own benefit. In promoting himself for a post, John Waterman, the Portland Democrat and editor of the *Weekly Times,* warned Lane, "Many of those whom are indebted to you for place and profit are at work secretly against your nomination."[4]

While the Clique and most Oregon Democrats applauded the president's appointments of Oregonians to positions in the Territory, they did not welcome his choice for governor, John Davis, a Democrat but an outsider. Their antagonism caused Davis to resign in frustration after only nine months in office. In his letter of resignation, Davis recalled an old adage, "It is manly to differ but childish to quarrel because we differ."[5] Resentment over presidential appointments was not new. In 1851, the recently established *Oregon Statesman* reported that a political gathering in Portland had adopted a resolution affirming that many "respectable" Oregonians were well qualified to fill territorial positions.[6] By 1854, the argument that power should be centered in the people of the Territory, not concentrated in the hands of federal officers regardless of their party affiliation, had become routine. Although himself one of the president's appointees, Nesmith even wrote Deady that Pierce's election had in fact hurt the Democratic Party in Oregon, because it had distracted some Democrats from the party's campaign for the election, rather than the presidential appointment, of officeholders in the Territory.[7]

With Davis's resignation, George Curry, then secretary of state, stepped in as interim governor. No doubt at Lane's urging, President Pierce confirmed Curry as governor and appointed Benjamin Harding to succeed him as secretary of state. In contrast to the experience of Gaines and Davis, Curry's appointment was embraced because he was an Oregonian,

After the territorial capitol building burned down in 1857, the legislature met in the Holman building in Salem until 1876. (Courtesy Oregon Historical Society, bb015010)

a Democrat, and a member of the Clique. Curry rose to the expectations of his fellows and held the office of governor until Oregon became a state. He was careful to respect the sentiments of the Territory's Democrats. Remembering the outrage that arose when Governor Gaines had the presumption to address the territorial legislature, Curry awaited an invitation. When it came, he responded with a speech affirming the Territory's voters' right to choose their governor and the other officials of the executive branch.

In light of Lane's role in his appointment, Curry became an even more ardent advocate for the delegate and his aspirations, rarely missing an opportunity to promote him. In 1856, when the federal government failed to provide protection from Native American hostilities in the Rogue River region, the settlers in the area were forced to go to war on their own. Curry traveled to Washington to secure compensation for the expenses of the war. Upon his return, he was highly complimentary of Lane's endeavors. "The delegate of the Territory was at his post, faithful and watchful; and it affords me pleasure to be able to bear personal testimony of his worth, ability and efficiency." Because of Lane's "unflagging zeal and indefatigable industry," Congress had directed the secretary of war to appoint a commission to address the expenses issue.[8]

With Curry as governor and Democrats in control of the legislature, the Clique might have been able to relax, secure in their status as the leading political force in the Territory. Instead a new challenge arose. The American party usually referred to as the "Know Nothings," had become a force back in the United States. Its aim was to keep control of the country in the hands of native-born citizens through the restriction of immigration and the denial to immigrants of the right to vote, hold office, or acquire public land. The party grew out of increasing resentment of foreign immigrants, especially the Irish and the Germans, who came to the United States in substantial numbers during the 1840s and 1850s. In a time of Protestant revival, the American party's fervor was particularly directed at Roman Catholic immigrants, claiming they could not be loyal Americans since they were actually the subjects of the Vatican. The Know Nothings established lodges, called "wigwams," and operated through clandestine meetings complete with passwords, oaths, and secret handshakes. Members maintained that they "knew nothing" of the party's activities, giving it the widely used nickname. Such was sentiment against immigrants that, by 1855, the American party was able to dominate political life in several states, including Massachusetts, Rhode Island, Connecticut, New Hampshire, Maryland, and Kentucky, and to elect their candidates to public office in many others.[9] When the Know Nothings first surfaced in the Oregon Territory, the party was embraced by some members of the old Mission Party still convinced that the Native American massacre of the Whitman missionaries in 1847 was inspired by Catholic priests.

The Know Nothing wigwams around the Territory were controlled by the Grand Wigwam whose constitution proclaimed:

> We believe in choosing and electing those men, for all offices of Honor, Profit or Trust, whom we know to have been born upon American soil, who have been brought up in politics purely American, and who understand those principles as they were understood by our Revolutionary sires. We will not believe that they ever expected, or intended that the patronage of our Local,

State, or General governments were to be placed in the hands
of foreigners, or that foreign influence should dictate in the
administration of American justice or assist in the framing of
American Laws. God forbid it! Let us also forbid it, and in thunder
tones protest against all such interference coming from what
quarter it may, either from Emperors, Kings or Princes.[10]

While some Oregonians were attracted to the antiforeign sentiment,
members of the Clique did not share their attitude. Well before the emer-
gence of the Know Nothings, Bush, in the *Statesman*, had written favorably
of immigrants and of their potential after they came to the United States
since they were provided with many benefits including fertile lands, river,
canal and railroad transportation, public schools, and freedom of worship. Once they arrived, they learned that "the idle, slovenly, and unthrifty
habits, acquired in Europe will not answer with us" with the result that
immigrants progressed both physically and mentally, proving that "there
is a special Providence in the great experiment, exhibited by our country
and her institutions for the welfare of the human race." He dismissed the
American party as "the most ridiculous piece of bigotry, intolerance and
stupidity grown persons were ever engaged in" and compared its premises
to the Alien and Sedition Acts, the series of four federal laws passed in
1798 that were initially directed at foreigners and, in defiance of the Bill of
Rights, criminalized any criticism of the government.[11]

Many historians have concluded that contemporary concerns about the
Know Nothings and their potential appeal to Oregonians were overblown.
Woodward, reflecting his own feelings toward immigrants, observed that
"the distance from the Atlantic Coast naturally excluded the undesirable,
floating element of foreign immigration which has readier access to the
East. Of the pioneer foreign born population of Oregon, which for the most
part was of a desirable nature, less than twenty-five percent came directly."
Immigrants in Oregon were, therefore, already "Americanized." While he
agreed with Woodward's point, James Hendrickson saw the introduction
of the party as having another objective. Other than the ongoing antagonism toward the Hudson's Bay Company and Roman Catholics who were
considered "un-American," Oregon settlers were not against foreigners.
They were attracted to the Know Nothings as formidable opponents of the
Democratic Party and of the Salem Clique. Patricia Knuth was of the same

opinion: The Know Nothings were a menace to a Democratic Party that was already "tottering."[12]

With the 1855 delegate election looming, the Know Nothings were just one of the challenges facing Lane. Hearing rumors of some disaffection with him in the Territory, Lane worked to maintain his relationships, sending reports on the accomplishments of the congressional session and observations about the international situation including his judgment that the revolution in Spain provided an opportunity for the United States to acquire Cuba. He did not hesitate to tout his relationship with President Pierce who took him to stay in the White House while he recovered from a serious illness. But, as he had before the 1853 election, Lane sent contradictory messages, sometimes writing of his desire to be reelected while at other times portraying himself as a reluctant candidate. Once again, his perceived ambivalence raised the aspirations of other politicians and promoted competition among members of the Clique. Deady wrote Nesmith that he had heard from an unidentified source that Nesmith and others were "distracting the party with your efforts for the delegateship." He added that the same source thought that "no one but Old Joe or another individual whose name modesty forbids me to mention can save the party."[13] Curry, always Lane's strongest advocate, was concerned about the consequences for the Oregon Democratic Party if Lane declined to run. He wrote Deady that he understood that Deady did not want the nomination, an understanding that was perhaps premature. If that were the case, Curry recommended Nesmith as the candidate who would have the broadest support of the Democratic Party unlike several others whose names had surfaced.[14]

Lane's most aggressive opponent within the Democratic Party was Orville Pratt. Joel Palmer, Lane's close ally for whom he had secured the appointment as superintendent of Indian Affairs, described Pratt in a March 1854 letter to Lane as still "humiliated, disgraced, his hopes and prospects blasted" nearly a year after the Senate's defeat of his Court appointment. From Palmer's perspective, Pratt's rejection was "an almost irredeemable injury done the democratic party." By August, however, Palmer was no longer sympathetic, warning Lane: "Judge Pratt is not your friend, of this I speak advisedly, nor do I believe he is a friend to any man longer than such friendship may be used to promote his own selfish, vain, and egotistical pretensions." Pratt, Palmer added, was publicly critical of

Lane whom he accused of neglecting the responsibilities given him by the Territory's voters.[15]

With a good deal of presumption, Pratt wrote Lane telling him that he was allowing his name to be put forward at the Democratic convention as a candidate for delegate: "May I not hope that this is agreeable to your feelings & that I shall have your support." Days later, Pratt presented an argument for Lane's withdrawal in his favor. He wrote to tell him that the *Oregonian* had alleged that Pratt had been dismissed from West Point for theft. To redeem himself, Pratt felt he needed to run for delegate. "There is but one thing in the way—your supposed wishes for a renomination to Congress next Spring and inasmuch as your friends are my friends and as we have always acted as one man—looking to one end, the advancement of true Democratic principles in the Territory." If they were both candidates at the coming convention, loyal Democrats would be divided. "Ought this not to be avoided? And cannot it be, by your early and decided action?"[16] Nesmith, amused by Pratt's "modest request," wrote Lane that Pratt could not win the nomination even with Lane's support. While he did not deny Pratt's contributions to the Democratic Party, he observed that Pratt's vanity as well as his "trying to make his private grievances an issue in the party" made him very unpopular, adding "this as a matter of course is *confidential*, as I harbor no enmity toward Pratt. I consequently have no desire to injure him."[17]

Despite such reassurance, Lane had begun to doubt that he had the unequivocal support of Oregon Democrats. His son Nat reinforced his concerns: "I discover that Pratt and other Democrats are trying to create a prejudice unfavorable to you, and to induce the Democrats to believe that you don't do as much for Oregon as might be done by one O. C. Pratt." He went on to tell his father that one of the arguments being used against him was that Lane was focused on getting the nomination for president. While Nesmith, Palmer, Curry, and "so far" Bush were supporting him, others, including Delazon Smith, would claim some votes at the convention. The problem was the Democratic Party itself: "I am tired of all such party organizations as those that have to use so much intrigue, lying and rascality as our would be leaders and rulers out here have to secure their own aggrandisement. I do think the democratic party in Oregon is made of the poorest hacknied rotten hearted set of Office Seeking Sons of Bitches I ever knew." In Nat's estimation, his father's chances of winning the election were small. "I wish you were in a condition to retire from Public life.

I would then suggest that we all emigrated to some quiet little valley in a pleasant part of California where we might cultivate the soil and have our little herd of cattle, horses and sheep and live a quiet happy life—and be free and far away from this Oregon democracy."[18]

As speculation regarding the nomination rose, Deady wrote Bush, who was still in the East, indicating his own ambivalence about a Lane versus Pratt race: "You recollect the story of the disinterested wife when the husband and bear fought." Still smarting from Bush's discouraging him from running for delegate in 1853, Deady added that Pratt had told him that, before the convention, Bush had argued for the selection of Lane rather than Deady. Pratt had acknowledged that he shared Bush's opinion but that Bush had said it first. Bush was undeterred. Having observed Lane in action in Washington, he sent letters to the *Statesman* enthusiastically supporting him to the point that Deady passed along a comment by one of Bush's friends: "'By the way what has Old Joe done for Bush that he is giving him such foolish puffs?'" The friend continued, "Bush has rendered himself rather ridiculous by the way he has been writing to his paper as to Lane.'" Bush's heated reaction led Deady to respond that the quote was accurate but he would not have reported it had he known that Bush would not take it as a "bit of fun." He cautioned Bush, who was about to marry, "If the temper you have displayed in your last is a fair specimen of the disposition you intend to exhibit around the domestic hearth, I tremble for the future peace and happiness of Madam B."[19]

While distracted by Pratt's efforts, Democrats were also increasingly uneasy about the Know Nothings and their appeal to the electorate. The Clique saw the party's introduction into the Oregon Territory as yet another of the machinations of that longtime opponent of the Democratic Party, the Whig Amory Holbrook.[20] The anti-Democratic opposition welcomed the prospect of a challenge to the party's dominance. Dryer made fun of the Democrats' apprehensions, writing that the *Oregonian* "knows nothing" of such an organization. Nat Lane intensified his father's anxiety when he wrote about the American party's organizational efforts in Portland and Oregon City. He expected that they would dominate politics in the Territory and might even capture the post of delegate.[21]

Curry assured Lane that he would get the nomination despite the signs of opposition, but he warned of the dangers of Lane's association with the Whig pioneer Jesse Applegate: "He ridicules you in his cups and he mortifies our friends out there and distracts the party by his boasts that he alone is your confidant, that none of our friends are deemed by you worthy to be such." Curry added: "It pains me to hear complaints made against you and believe me that I do not hear them silently. . . . Yet it is so easy to find fault that were Jesus Christ himself in your place I am quite certain he could not give universal satisfaction."[22] After his return to Salem, Bush wrote Lane that Pratt had come to tell him of his ambitions but that he had told him not to waste his time as Lane would not decline the nomination. Bush added that he was not Pratt's enemy and still credited him for his earlier service to the party in the controversy over the location of the capital. Joel Palmer wrote Lane that Bush's support for him seemed genuine and that Pratt was the only declared candidate. Nesmith was out of the picture while Deady remained noncommittal.[23]

Nesmith, too, was reassuring. When Lane wrote that he had heard from a contact in the Territory that Oregon was turning against him, Nesmith responded that Lane's informant, while "an excellent man and incapable of a dishonest act," was "rather domestic in his habits and consequently has but little opportunity for knowing public opinion." Like Curry, Nesmith cautioned Lane about his prospects among Democrats in the Umpqua region because of his relationship with Applegate who was showing off Lane's very complimentary letters promising federal appointments and grants while at the same time "he laughs at your credulity in attempting to buy up his influence, and sayes that he would not vote for you to save your life." Despite the declarations of support, Lane's fears about the commitment of the Clique were reinforced by the ongoing criticism of presidential appointments he received from others. Fred Waymire persisted with his complaints: "We are left now in entire darkness, as to who caused these *names* to be *selected* to the exclusion of your *best friends*; who laboured both night and day to secure your nomination and election as Delegate to Congress." Waymire accused Lane of succumbing to the demands of individuals "who would rather have office, than maintain the honor of the Democratic party!!"[24]

Within the Clique, speculation about the approaching election was unending. Deady wrote Bush that he thought Nesmith might support Pratt at the convention. Palmer wrote Lane that Delazon Smith was supporting Pratt. Others in Lane's territorial network only increased his alarm. He complained to Bush about reports from southern Oregon that "my very especial friends, Pratt and Deady," had been campaigning in the south, Pratt promoting himself for the office of delegate and Deady "carelessly saying that he did not care who should be selected, so that it was not *Lane. If this is so is it not queer? What have I done to bring down upon my head the wrath of those I have loved and served.*"[25] Pratt had certainly not given up. He demanded that Lane stop "pressing our democratic friends for a third nomination to Congress notwithstanding the wish of some of them, unembarrassed by your requests, to give me, after six years somewhat thankless service in Oregon as a Democrat, a chance for approval by the people through the ballot box."

Lane was certainly not persuaded by Pratt's arguments. He went on the attack. In a letter to Nesmith, he angrily accused Pratt of cheating the soldiers during the American Indian Wars: "Think of him trying to speculate off the poor soldier who bared his breast to a savage and endured the privations and hardships of a campaign while he was sitting comfortably by the fire side enjoying the fat of the land."[26]

Beyond the emerging divisions within the Democratic Party, the Know Nothings still loomed. Bush's earlier complacent attitude changed when he witnessed the party's successes in the East during his 1854 visit. Once back in Oregon, he launched an effort to expose and discredit the party through a series of *Statesman* articles in which he revealed the names of members, the substance of their meetings, and the various mechanisms used to conceal the workings of the party. He noted that Whigs made up the majority of the membership and condemned the few Democratic members to oblivion. Later investigation established that Bush's source was a *Statesman* printer who infiltrated the Salem Wigwam.[27] The Know Nothings reacted quickly to his critique. Members threatened Bush, demanding the name of his informant. For some weeks after the first article was published, armed friends accompanied him when he was out in public. Nesmith wrote Lane of one incident: "About twenty of them surrounded Bush and myself on last Monday evening, and threatened to eat us up. We drew our revolvers. Those heroes cooled down and looked very foolish."[28]

During the December 1854 legislative session, Delazon Smith with Bush's guidance introduced a bill requiring that citizens announce their votes in a public forum or submit a list of their votes to a judge who would then proclaim them to assembled voters. The concept, known as viva voce, was not a new one. Since US independence, it had been tried and then abandoned in the states of Kentucky, Georgia, New York, Maryland, Arkansas, and Pennsylvania. In Virginia, viva voce survived into the Civil War.[29] With opposition from Whigs, Know Nothings, and even some non-Clique Democrats, the viva voce law barely passed: fourteen votes to twelve in the assembly and five to three in the council. But Bush reveled in his victory: "What Democrat does not feel proud in the consciousness that he is pure and free from niggerism, Know Nothingism, and all the other isms of the day? Who had not rather be a straight forward, consistent, fearless Democrat, than a shame-faced Know Nothing, skulking around from one garret to another in the darkness of the night."[30]

In the *Oregonian*, Dryer responded that "a native born American, made free by the best blood of the revolutionary sires, and educated under laws and institutions truly American, should be able to vote in accordance with dictates of his own conscience, in spite of the objections of the democrats." He dismissed viva voce as nothing more than a ploy of the Salem Clique: "They have said, in plain terms, that 'we are your owners,' and *we* will drive you with the *viva voce* system, as we drive cattle into the corral with the *lash*." Dryer's reaction may have been influenced by his own prejudice against foreigners. The same issue of the *Oregonian* featured the masthead "Put none but Americans on guard! Americans in sympathy, feeling and sentiment! Americans by the provisions of the Constitution of the United States."[31]

Despite Bush's exposé and viva voce, Democrats cautioned Lane about the American party's potential impact on the approaching election as well as Whig complicity with the party's efforts. Nesmith warned: "The Whig leaders have made every exertion to spread it throughout the country. And I regrett to say that their efforts are being crowned with success. They number now 300 in Portland, 150 in OC, 100 in Lafayette, 90 in Salem." The Know Nothings were putting together a Territory-wide party organization aimed at winning the coming election and "there is reason to fear that they may be successful." Nesmith wrote that Lane's friend Joel Palmer had become a "traitor to his party, his friends, his God and his country" because of his support of the Know Nothings and added that Dryer was a member and that Waterman of the *Times* was also a supporter. Nesmith understood why Whigs and disaffected Democrats would support the Know Nothings but questioned the support it was getting from some in the Clique wing of the Democratic Party: "Why the treason should extend to the Ins is more than I can account for." Rumors of Joel Palmer's membership in the

American party led to a petition to the president that he be removed from his post as superintendent of Indian Affairs. Although Palmer wrote Lane in defiant denial, he later admitted to Nesmith that he had joined the party out of curiosity but then regretted it.[32]

While the Democrats would not formally select their nominee until the April convention, the former governor John Gaines emerged early in 1855 as the Whig nominee. In January, the wife of George Williams reported to Bush that Gaines had confronted Lane and that they had fought. Gaines retreated, his face covered with blood. Bush passed the information on to Deady, cautioning: *"But she is a woman and can't tell much about it."*[33]

When attacks on the Clique became the central focus of Gaines's campaign, Bush flew to its defense, denouncing the "mad dog cry of clique and dictation at the Seat of Government."

> There are some half a dozen democrats holding office, and on that account reside at Salem, the seat of government. They are from almost as many different counties in the Territory and will probably return to those counties again when they go out of office. The Democratic party has placed them in these positions, and requires and expects from them in return, that, as individuals and officers, they will faithfully exert their abilities for the success of democratic measures throughout the Territory. In doing this, they exercise more or less influence in the administration of the party; this results from the necessity of things and is not expected to be otherwise. While in the discharge of these duties, however faithfully, honestly and disinterestedly, it often happens that some disappointed demagogue or light-metalled politician, who conceives himself overlooked in the distribution of party favors, takes up the trade of sham patriotism.[34]

In the run-up to the convention, Bush was Lane's steadfast supporter and dismissive of Pratt. As the convention approached, Bush reassured Lane that, despite the "very ungenerous course" Pratt was pursuing, Lane's friends were laboring on his behalf and "the indications are that you will be nominated, and I have great confidence that you will be." The information he gathered through his Territory-wide network was valuable even when it was not encouraging to Lane. The Know Nothings remained a concern.

Delazon Smith shared with Bush "very private information" that the party's membership would exceed five thousand by the time of the election. His source told him that Judge Williams was friendly to the party and that "Judge Pratt applied for admission but was refused." Smith added that another of his informants reported that Pratt had joined the party while in California.[35]

Bush's support was not entirely disinterested, as he saw a connection between Lane's success and his own campaign for reappointment as public printer, which was being challenged by Waterman and the *Times*. Deady certainly did not share Bush's enthusiasm for Lane but understood the importance of his reelection to Bush: "I suppose you begin to feel a deep interest in the result of this delegate question, and I conceive that your own fortunes will be materially affected by the issue of it." Although Bush was, Deady teased, a "miserable man," he promised his support: "Rather than see you worsted in the fight I would do a good deal that otherwise I might leave undone. In short I am your friend, and *on that account* shall do more if in my power, to forward your views than I have given you reason to expect."[36] At the time a judge of the territorial court, Deady had little to say about who would be chosen public printer. Still his relationship with Bush apparently required such reassurance.

Pratt had not abandoned his aspirations and was in fact quite confident. Bush wrote Deady that Pratt had graciously informed him that he wanted it "understood that the friends who favored Lane to him now should not be forgotten in the hour of his triumph." Delazon Smith warned Bush not to allow Pratt and his supporters "to denounce and slander" Lane. While convinced that Bush would once again be chosen public printer, Reuben Boise was not confident of Lane's nomination and very concerned that the Democratic convention would be divided.[37]

Lane's insecurities were heightened when Bush passed along a critical letter from Nesmith. Lane immediately wrote Nesmith to defend himself. He added: "I must confess that I feel mortified, pained, yea hurt, to find you dissatisfied with me. You have my friendship & confidence to an extent that but few have. If you shall act lukewarmly, it will hurt. I will not allow myself to believe that you will do any such thing." The letter was addressed to "Gen'l J. W. Nesmith" and, in a departure from Lane's earlier correspondence with Nesmith, had the salutation "Dear Sir" rather than "Dear Friend."[38] Nesmith was not apologetic although he was well aware that another Lane victory would follow. While there was some unhappiness with Lane in the southern counties and despite his own misgivings regarding Lane, Deady was sure that he would prevail at least for the time being: "Old Joe will yarn them out of it for the present in some way. He is par excellence in humbug. The only difficulty about that system of tactics is, that as time rolls around his yarns come home to roost occasionally." In his next letter, Deady protested Lane's failure to defend Democrats from attacks by the opposition.[39] Other delegates to the convention shared Deady's reservations but Lane overcame both those trepidations and Pratt's efforts and was renominated. In his disappointment, Pratt left Oregon for San Francisco where he practiced law and later became a justice of the District Courts of San Francisco and San Mateo.

Lane's nomination did not convert Deady to his cause. After the convention, Deady angrily complained to Nesmith about Palmer's retention as superintendent of Indian Affairs. Despite the Clique's objections to Palmer, Lane had chosen to protect a loyal disciple: "Hereafter the test of a man's standing in the party and political worth, will not be fealty to Democratic principles and the party which maintains them, but fidelity to the personal interest of Old Jo. . . . To say the least of it is a d—-d shabby conclusion for a campaign conducted and won by the Statesman." Deady believed that Lane considered having him removed from the Bench because he thought Deady had opposed him. "I would today prefer to have honestly opposed his nomination and been turned out, than to retain the office on servile condition of approving his conduct and aiding his ambition in all cases without reference to right or wrong." Deady concluded his letter with the observation that if the Democratic Party was to "sink into a mere personal party, where the soulless Flunkey who sings old Jo's praise loudest and longest is alone to be elevated and honored, I think the institution had better be abolished, to make room for the divine right of Kings." He intended to confront Lane before he returned to Washington, "Then let him procure my removal if he dares and be d—d to him."[40]

The Lane-Gaines contest was decidedly more contentious than the 1853 delegate race had been. After witnessing a debate between the two candidates, Deady reported to Bush and to Nesmith. Lane's speech was "the same old story about the Oregonians being the bravest, handsomest, most generous, most intelligent, most patriotic people in the world. How he loves them all and every part of them. What he had done for them and what he intended to do for them." While both Lane and Gaines "kept up an appearance of good humor," in one exchange each referred to the Rogue River War of 1851 as the "Squaw War" and accused the other of having taken "a turn at the squaws." While he dismissed the anti-Catholic provisions in their platform, Gaines defended the Know Nothings, declaring that only Americans should rule America. Immigrants were, in Gaines's opinion, the "sweepings of Belfast, Cork, the Hanseatic towns, Hamburg, etc." Deady told Bush that Gaines had said he would not touch the *Statesman* with a ten foot pole and had asserted that Lane enjoyed no respect from a majority in the Congress and it "would be no use to send him there."[41]

From Jacksonville, Joseph Drew warned Bush that "the *Clique* must not rely upon this county to secure old Jo's election." Since they had helped Lane get the nomination at the Convention, local Democrats seemed to feel they had done their part and could not be counted on to go to the polls. Drew thought Lane would be fortunate to get a hundred-vote majority in Jackson County but expected him to win easily in Douglas and Umpqua Counties. He attributed Lane's good prospects in Douglas County to the fact that Lane's home was located there and that there were "more damned fools in Douglas County than any where else in the Territory." Drew's judgment might have been affected by Lane's getting someone else appointed collector at Port Orford, a position Drew had expected to be his own.[42]

In anticipation of Lane's victory over Gaines, Deady sent Bush and copied to Nesmith a poem he had written:

> Now glory to the "Salem Clique," by whom "His Honor" died,
> And glory to the "Scribbling Chick," whose goose quill pierced his
>   side.
> Now scattered wide the speckled band who boasted rather soon
> Our good old Clique to them should yield before the Ides of June.
> From "Joshua broak" to "Single bow" they scamper hither and yon
> And leave the ship to the Salem Clique by whom 'twas fairly won.[43]

Drew's discontent and Deady's derision notwithstanding, the Clique under Bush's leadership remained committed to Lane. The *Statesman* regularly countered the *Oregonian*'s blistering attacks. As George Williams remembered, both newspapers "exhausted the vocabulary of invective and abuse." Lane again demonstrated his mastery on the campaign trail and won the June election handily. Still his insecurities remained. Strangely enough, given Deady's well-known skepticism about him, Lane showed Deady a letter he had received before the election from Jesse Applegate who wrote that Bush had planned to eliminate Lane and Pratt and elect Deady.[44] There is nothing to indicate that Applegate was correct, but Lane required reassurance which Deady apparently provided.

Bush had his own issues with Lane over government appointments, particularly one he wanted for his father-in-law. He wrote Nesmith asking that he confront Lane and tell him that "something has got to be did." Despite such concerns, Bush began promoting Lane for the presidency whether out of genuine conviction or the Democrats' dependence on Lane for government favors or both. When some of his compatriots objected, Bush responded with harsh letters to Deady and to Joseph Drew. Drew replied that he and Deady "regretted that a few plain words relative to your candidate for President should have so disturbed your usual equanimity. We were flattering ourselves that we considered matters dispassionately as they came to our knowledge, and never for one moment imagined that any one could esteem us 'unreasonable grumblers.' It pains us to think that the favorite of the democracy of Oregon is so much disposed to flattery and to humbug. . . . The truth is that we still think (and we have good cause to think so) that the 'Old Statesman' is too much inclined to listen to softs and Whigs." Bush responded, "I think you are the most sensitive gentlemen I have come in *collision* with." Bush did not abandon the cause and repeatedly ran his endorsement in the *Statesman*: "For President in 1856 GEN. JOSEPH LANE."[45]

In the midst of the delegate campaign, another issue had arisen. In what some have seen as an attempt to lessen the influence of the Clique, the capital was moved to Corvallis in 1855. Bush moved the *Statesman* to Corvallis but was unhappy with the town. He found its inhabitants "the most tackiest, picayune, grabbing people it was ever my lot to fall amongst."[46] He had hardly arrived before he began working to return the capital to Salem through his editorials and his entreaties to Lane for a reversal of the decision. Deady encouraged his efforts, recommending "an article in a temperate tone, upon the Seat of Government question, embracing not only the legal question . . . but 'where it *ought to be*.'" After the Department of the Treasury refused to allocate funds for the necessary construction in Corvallis, perhaps in response to Lane's efforts, the capital and the *Statesman* returned to Salem in December. Not long after, the Salem capitol building and all of its contents were destroyed by a fire that many saw as the work of a Corvallis-inspired arsonist.[47]

While elections and government appointments were issues throughout the territorial days, another significant concern was the matter of the Native American population. When the early pioneers began their migration during the 1830s, Native American numbers in the Willamette Valley were already small due to the diseases that had decimated the native population. Native Americans were much more numerous in the eastern and southwestern parts of the Territory. There hostilities broke out as more and more settlers arrived, attracted by the Donation Land Law that offered them free land, land that the Native Americans already considered their own.

During his brief 1847 term as the Territory's governor, Joseph Lane made concerted efforts to reach some sort of understanding. He met a number of times with different Native American groups but had little to offer them. While he reassured the settlers that any injury to them would be met with "sudden and severe chastisement," Lane advised the federal government that, since white migration had deprived Native Americans of their land and the game that was their subsistence, the solution was to buy their land and relocate them in areas away from the settlers. "Indeed the cause of humanity calls loudly for their removal from causes and influences so fatal to their existence."[48]

In 1853, after he became delegate, Lane petitioned President Pierce to appoint his friend and supporter Joel Palmer superintendent of Indian Affairs. The president obliged. In the face of continuing violence, Palmer sought permission to negotiate treaties with the native people. Both Judge Orville Pratt and the Territory's attorney general Benjamin Harding refused to grant him that authority. Nevertheless Palmer persisted, although his efforts to reach a resolution along the lines that Lane had recommended earned him no support either from the government or from the white settlers. In 1854, Palmer successfully negotiated a treaty with the Tualatin tribe that, in return for the tribe's turning over 1,476 square miles of land, promised each family forty acres on the reservation that was yet to be established, as well as grants of supplies for some years. He defended the agreement to Lane: "The provisions of this Treaty may be thought by some as too liberal towards these poor degraded beings, and that they are not entitled to the consideration given them. Their very weakness and ignorance is one of the reasons why we should liberally provide for them." But, as the *Statesman* reported, Lane no longer favored an accord with the Native Americans.[49]

Another important influence in the settlers' relationship with the Native Americans was the presence of the missionaries, who had been sent by religious congregations in the East to convert the Native Americans to Christianity. With few exceptions, the clergymen became powerful figures in the white communities, particularly in the Willamette Valley. They did not hesitate to demand that settlers adhere to church policies. A case in point was an order prohibiting merchants from opening their stores on Sunday "on pain of forfeiting their licenses" since "desecration of this holy day tends to retard civilization among savages." That the clergy could threaten to take away the businessmen's licenses reflects the strong support that they commanded from civil authorities. In this instance, the Office of Indian Affairs in the federal Department of the Interior reinforced the Sunday-opening prohibition. The Office's order proclaimed a high-minded policy toward the Native Americans. The government, "while constantly endeavoring to promote their physical well-being, has looked earnestly to the accomplishment of a higher & nobler object. It has sought to improve their social condition; to advance their political prosperity; to diffuse knowledge among them; to super induce an habitual observance of morality; and to make them participants in all the advantages and blessings of Christian civilization."[50]

Members of the Clique played roles in the different aspects of relations with the Native Americans. James Nesmith led troops in the Cayuse and Rogue River Wars. He was appointed US marshal responsible for overseeing the protection of the settlers and later became superintendent for Indian Affairs. Lafayette Grover led a company of volunteers in the 1851 Rogue River War. As leaders of the territorial legislature, Matthew Deady, Benjamin Harding, Fred Waymire, and Grover wrestled with the challenges that the wars presented. Grover was appointed commissioner to audit the claims for federal payment to the territorial government to meet the expenses of the wars. The judiciary as well grappled with Native American issues. Judges Orville Pratt and Reuben Boise were several times called upon for decisions on matters pertaining to the native population.

While fears for their safety from Native American hostility preoccupied settlers, Matthew Deady dismissed the danger: "A street mob in New York which scarcely makes an item in the morning papers often equals the whole affair as yet in the destruction of life and property." In his eyes, war against the Indians was not the answer: "The Indians will not be exterminated except through the operation of natural causes, which will hardly complete their work of decay and extinction in our day. In the meantime the foundation has been laid in blood and treachery for a lasting enmity between the races."[51]

The federal government did station troops in the Territory but the people often had little confidence in the protection they offered. When officials in Portland responded to local anxieties by creating night patrols, Asahel Bush was not above suggesting a lack of courage on the part of Portland men. Thomas Dryer accused him of malicious slander: "In the midst of an Indian war raging all around us, this contemptible backbiter, practiced libeller and cowardly calumniator, Asahel Bush, seeks to plant a poisoned dagger into the public mind for party purposes."[52]

Eastern criticism of aggressive action against the Native Americans prompted a response from Governor Curry:

Some of the newspaper editors of the refined east, where the chiefest danger to life arises from voluptuous living, who know the Indian character only through poetry and romance, who seem to care more about cultivating treasonable machinations, and fostering disaffection to the Union, than the advocacy of truth, have filled their columns with wholesale denunciation of their fellow citizens, inhabiting an isolated portion of the Country, who resorted to arms in defence of life and property, rather than risk the general ruin and butchery by remaining cowardly inactive. It is painful to conclude that the success of the whites, in repelling the attacks of the ruthless invader, was less gratifying to such mental organizations than would have been the depopulation of both territories by Indian conquest.[53]

Neither did subsequent government efforts to placate Native Americans meet with support in the Territory. Dryer, in the *Oregonian*, took issue with "the Indian agents, superintendents, and officers of the general government" who had identified with the Native Americans rather than with the settlers, stating: "And now again these red devils have recommenced the work of murder, rapine, and destruction against their allies, friends and supporters, by another exhibition of their natural instincts and designs." Dryer judged US government policies "radically wrong. It is far cheaper to whip them at once and bring them into subjection, than to feed, clothe, and fight them for years in succession."[54]

For the most part, Bush agreed. His editorials consistently opposed any recognition of Native American rights. In 1858, the treaties negotiated by Palmer, setting aside land for Indians in central Oregon, were before Congress for ratification. Bush objected that such treaties "value the degraded and bestial savages, at least in their own estimation, to a political equality with the whites."[55] Despite Bush's opposition and the objections of many settlers, the US Senate passed the treaties in 1859, resulting in the creation of the Warm Springs Indian Reservation.

CHAPTER FIVE

"Is the introduction of slavery into Oregon practicable? And will it prove profitable?"

—Asahel Bush, *Oregon Statesman*

Through the 1850s, while elections and other issues occupied the Clique and the Democratic Party, resentment over the president's power to appoint the members of the executive and judicial branches of the Territory's government grew. The conviction that statehood was the only way to address the problem became more and more common. In fact, the statehood aspiration was not new. In 1850, Thurston had expected that statehood would follow from his efforts to organize the Territory's Democratic Party.[1] At a Portland meeting the following year, Democrats passed a resolution stating that many men in Oregon were "capable of discharging the duties devolving upon the judges as well as filling any other office under the territorial government, who would either discharge the duties or resign the office."[2] Dryer responded with an immediate attack on the resolution and its sponsors, charging that the measure was the first step in a Democratic plan to establish a separate republic independent of the United States. Ignoring Dryer's allegation, Bush weighed in: "Would any of the States willingly consent to yield the election of governor and other state officers to the Executive of the United States? Far from it."[3]

His constituents began to put pressure on Delegate Lane. Benjamin Harding, then speaker of the assembly, wrote to complain about the behavior of federal appointees. "It is confidently expected that you will early endeavour to have those matters made right. Your well known integrity, promptness and energy are a sufficient guaranty to us that you will do so." From Washington, Lane wrote Bush in support of his editorial, asserting that "as a Democrat I have ever believed in the Democratic doctrine that the people are capable of self government" and should be entrusted with the right to elect their own officers. "Are the people of Oregon less capable of exercising this prerogative than other American Citizens? Are they not as intelligent, as patriotic, as law-abiding & as capable of protecting their just rights, as the citizens of any other community?"[4]

During the 1851–1852 session of the Democrat-dominated territorial legislature, both the assembly and the council passed a resolution that, should Congress adjourn without an amendment to the Organic Act allowing election of territorial officers, the speaker of the assembly should announce that within the next sixty days, there would be an election in which the people would decide whether or not to elect delegates to a convention that would write a constitution. On the other hand, the Whigs, enjoying their position of power in the Territory with the Whigs Zachary Taylor and then Millard Fillmore in the White House, supported the status quo with the strong endorsement of the *Oregonian*. An exception was the Whig Jesse Applegate, who wrote the *Statesman* in favor of a change "allowing to the people the political rights enjoyed by those of the states of electing their own officers instead of having them imposed upon them by the Federal Government."[5]

Even after the Democrat Franklin Pierce won the presidency in 1852, Democratic leaders were committed to the belief that self-government could only be accomplished by Oregon's becoming a state. They put a proposition calling for a constitutional convention on the ballot in the May 1854 election. The measure was opposed by the Whigs who held out hope for the election of another Whig president to restore their dominance in the Territory. Bush reminded the citizens of Oregon that they had the opportunity to "take the first step toward statehood." While expressing his own reservations about the measure's chances, Grover wrote Deady to check on voter sentiment in Douglas and the other counties in the southern part of the Territory. Deady's response was not encouraging. Governor Davis was far more optimistic, writing Lane that he had no doubt that it would "carry at the next election by a large majority."[6]

The Territory's voters confirmed Grover and Deady's skepticism, defeating the proposition handily. In a letter to Lane, Pratt attributed the defeat to neglect: "Democrats too generally, I regret to say, turned a deaf ear to all considerations in its favor & were *indifferent* whilst the Whigs almost to a man fought it with system & with far more than their usual zeal."[7] Dryer in the *Oregonian* relished the setback but, with the expectation of further efforts for statehood, urged the formation of an organized opposition: "Let them understand that your votes cannot be obtained for a measure which must inevitably be destructive to the masses of the people, merely to pacify the morbid appetites for office and power on the part of a few party hucksters."[8]

Bush, absent from Oregon at the time, reacted to the proposition's failure in a letter to the *Statesman.* He explained the voters' decision as the result of a counter-movement proposing a state comprising southern Oregon and some California counties rather than statehood for Oregon with its current boundaries. A reflection of the rising national debate over slavery, the plan had surfaced in southern Oregon during 1853 when a convention in Jacksonville embraced the creation of a Jackson Territory proclaiming "we will use every exertion to prevent the formation of a state government in Oregon with its present boundaries." The concept attracted some adherents particularly among slavery advocates who envisioned the Jackson Territory entering the Union as a slave state. Its proponents even presented a memorial to the territorial legislature. Although the separate state movement did not disappear, it failed to gain any support in northern California.[9]

The Democrats persisted. At the party's convention in April 1855, they passed a definitive measure: "Resolved, That in the opinion of this convention the time has arrived when Oregon should assume the position of a sovereign state; that the numbers, wealth and intelligence of the population entitle her to become the latest and brightest star of the Union, bearing the farthest westward the standard of the Pacific." When Alonzo Leland, then editor of the *Statesman*'s Portland rival the *Democratic Standard*, opposed the convention resolution and called for a delay in any effort toward statehood, Bush condemned "the iscariotism of the *Standard*."[10] In June, the Democrats managed to place another proposition for a constitutional convention on the ballot. The measure included a provision that the members of the assembly would serve as delegates. Again the voters turned it down, although by a smaller margin. Bush attributed the loss to the sense in some counties that they were under-represented in the assembly and thus would have a weak position in the convention.[11]

After the defeat, Leland in a *Standard* editorial presented an alternative to statehood that came to be known as the "Pacific Republic." He

maintained that Oregon should not involve itself in the divisive controversies over slavery in the United States but instead separate itself from
the Union, just as the American colonies had separated themselves from
England. The Rocky Mountains formed an "unmistakable boundary"
established by "an over-ruling Providence." Dryer feigned surprise and
indignation, attributing the sentiment to all Democrats:

> Although the party in power in this territory have had everything
> in their hands for the last three years, and although the leaders
> have been able, under their hypocritical cry of Democracy, to
> create, deceive, and gull the majority to sustain their measures,
> and to elevate an unprincipled set of demagogues to office and
> power; although their pensioned newspapers and party hacks
> have denounced for years the great fundamental principles of
> Americanism, yet we are not prepared to see them at this early
> hour throw off the mask, and declare in favor of a Revolution, and
> a separate government here, but nevertheless they have done so.

The *Statesman* dismissed Dryer's comments but reported that an
anonymous source in San Francisco had shared a supposed plan for just
such a new republic to consist of ten states formed from California, the
Oregon and Washington Territories, and parts of what are now the states
of Utah and New Mexico.[12]

Frustrated by the continuing opposition to statehood, Delazon Smith
wrote an article for the *Statesman* analyzing the voters' decision and proposing another approach. The Democrats should put together a slate of
Democratic candidates in the next legislative election who supported a
convention. Given the dominance of the party, they would have a majority
in the assembly and could then call for a constitutional convention, with
the members of the assembly serving as delegates. Bush rejected the idea:
"We do not expect or desire to see the question of a Convention made a
party test." Such a process, he maintained, would give the Know Nothings
too much say in the convention because they would be over-represented.
Bush cautioned that, while he supported statehood as soon as it could be
achieved, "being firmly of the opinion that the freedom, growth, and substantial interest of Oregon would be promoted by it," it would be a mistake
to again put the issue before the voter "in the face of probable defeat."[13]

Boise too opposed Smith's plan: "I have talked with a good many men of influence relative to this matter and all concur in the opinion that it would be hazardous to go forward and form a constitution without first submitting the question of Convention or no Convention to a vote." He favored a special election in the spring of 1856 with the understanding that delegates would be chosen at the general election and that the voters would then have the opportunity to approve or disapprove the convention's product at another special election. He was convinced that, if the proposition was presented in a special election, supporters would come out to vote and those indifferent to the proposition would stay home.[14]

The legislature agreed to Boise's plan and scheduled a special election for June of 1856. Meanwhile the debate continued. When the opponents of statehood, including the *Oregonian,* argued that Oregon was not sufficiently populated and prosperous to support statehood, Bush meticulously picked apart their premise, citing the costs of government in various states and listing the populations of the current states at the time they joined the Union.[15] In the end, however, Boise's plan failed to attract sufficient support from the Territory's voters although the margin of defeat was substantially smaller, only 249 votes. Despite the Clique's supposed dominance in Salem, voters in Marion, Yamhill, and Washington Counties remained opposed while those in Lane, Douglas and Linn Counties favored a convention.[16]

Bush interrupted his campaign for statehood to turn to another matter, one of significance to the Clique. In the fall of 1856, for reasons that are unclear, he attempted to sell the *Oregon Statesman.* After discussing the matter with Nesmith and Harding, he offered the paper to Deady, assuring him that he would make money with the paper and that Nesmith would partner with him, providing the necessary capital: "It is no flattery to say you are the best newspaper writer in Oregon, and you can keep and make the Statesman the best property in Oregon, in a pecuniary view." Deady responded that he would prefer that Bush remain the owner and editor: "I could not be induced to take it upon any other principle than to prevent its falling into more unacceptable hands." Notwithstanding the close relationship evident in their correspondence, Deady was cool to the idea of a partnership with Nesmith. Besides, he wrote, he had spoken to his wife about the project and "she thought the paper was bad enough now, but if Nes and I went into it, its morals would be intolerable."[17]

Abandoning his usual teasing, Deady was complimentary of Bush's management of the paper: "You have in the main made it useful and subordinate to the common good, and although compelled to make some very short tacks, yet you have made them with such consummate skill and adroitness as never to lose your distance or position." He was also complimentary of Bush's editorial skills. "Since when you first began the Statesman, you have done your share of beheading, lampooning, amputating and other rough butchery."[18] Although the Clique made every effort to keep the question of a sale confidential, others got wind of it. Deady described one exchange with "Intrusts" who said "that Nes and myself were the controlling influences of the Statesman. I told him that Bush controlled the Statesman as much as ever one man did a paper, but *I* was neither afraid nor ashamed to be so considered." Rumors of a sale persisted for months, leading Bush to respond: "The Oregonian pretends to have heard a report to the effect that the Statesman office has been sold. The intelligence is news to us; if anybody but ourself has any interest in the Statesman, we have not been advised of it. And when ever it is sold we think we shall know it."[19]

That distraction dealt with, the Clique returned to political matters. The slow and tortuous, and as yet unsuccessful, process of convincing the Territory's voters to support statehood would be more than matched by the challenge of getting Congress to approve it. There the issue was slavery and the balance between slave and free states in the Union and more specifically in Congress itself. The question had surfaced each time new territories were added to the Union. The Ordinance of 1787 banned slavery in the newly acquired Northwest Territory, which included the future states of Ohio, Indiana, Illinois, Michigan, Wisconsin, and part of Minnesota, effectively setting the Ohio River as the northern boundary for slavery. In 1820, the Missouri Compromise set the border between slave and free states within the lands of the Louisiana Purchase. Similarly, Congress applied the painstakingly constructed Compromise of 1850 to the lands won by the United States in the Mexican-American War. Finally, the Kansas-Nebraska Act of 1854, fashioned by Democratic Senator Stephen A. Douglas of Illinois, abolished the Missouri Compromise and established "squatter sovereignty," whereby the inhabitants of a Territory or state could decide whether or not to allow slavery.

The ongoing national debate between proponents and opponents of slavery generated widespread fear for the viability of the Union. In

November 1850, Thurston wrote a letter using the pseudonym "Jefferson," for the not-yet-existent *Statesman*. He carefully surveyed the southern states and reported on current opinion in each, sometimes with rather extravagant language: "In Missouri, Old [Thomas Hart] Benton, true to his instinct for fight, felt his way to the pillars of the disunion temple and, bringing his giant strength to bear, has prostrated it in a heap of ruins, himself standing erect amidst the crumbling fragments around him." He reassured the people of the Oregon Territory that "the dissolution or secession cause at the South is rather on the wane."[20] Thurston's optimism proved to be misguided as the tensions only heightened. Joseph Lane weighed in on the issue during his first term as delegate to Congress. Himself a committed supporter of slavery, he warned that "sensible people in the free states should leave it alone as the Constitution had done, because it could never be agitated without endangering the integrity of the Union."[21]

While there were certainly noteworthy exceptions, American settlers had consistently opposed slavery in the Oregon Territory. When they created a provisional government through the Organic Act of 1843, they approved an antislavery law on the basis of the Ordinance of 1787 and its prohibition of slavery in the northern territories. The provisional legislature reiterated the ban in 1848. The implications of that proscription were soon addressed by the judiciary. After Nathaniel Ford brought his slaves to Oregon in 1844, one of them, Robin Holmes, fled with his wife and child. When Ford refused to release Holmes's other children, Holmes appealed to the courts with Reuben Boise serving as his attorney. Later in the proceedings, Matthew Deady took over that role. Although Deady favored slavery, he maintained that, in light of the Territory's law prohibiting slavery, Ford had no right to the children. The legal process proved to be long and tedious. Hearings began in April of 1852. As associate justice of the territorial Supreme Court, Orville Pratt was the presiding judge, the first of four judges to hear the case. In the course of the trial, Joseph Lane was deposed and supported Nathaniel Ford's position that the Holmes children were his property. In July 1853, the newly appointed chief justice of the territorial Supreme Court, George Williams, ruled that slaves became free when they entered the Territory because there was no law permitting slavery. His decision precluded any subsequent effort to enforce slavery through the Oregon courts, even after the US Supreme Court's 1857 Dred Scott decision, which upheld the rights of slave-owners in similar situations.[22]

Over an extended period of time, Bush presented *Statesman* readers with a variety of opinions about slavery. In 1851, he printed, without comment, a long treatise from a Virginia newspaper, the *Richmond Examiner,* promoting slavery as the "highest and happiest" condition under which "Negroes" could live. Later that year, he maintained that the Donation Land Law applied only to white settlers. In 1854 he wrote in support of the Kansas-Nebraska Law, describing it as a successful effort "to apply to one of the most dangerous elements of our confederacy a policy which Jefferson had declared in our federal relations more than fifty years before. It was another development of the great democratic theory and one of momentous importance in the future peace and harmony of the Union."[23] In a July 1854 letter to George Rhoades, an acquaintance who was a merchant in Philadelphia, Lafayette Grover outlined his thoughts on the subject:

> As to the Nebraska bill, the people this way think it all right.
> Knowing what I do of the spirit and development of western
> territories, I think the principles of non-intervention, established in
> the organization of Nebraska and Kansas, will result in favor of free
> soil. I do not believe there will ever be a single slave state organized
> west of Missouri. In Oregon the people not only would exclude
> slavery but they have, by law, *excluded negros* from settling here.
> Our pre-emption and donation land laws are fatal to the institution
> of slavery. Western settlers, under these laws, are actual cultivators
> of limited quantities of land—laboring men whose interests are
> opposed to negro service. The laboring classes of white men from
> the south, who are found numerously in the western territories, are
> the most uncompromising enemies of slavery found in the Union.
> Therefore I think, by no possibility will slavery be extended north
> of 36°20 and as our country enlarges south, the same influence will
> govern, as far as the continent is concerned, but when we get Cuba
> it may remain a slave state. It appears to me that there has been
> more noise than necessary about this Nebraska question.[24]

Bush agreed that, because slavery was not suited to the new territories, settlers would oppose it. Further he expected, with undue optimism, that the repeal of the Missouri Compromise would "mollify the South, which, being no longer on the defensive, would inaugurate a policy of gradual emancipation."[25] But the contest over slavery in Oregon had hardly begun. After the passage of the Kansas-Nebraska Act in 1854, Clique member Delazon Smith introduced resolutions in the territorial legislature to the effect that the act repealed the ban on slavery in Oregon, and he called for a vote on the issue in line with popular sovereignty. Although he personally favored slavery, Smith believed that, because Oregon's climate and soil were inconsistent with a slave economy, voters would reject it. Bush agreed that current sentiment was antislavery but was concerned that the "fanatics and nigger-struck dames" of the abolitionist movement would cause a backlash among voters who would then support slavery.[26]

In his correspondence with Bush, Lane reported the debates over slavery in Congress: "Abolition antecedents have well nigh broke us down, and I don't like abolitionism in any shape it can be presented." When the National Democratic Convention declined to renominate his friend, Franklin Pierce, for the presidency, Lane turned his support to the party's nominee, James Buchanan, writing Bush: "Buchanan will and must be elected—upon it depends the existence of this union, the union of the states." Although a northerner, Buchanan was very much committed to the institution of slavery while his Republican opponent, John C. Fremont, had a record of opposition to slavery. The issue surfaced when Lane's bill for statehood failed to pass. While the excuse given by its opponents was the Territory's small population, the underlying reason was the fear of the Whigs in Congress that, since the Territory had always elected Democrats as delegates, voters in the new state would elect Democrats to represent it in the House and the Senate, Democrats who would support slavery. For Lane, the issue was a distraction: "Nothing has been done but talk about niggers, niggers . . . this useless waste of time"[27]

Regardless of their opinions about slavery in Oregon, members of the Clique were leery of the abolitionist movement. As it gained strength, its implications for the unity of the country dominated the national discourse. While abolitionists strongly advocated for their cause, political leaders stepped much more carefully, fearing that the movement would unite the South behind slavery. Thus, while opposing slavery in the territories and in new states, politicians generally did not espouse the end of slavery in the South. Even when the Civil War came, President Abraham Lincoln addressed Congress and maintained that he had "no purpose, directly or indirectly, to interfere with slavery in the States where it exists." Most northerners agreed with him.[28]

The distinction carried over to Oregon. In 1854, the Methodists founded the *Pacific Christian Advocate* in Salem and chose Thomas Pearne as its editor. Pearne, in the *Advocate,* became the Territory's most vehement spokesman for the abolition of slavery in the United States. Others shied away. When charged with being an abolitionist, Dryer was vehement: "While we oppose slavery, we deny being an abolitionist in the modern sense."[29] Bush consistently opposed slavery in Oregon, but he was equally adamant in his criticism of the abolitionists, maintaining that interference with slavery in the South would only strengthen proponents of the institution. Deady, who favored slavery, played to Bush's sensitivity about the issue when he warned: "There seems to be an impression going around that you are secretly an abolitionist." Oddly enough, despite his own proslavery sentiments, Delazon Smith admired Pearne as a good reporter, "the best in the country," and wrote his wife that he regularly bought eight copies of the *Advocate.*[30]

The prospect of Buchanan's victory in the 1856 presidential election brought Dryer to a change of heart regarding statehood. Although he opposed slavery, he wrote that if slavery had to come, it should be the choice of the people of the Territory, not the national government. While he had not abandoned his conviction that local Democrats would fight for slavery, he had come to prefer that battle to the possibility that the federal government, under Buchanan, would impose slavery on Oregon as a prerequisite for statehood. Buchanan's subsequent efforts to force the proslavery Lecompton Constitution on the Kansas Territory bolstered Dryer's fears. Deady saw an opportunity to ridicule Dryer and encouraged Bush to "shew up the inconsistency of the new friends and old enemies of the movement" toward statehood in the *Statesman.*[31]

Whatever Dryer's opinion, neither the Democratic Party nor the Clique itself was united on the questions of slavery or exclusion. According to one scholar, "Most Democratic leaders were as ardently opposed to slavery in Oregon as any 'Black Republican'; Asahel Bush of the OS, LaFayette Grover, and George Williams were vocal in their rejection of the institution in that region. They were equally opposed to anything that smacked of abolitionism." While that was certainly true, the writer's other assertion, that Lane and Deady "favored Oregon's admission as a slave state not so much because they wished to plant the institution there as because they wanted to add two more votes in the U.S. Senate to the pro-slavery side" is false. Although the makeup of the Senate was indeed a consideration, both men believed slavery to be essential to Oregon's future prosperity and to the wellbeing of its citizens.[32] When a bill reinforcing the exclusion laws came to the floor of the territorial assembly in January 1857, Delazon Smith rejected it as unnecessary since large numbers of blacks would never come to Oregon. On the other hand, he argued that Oregon needed some blacks: "We want laborers here. Oregon wants working men. We want negroes in every town. They do not come in competition with any class of white laborers. We want barbers, waiters and boot-blacks everywhere. If your wife is sick, you want their help . . . There are not more than fifty negroes in Oregon. They all behave well. They are law abiding people so far as I know." Despite his support for the institution of slavery in the South, Smith dismissed it as unsuited to Oregon: "Would you establish slavery here?—In Oregon?—Oregon! In the far northwest—surrounded by free territory—with climate and soil not adapted to it—with a large proportion of its people from Northern States and opposed to it inherently and by education! It could not be done.[33]

The discussion carried on for months in the *Statesman*. In a letter to the editor, F. B. Martin of Yamhill County advocated slavery as a way to address the declining value of agricultural land, while Thomas Norris warned that Oregon's location would make escape too easy.[34] The risk that the question would splinter the anticipated constitutional convention led Bush to print Lafayette Grover's letter outlining a plan that the constitution's framers eventually adopted:

> The question of African slavery and the question of the admission of free Negroes will come up in the formation of a State government for Oregon. I believe the proper way to dispose of these questions will be to submit them to a direct vote of the people in a schedule appended to the constitution at the time they pass upon its adoption. That vote will determine whether or not slavery shall become a part of that constitution—whether or not free Negroes shall be admitted.[35]

Grover opposed slavery and added that exclusion of blacks would spare Oregon the troubles now engulfing the South. Again invoking the Kansas-Nebraska Act and its implications, Bush supported Grover's proposition: "We are heartily in favor of leaving the settlement of that question [slavery] in the Territories to the citizens thereof, as entirely as it is left to the citizens of the States." He went on to apply the principle of "squatter sovereignty" to the broader and more pressing issue of territorial self-rule, maintaining that "the people of the Territories should choose from among them their Governor, their Judges, and all their officers, and that they should make their own laws, subject to no disapproval by a distant, and essentially foreign power.[36]

Dryer had no doubt as to Democratic intentions:

We have ever regarded the *Statesman* as a pro-slavery paper which would be found doing battle in favor of slavery whenever its services were needed to carry it through . . . This little family quarrel between all these democratic organs [*Messenger, Times, Standard, and Sentinel*] is a ruse on the part of Bush for his own purposes, however honest the others may be. Bush has the party in his hand or under his thumb, and can do as he pleases with them. The others may whistle while he sings. They may shake the bush but Bush will catch the bird.[37]

As the intensity of the slavery debate heightened, a new political force had appeared in the Territory. From its founding in Wisconsin in 1854, the Republican Party with its strong stand against slavery in the Territories soon spread across the country. The Oregon Republican Party was established at an Albany convention in August of 1856. The members proclaimed their platform: "*Resolved,* That we fling our banner to the breeze inscribed, free speech, free labor, a free press, a free state, and Fremont."[38] The *Oregon Argus*, the newspaper founded in 1855 by William L. Adams, became the voice of the Republican Party and its commitment to "free labor, out of love for the teeming millions of poor white laborers."[39] This third strong voice in the debate served to harden the stances of the other parties. Dryer, still hoping for a Whig resurgence, was skeptical of the new party and its role in Oregon. He rejected the idea that the Republicans were in the forefront of the antislavery cause while he remained convinced that the Democrats, led by Bush, sought to impose slavery on Oregon.⁴⁰ Bush warned Democrats not to abandon their party in favor of the "Negro equality movement," as he characterized the Republican Party.

Of much greater concern to Bush and the Clique than the Republicans was the growing evidence of rebellion within the Democratic Party. Leland and the *Standard* attacked the Clique and its adherents with increasing vehemence, evidence that the Softs were gaining greater power in the Portland area and beyond. Resentment at the Clique's exclusive control of executive appointments during the Pierce administration, an important factor in its dominance, manifested itself. The power of the dissidents was evident during the 1856–1857 legislative session when they refused to follow the mandate of the caucus. At first Dryer embraced the movement but then backed off. Bush was quick to detect his change of heart. Dryer, he observed, had discovered that the anti-Clique Democrats, or as Dryer called them, the "real democrats," were not the allies he had hoped for. "It is all very well for the opposition to stand off at a distance and applaud the conduct of Bull-heads and Tender-feet who are endeavoring to destroy the democratic party while professing to belong to it, but Dryer will find them troublesome bed-fellows when he comes to 'bunk' with them. Ten to one he'll pray for deliverance, and wish them out of his party."⁴¹

Bush certainly wished them out of his party. In his eyes, an independent democrat was "one who votes for the meanest kind of a Know Nothing, nigger-worshipping apostate from the Democratic party." Nor did he support the abolitionists, whom he identified with the Republican Party. He maintained that the "insane agitation of the question by a few anti-slavery advocates among us" had actually increased sentiment for slavery in Oregon by as much as three hundred percent. He repeatedly argued that the question was not an ethical one, asserting that not five hundred voters in Oregon would be persuaded by that argument. Rather, "the only real questions are, is the introduction of slavery into Oregon practicable? And will it prove profitable?" When it came to the larger question of the controversy over slavery and its implications for the unity of the country, however, Bush was adamant, assuring his readers that "the people of Oregon are eminently National in their sentiments and attachments, and whether she enters the Union slave or free, she will be a conservative National State, and in every emergency will stand by the Union and the constitution as they are, with the compromises upon which they were formed and upon which they rest."[42]

Focused on the platform the approaching convention would adopt, Bush applauded the resolutions agreed upon by Democrats in preconvention meetings in Marion, Lane, Yamhill, and other counties: "In the language of Vice President Breckinridge, uttered in a speech during the last Presidential canvass, they declare that the Democratic party is neither a pro-slavery or an anti-slavery party, but that it is a party of the constitution, which will defend the constitutional rights of all sections, States or individuals, and leave the people of each State and Territory to regulate their domestic institutions in their own way, and to their own liking."[43]

When the convention convened, the delegates agreed on a platform that reflected the Breckinridge comment as well as Clique attempts to downplay the divisions within the party: "Each member of the Democratic Party in Oregon may freely speak and act according to his individual conviction of right and policy upon the question of slavery in Oregon, without in any measure impairing their standing in the Democratic Party on that account. Provided, that nothing in these resolutions shall be construed as toleration of Black Republicanism, Abolitionism, or any other faction or organization arrayed in opposition to the Democratic Party." The platform also endorsed Grover's plan that the proposed constitutional convention not address the questions of slavery and exclusion but leave those to the voters.[44]

Some in the East were not convinced. Bush printed various extracts from "abolition papers," including one from the *New York Tribune* that he characterized as a "frantic abolition sheet." The *Tribune* writer reported that he had recently received letters indicating that Oregon, widely expected to be a "free" state, would instead pursue admission as a state in which slavery would be legal.

> The sham Democratic party, under the leadership of Lane, is completely ascendant in that Territory. The larger part of the late Whigs, of whom many emigrated from slaveholding States, have become his supporters. The triumph of Buchanan in the Presidential election is commonly regarded throughout the Territory as a triumph of the policy of Slavery Extension; and as a very considerable part, perhaps a majority, of the people of

Oregon came thither from slaveholding States, principally from Missouri, they are beginning to claim the right of introducing slavery and, in spite of the prohibition contained in the Territorial act, of legalizing it by the State Constitution. It would hardly pay, at the present extravagant price of negroes, to import them into Oregon; but as in Utah, so in Oregon, a domestic supply might be obtained from among the Indians.

In fact, the *Tribune* writer concluded, his sources indicated that a large number of the "leading Lane politicians" had taken Native American women as their wives.[45]

For Dryer, the Democratic platform merely reinforced his conviction that the party with "Lane at its head and Bush at its tail" was united in its intention to impose slavery on Oregon by exercising a command "as tyrannical and absolute as that instituted by Loyola for the government of the brotherhood of the 'Order of Jesus,' or Torquemada in the days of Ferdinand and Isabella." But, while maintaining the dominance of the Clique, Dryer provided his own analysis of the growing divide within the Democratic Party:

One party, styling themselves the *hards*, have established and are using all means to maintain their ascendancy, claiming that thorough party organization must be maintained "at all costs and all hazards"; deciding that party caucuses ruled by themselves can do no harm, that all opposition must give way before the determinations of their Jesuitical and inquisitorial combination, and that whosoever shall dare question the authority of their self-exalted few, shall be denounced as political heretics, for whom there can be no forgiveness, to be placed under the bad of the inquisition, against whom the bull of excommunication is to be hurled; in short, damning them both politically and socially.

The reputation of such offenders, both as politicians, as men, or as citizens, is to be annihilated—for what? Because the *softs*, as they term them, dare assert and maintain the power and rights of the people; because they have dared to say to this self-formed, all-absorbing political clique: "Who made you kings that you should rule over us?"—because the so-called *softs* dare

further maintain that all representatives of the people shall obey
in their representative capacity the instructions by their several
constituencies; that in the absence of all particular instruction,
each representative shall have free right of opinion and action
in all matters, accountable only to the people he represents;
that violations of party principles and usages by a representative
must be adjudged by the people he represents, not by a clique or
caucus composed of representatives of other constituencies.[46]

In the face of another election to let the voters decide whether to have
a constitutional convention and, if so, to choose delegates to that convention, Dryer promoted himself as a candidate for delegate "independent of
all parties, factions, cabals, cliques or combination of men." Anticipating
the power of the Clique in any constitutional convention proceedings, he
called for resistance: "Will the people submit to this longer? Have they
lost their manhood?" He warned that Lane and Deady, in their ambition
to become senators whenever Oregon was admitted to statehood, would
"get the fattest offices and *farm out* the balance to their devoted followers, leaving the great mass of the people to feed upon the husks."[47]

Along with the statehood/constitution question, voters in the coming election were again selecting a delegate to Congress. With less of the
pretended hesitancy that had been his custom in previous elections, Lane
pursued renomination. His national profile had been raised by his role in
the infamous caning of the senator from Massachusetts, Charles Sumner.
The Congress was divided over whether Kansas would be admitted to the
Union as a slave or a free state, with the Senate favoring a free state and
the House a slave state. In Kansas, fighting broke out between the opposing sides. Sumner made a long and impassioned speech attacking the
proslavery forces and reviling the senator from South Carolina, Andrew
Butler, who supported them. The following day Representative Preston
Brooks of South Carolina, a cousin of Butler, attacked Sumner with a
cane on the floor of the otherwise empty Senate. Sumner was seriously
injured. Not surprisingly, the incident became a national sensation. Lane
was a vocal defender of Brooks and, in letters to Bush, minimized the
seriousness of Sumner's injuries. Bush gave the incident little attention
in the *Statesman* while the *Oregonian* devoted considerable space to the
confrontation and to Lane's defense of Brooks.[48]

To reinforce his standing in the Territory, Lane repeatedly assured his constituents of his efforts in pursuit of statehood pointing to his 1854 memorial to Congress that passed the House but was tabled by the Senate. When the 1856 proposition was defeated by the voters, he expressed his regrets to Grover and assured him that he had another plan, "a bill for holding a convention and the formation of a constitution and for admission into the Union." With his usual solicitous attention to the interests of important constituents, Lane added, "Allow me to express the hope that your company organized for the manufacturing of the wool of Oregon may succeed to the fullest of their wishes."[49]

One member of the Clique was not easily courted. Deady derisively commented to Nesmith: "I see the Genl has thought of resigning and coming to the rescue of Oregon, and for fear the world may not appreciate the pecuniary loss of this contemplated magnanimity we are treated in advance to arithmetical calculations showing it would involve the loss of $10,000. Oh! Perfection of humbug." Deady compared Lane to Cesare Borgia "pushing his fortune in the year of grace eighteen fifty six in the shallow puddle of Oregon politics, much after the manner of the wily Italian in the sixteenth century. May his latter end be as near his just deserts."[50]

Deady was also very critical of Bush for his support for Lane, which he attributed to Bush's desire for the surveyor general position for his father-in-law in preference to Lafayette Grover whose name had also been mentioned for the post. He wrote Nesmith about an article in which Bush included "a little of the Lane litany" referring to him as the "'man of the people,' 'Star of Democracy,' 'Ark of the covenant,'" and as the "luminous expounder of 'the true principles of the Government.'" Deady added, "I hope he will get his reward, and it is quite as well that it don't depend upon me."[51] But whatever the differences between them regarding Lane, Deady continued to be complimentary of Bush and of the *Statesman*.

Lane's pursuit of another election victory proceeded: "Now I pledge you my word that I would rather succede in procuring favorable action on matters relating to our interests than to have fifty years added to my life." When he failed, the "Black Republicans" were to blame. Through letters to Bush in the hope for complimentary articles in the *Statesman,* he reported his success in securing appropriations for roads, mail delivery, and reimbursements for the expenses of the American Indian Wars.

He promoted Nesmith for a presidential appointment to the position of territorial superintendent of Indian Affairs. For reasons that are unclear, the appointment was blocked when it reached the Congress. Despite the demands of his electoral campaign in Oregon, Lane remained in Washington, explaining to Bush, "Nes. is in trouble and I have all my life made it a rule to never desert a friend."[52] Nesmith was skeptical and, when finally confirmed for the position, not particularly grateful, writing Deady, "I don't believe a damned word of what the 'Senett' says about the charges against me in Washington. . . . I am inclined to think that he has manufactured the things for the purpose of magnifying his efforts on my behalf."[53]

Lane's first hurdle was securing the Democratic nomination at the convention. He modestly assured Bush, "Now my friend as to myself, let my friends do just what they may think best for the party & the country, and I shall be content."[54] Some of those most loyal to Lane warned him that he could not count on the Clique. His son-in-law Lafayette Mosher wrote Lane that Deady was their preferred candidate. Delazon Smith wanted the job himself and argued for the concept of rotation in office. In the end, however, Smith promised Lane his support. Expecting Lane's nomination, Dryer carried on a series of attacks in the *Oregonian* accusing him of being ineffective in his role as the Territory's advocate in Washington.[55]

Despite the divisions within the party, Lane won the nomination and prevailed in the June election over his little-known opponent, the independent Democrat George Lawson. Although he had supported Lane, Bush was concerned about the future of the Democratic Party. He warned of the danger of "personal parties" devoted to the political success of a particular man rather than the overall success of the party: "Not infrequently in this way a great party, founded upon principle and held together by common and concurrent opinions upon governmental questions, is distracted and rent asunder by issues and contests upon men." He pointed to Senator Thomas Hart Benton, "a man of great talents and political merit," who had turned the Democratic Party in Missouri into his personal party. While his party was successful initially, in the long term, "the consequence was restlessness and impatience on the part of other meritorious and talented men of the party in Missouri for a long series of years, and finally intestine war of a most malignant character, in which measures and principles were ignored, and persons only dealt with, at last resulting, as everyone saw it would, in the success of the men and measures of the opposition."[56]

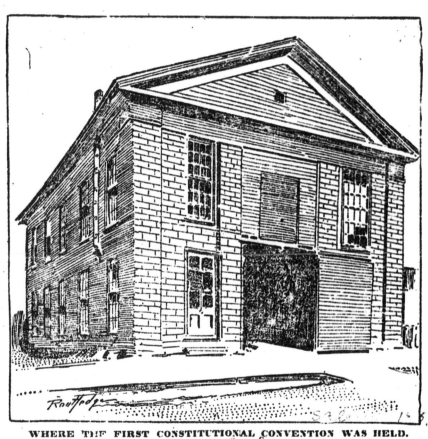

WHERE THE FIRST CONSTITUTIONAL CONVENTION WAS HELD.

The Salem meeting place of the constitutional convention.
(Courtesy Oregon Historical Society, bb010501)

CHAPTER SIX

"A word to the wise is sufficient," or "Is as good as a wink to a blind horse," whichever you think most applicable.

—Matthew Deady

In June 1857, the Oregon electorate finally supported statehood by a vote of 7,617 to 1,679 and called for a constitutional convention. They elected sixty delegates of various affiliations: Hard and Soft Democrats, Whigs, Know-Nothings, supporters of the temperance movement, and one Republican. The chosen included justices on the territorial Supreme Court, current and former legislators, federally appointed office-holders, and other well-known personages. Most were farmers or lawyers by profession.[1] While the forty-four Democrats handily outnumbered the sixteen opposition delegates, the division within the party threatened to minimize their influence over the proceedings. Members of the Clique who were delegates to the convention included Matthew Deady and Stephen Chadwick representing Douglas County, Lafayette Grover for Marion, Delazon Smith for Linn, and Reuben Boise and Fred Waymire for Polk. Without declaring a party allegiance, Thomas Dryer won a seat for Multnomah County, a victory one observer much later attributed to the even balance of the parties in Portland and to Dryer's "amiable qualities."[2] Multnomah County voters also chose another independent, David Logan. The Soft Democrat A. L. Lovejoy was elected to represent Clackamas County and the Whig Jesse Applegate for Umpqua County. John McBride of Yamhill County was the lone Republican in the convention.

In declaring his candidacy for a seat in the convention, Deady had announced that he would support a constitutional provision allowing slavery. His attitude toward slavery has been characterized by historian

Dorothy Johansen as "Jeffersonian" in that he favored an agricultural society with its virtues of independence and self-reliance providing, in Deady's words, the "true and solid wealth and happiness of a people." Slavery would enable people to remain on the land rather than fleeing to the cities where they would become "in some instances purse proud millionaires, but more frequently sharpers, thieves, rowdys, bullies and vagabonds."[3]

Deady's stand prompted Dryer to warn that the "church of latter-day democrats," under Deady's command, intended to impose slavery on Oregon. He pointed to a significant danger, that if Oregon came into the Union as a slave state, supporters of slavery would control the US Senate. Despite the very public divisions within the Clique over the slavery question, Dryer remained convinced that they had "asserted the right of a *political inquisition* and entered into a secret *conspiracy* to *first* make slaves of the white men in their party, preparatory to Oregon becoming a slave State of the Union."[4]

While it was true that Deady and Lane favored Oregon's coming into the Union as a slave state, other prominent Democrats were opposed. At Bush's invitation, Deady's colleague on the territorial Supreme Court, George Williams, wrote a detailed letter on the subject for the *Statesman*. He prefaced his examination of the issue by calling for "good feeling and moderation" and by defending slavery and its proponents in other parts of the country, adding that he considered slaveholders to be "high-minded, honorable, and humane." His letter carefully presented historical opinions: that Thomas Jefferson had opposed slavery north of the thirty-first parallel, that the Oregon pioneers had rejected it in 1843, and that in 1850 Whig senator Daniel Webster of Massachusetts held that God had "fixed the natural limits of slavery southward" of Oregon. Asserting that Oregon, at least for the time being, needed more settlers and workers, he echoed former Virginia senator John Randolph's observation that slave labor was "demonstrably the dearest of any," noting that several northern states, including New York, Pennsylvania, and Massachusetts, had tried slavery and found it "detrimental to their interests."

Williams argued that, because he is motivated by economic concerns for himself and his family, "one white man is worth more than two negro slaves." Importing slaves from the South would be more expensive than hiring white workers. With free California to the south and wilderness to the north and east, slaves could easily flee Oregon. By comparing the growth of the population in the contiguous states of Indiana and Kentucky, one free and the other slave, Williams dismissed the notion that slavery was the most effective way to provide a workforce. Besides, "suppose a farmer has slaves to do his work, and sons to rear. Will those sons be as industrious as they otherwise would be, and is any father willing to have his children grow up without habits of industry?" In summation, Williams declared slavery unsuitable for Oregon because of its geography, its need for settlers, and its economy, present and future.[5]

In presenting the letter, Bush described it as "written in a spirit of inquiry and moderation, and if his facts and arguments do not convince the reader's judgment, the spirit and manner of this letter must command his approval." But not all of the *Statesman*'s readers approved. James M. Pyle, a supporter of slavery, wrote Deady urging him to "demolish the alpine mountain of *highflanuten* and *poppycock* which your honorable associate has oiled up to frighten the little fishes with."[6] Deady instead refused Bush's invitation to provide the *Statesman* with a response to Williams's letter. When Bush admonished him for his proslavery stand and the danger that it would shatter the Democratic Party organization in Oregon, Deady responded angrily: "Why not sneer at Lane who has said in these parts during the canvass that he was in favor of Slavery in Oregon, and in a speech at Winchester said that he doubted whether a man could be a good Democrat and vote against Slavery in Oregon."

Despite this exchange over the slavery issue, the relationship between Deady and Bush remained close. In the same letter, Deady complained that Bush did not write him often enough. Attributing Bush's neglect to the time taken "talking fun and nonsense and playing boyish pranks about the 'Clique room,'" Deady jokingly warned that "the Salem part of the Clique are getting a reputation for frivolity and light-mindedness rather unbecoming the rulers and leaders of a grave and earnest people. 'A word to the wise is sufficient,' or 'is as good as a wink to a blind horse' whichever you think most applicable."[7]

In his 1901 *Oregon Historical Quarterly* article, George Williams asserted that he was the only Democrat to address the slavery issue publicly: "Many democrats in private conversation expressed their opposition to slavery, but they spoke with 'bated breath and whispering humbleness' for the dominating spirit in the democratic party was favorable to slavery." Williams's claim was patently false. Bush was quite explicit and quite public in his opposition to slavery in Oregon. In fact, despite their acrimonious exchanges, Bush and Dryer held essentially the same opinion regarding the introduction of slavery into Oregon. Both men were opposed to it not on moral grounds but because of their conviction that it would not benefit Oregon economically or otherwise.[8]

The constitutional convention convened in Salem on August 17, 1857. Some observers remarked on the importance of the location as the home of the Salem Clique. A reporter covering the convention, Patrick Malone of the *Sacramento Daily Union* wrote that Salem was a town "inconsiderable in point of numbers . . . but territorially omnipotent in point of political power. It is to Oregon what Rome is to Christendom—the point from which emanate mandates that are felt to the outside rim of its jurisdiction."[9]

Because the official *Journal of the Proceedings* is a very sparse record of the debates, Charles Carey in his history of the Oregon constitution includes the much more extensive reports of the *Oregon Statesman* and the *Oregonian.* As the convention progressed, the *Oregonian* provided the more comprehensive coverage. Afterward, Dryer wrote that "we only did our duty" while the *Statesman* in failing to hire a shorthand reporter demonstrated "the illiberality, the thorough selfishness and disregard for its readers' correct instruction, which Bush is capable of, when money, his sole and only God, is to be saved by it."[10]

Before, during, and after the convention, Dryer maintained in the *Oregonian* that the Clique had predetermined the provisions of the constitution. He compared its members to Hannibal, Nero, Robespierre, Judas Iscariot, and Benedict Arnold: "But none of these have ever attempted a political tyranny equal to that of the Salem inquisitors, self-christened and self called 'the democracy of Oregon.'"[11] In fact, the debates, in the official and even in the *Oregonian* reports, indicate that the Clique delegates were by no means in agreement on questions of both procedure and substance.

The specifics of organization were the first priority of the convention. Before the delegates gathered, the Democrats had caucused and agreed to support Matthew Deady as the presiding officer. The delegates elected him by a vote of thirty-nine to fifteen with Dryer among those voting against him. Deady himself, along with three other delegates, voted blank. The convention then elected a secretary, an assistant secretary, a sergeant-at-arms, and a doorkeeper. With the exception of John Baker who was nominated for doorkeeper by George Williams, each of the winning candidates was nominated by a member of the Clique. In most cases, the opposition voted blank. Asahel Bush was elected printer by a vote of forty to two with thirteen delegates, including Dryer, voting blank. After considerable discussion, eleven standing committees were appointed. Members of the Clique chaired six of them: Reuben Boise the Credentials, the Legislature, and the Seat of Government Committees; Delazon Smith the Committee on Suffrage and Elections; and Lafayette Grover the Rules Committee as well as the Bill of Rights Committee, which was formed later in the proceedings.[12]

Delegates debated a number of rather trivial questions: whether delegates should take an oath to support the US Constitution, whether delegates should be referred to as "the honorable," whether each member should be required to explain his vote for or against each officer and so on. A much-argued procedural matter was the length to be allowed for individual speeches. When the Rules Committee's report included a provision limiting floor speeches to forty minutes, several delegates protested, most passionately Delazon Smith: "Why, sir, I could not begin to have a good sweat on by that time. Some men can not get their minds off freely until they get warmed up. I am among the number. And right in the midst of my progress the hammer of the speaker falls, and I am cut short. As well to be cut off at the knees. I would rather not speak at all." Smith added that the people had not sent them to Salem "to hold a Quaker meeting." In a rare instance, Dryer agreed with a member of the Clique, saying that the provision "savors too strongly of the rules adopted by boys' debating societies." Despite their objections, the motion to strike the forty minute limit was defeated thirty-four to seventeen. Boise and Smith voted to strike it while Chadwick, Waymire, and Deady voted to retain the rule. In the course of the convention, as time grew short and delegates grew impatient, the limit would be lowered to twenty minutes and finally to five minutes.[13]

The first substantive controversy arose over whether or not a Bill of Rights should be included as a distinct part of the Oregon Constitution. During the extended debate, some dismissed the necessity since the Constitution of the United States had been amended to include the Bill of Rights. Delazon Smith argued for the inclusion of a Bill of Rights. While a number of states did not have a Bill of Rights in their constitutions, the majority did. He particularly pointed to Indiana's constitution whose Bill of

Rights was "gold refined," because it affirmed not only the right to life, liberty, and the pursuit of happiness but also included a declaration of other rights that had emerged in the seventy years since the adoption of the US Constitution. George Williams argued that the concept of a Bill of Rights originated with the Magna Carta when "the government was independent of the people and possessed absolute power over them." In Oregon, the people were independent, "there is no king to declare against; no power above them to curtail their rights." He maintained that limitations on the powers of government should be incorporated into the articles on the executive, legislative, and judicial branches.[14] To the delegates' amusement, Fred Waymire presented another argument in favor of a separate Bill of Rights: "Put a good bill of rights right in the beginning of the constitution, and the voters would read that, and vote for the whole constitution without ever reading the constitution at all." Whether or not Waymire's proposition influenced the outcome, the convention incorporated a Bill of Rights as Article I of the constitution. Much later, in his memoir, Lafayette Grover claimed credit as its author.[15]

Section 5 of the Bill of Rights prohibited the use of tax dollars to promote or support any religion or religious institution and specifically banned "the payment of any religious services in either house of the Legislative Assembly." A delegate proposed an amendment allowing the payment of a chaplain to serve the legislature. Deady objected that paying a chaplain violated the separation of church and state. He rejected the argument that without such a provision, the voters would not approve the constitution. Waymire agreed: "The people of this country were composed of every shade of opinion upon the subject of religion, from the half-crazy religious fanatic to the unbelieving atheist. And we had no right to compel by law the support of any from the pockets of all." When P. R. Marple of Coos County argued that such an amendment was necessary to avoid the fate of France with its revolution, Grover said he saw the French Revolution differently. The stance against religion came because "the public mind had become demoralized by a union of church and state, promulgation and enforcing forms rather than faith, conventionalisms rather than true morality."[16]

In an attempt at compromise, Boise suggested that the article be amended to prohibit the use of public funds "for the benefit of any religious or theological seminary." He was willing to allow the payment of the chaplain for the legislature as chaplains to penitentiaries were paid but would leave the question to the legislature. Deady responded:

> Were I a member of the legislative assembly and the question was to arise whether a chaplain be invited to officiate in that body, I should be governed by considerations of this nature: I would ask if he was a holy man, a man of practical piety, and one who had at heart the good of his fellow men; if he possessed those qualifications I should vote to invite him. But if he were one of those stump pulpit orators and fanatical demagogues with which our generation is cursed, I would vote against him; a pious and good man would not be insulted by being asked to pray without pay.

Waymire added "Suppose a Roman Catholic should be elected chaplain; every other religious denomination in Oregon would be in open rebellion. Every one here knew that. Yet you taxed Roman Catholics to pay for Protestant chaplains, and why not tax Protestants to pay Roman Catholics." In the end, the convention approved the amendment that Boise had presented: "No money shall be drawn from the state treasury for the benefit of any religious or theological institution."[17]

Early on, the delegates accepted the proposal that Grover had outlined in his March letter to the *Statesman:* that the questions of slavery and exclusion be submitted to the voters. Grover was appointed chair of the committee formed to devise the procedure for the referral. Jesse Applegate introduced a resolution that in light of the planned referendum "the discussion of the subject of slavery by this body is out of place and uncalled for, and only calculated to engender bitter feelings among the members of this body, destroy its harmony, retard its business and unnecessarily prolong its session." While proclaiming "I would as soon sever my right hand as to vote for a constitution that would either inhibit or adopt slavery here," Delazon Smith opposed any restriction on the convention's debates and particularly on the issue of slavery. Dryer agreed, "Is that freedom of speech? Is it freedom of thought? Is it manly? Is it bold? Is it the principle that governs the rights of American freemen in deliberative bodies?" On the other hand, Waymire and Chadwick supported Applegate's resolution, Chadwick saying that the convention had no right to discuss the issue.

"Upon the question of slavery, it is none of your business how I shall vote, and none of mine how you may choose to record your vote." He was concerned that a discussion in the Convention would compromise the people's independence when they voted on the matter.[18] The preceding is the *Oregonian's* account of the debate. The *Statesman* account is shorter but interestingly enough records Dryer's statement that he "wanted no man to steal a senatorial robe on this floor by dodging the nigger question. He wanted every man to show his hand—to either serve God or Mammon. General Lane, the great bell-wether of the democratic party had dodged. He did not dare to say to the South that he was opposed to slavery, and he did not dare to say to the North that he was in favor of it."[19] That he published Dryer's remark reflected Bush's growing disaffection with Lane.

Another question that divided the Clique delegates was that of Chinese immigration. The Chinese presence in the Territory had become an issue early in the decade when numbers of Chinese came to work in the southern Oregon mines. The argument ensued when William Watkins of Josephine County made a motion to add exclusion of the Chinese to the proposition on black exclusion that was to be submitted to the voters. He maintained that, in his region, the Chinese were no different than slaves, "they were bought and sold to one another, and to white men." He predicted that if more Chinese came to his county "in five years no white man would inhabit it," because the Chinese worked so cheaply that whites could not compete with them. Grover opposed submitting the question to the voters, arguing that two thirds did not know anything about Chinese immigration. He preferred adding a clause excluding them to the constitution. Boise agreed that the people were not prepared to deal with the question but favored passing it along to the legislature. Waymire opposed exclusion. His constituents wanted more Chinese, "They made good washers, good cooks and good servants." Deady wanted the question submitted to the voters since he "saw no reason for making a difference between Chinamen and negroes. The negro was superior to the Chinaman, and would be more useful." Dryer said he "would vote to exclude negroes, Chinamen, Kanakas, and even Indians. The association of those races with the white was the demoralization of the latter."[20] While the question of Chinese exclusion was in the end left to the legislature, Section 6 of Article II of the Constitution declared that "no negro, Chinaman, or Mulatto shall have the right of suffrage."[21]

Other questions arose. When Deady proposed an amendment to Section 8, the "freedom of speech" portion of the Bill of Rights, to protect public figures from libel in the newspapers, Dryer predictably disagreed: "If the amendment is adopted, a man may be put up for office who is the veriest villain and a disgrace to the community, yet no public newspaper could denounce him. . . . An editor of a public newspaper is the guardian of the public interests." Deady characterized the press of Oregon as "a running sore on the community," a declaration that must have unsettled Bush. Dryer responded that the judiciary was "a running sore on the community." In its final form, Section 8 protected freedom of expression but cautioned that "every person would be responsible for the abuse of this right," meaning that the speaker or writer could be sued and would have to defend his statement in court.[22]

Clique members disagreed on the proposed constitutional provision meant to protect for a woman "the property and rights she had at the time of marriage or obtained afterwards, by means of which the husband was not the meritorious cause." Deady favored striking the section because it "only tended to family alienation and jars." Williams agreed: "In this age of woman's rights and insane theories, our legislation should be such as to unite the family circle, and make husband and wife what they should be—bone of one bone, and flesh of one flesh." On the other hand, Boise and Smith favored the provision, as did Waymire: "If the gentlemen who were in favor of striking out this provision had girls old enough to marry he thought they would take the other side of the question. How many men had already in this country married girls, used them for a year or two, spent all their property and put off to the states." The motion to strike failed, twenty-two to twenty-seven.[23] The question of women's suffrage did not come up in the convention proceedings.

The draft constitution included a provision for common schools, which the delegates, including those from the Clique, generally supported. The "boss" of the Clique did not: "We regret the introduction of that provision in the instrument. Not that we are opposed to common schools in the abstract, for we are not. But Oregon is a very different country. Oregon is too sparsely populated. In our opinion we now have and under the present system for years to come will have schools inferior to those which would spring up under the voluntary system."[24] The same provision called for a state university to be financed by the profits from the sale of state-owned lands. Deady opposed the public university: "Experience had demonstrated that state universities were of very little use to anybody. That they better be left to private enterprise." Smith and Waymire disagreed, supporting the university to provide students a broad education and keep young people from leaving Oregon. In the end, the establishment of a state university was delayed for ten years.[25]

Bush did not hesitate to share his opinion on issues beyond common schools. Continuing pressure from the temperance movement and its promotion by the Salem newspaper the Methodist-influenced *Pacific Christian Advocate* brought the prohibition of alcoholic beverages to the table. Some delegates proposed including it in the constitution, while others called for it to be submitted to the voters and still others that it be left to the legislature. Bush attacked the *Advocate's* position and prohibition itself, saying that prohibition laws required search and seizure clauses that would be unconstitutional and that, without them, the law would be a "dead letter." In its final form, the issue of prohibition was not addressed in the constitution.[26]

Perhaps the most contentious debate among members of the Clique was over Article XI regarding corporations. Deady opposed corporations as they were "generally got up by some smart gentlemen running around among the farmers and representing to them some glittering schemes where hundreds of thousands of dollars may be made. They get the farmers to subscribe; they get themselves elected managers, and they keep managing the concern until everything connected with it is managed into their own pockets or gone to ruins." Boise supported him, pointing to New England where, because of corporations, "the people had fallen from the ancient dignity which they once had." Now Massachusetts lacked the "intellectual power and strength of mind and moral force, that there was in it before the corporations had drawn off from the healthful pursuits of country life, the young women of the country."[27]

Grover, founder and majority stockholder of the Willamette Woolen Manufacturing Company, objected that corporations were necessary to finance internal improvements and disputed Boise's contention that corporations destroyed a society: "It has been said that corporations tended to the degeneracy of a people. How did England, with her manufactures and great internal improvements, compare with Russia, which had not opened her country to internal improvements? How did she compare with southern Europe, which was in a like condition? Where you found not arts and manufactures, you found a degenerating people." Stephen Chadwick pleaded, "Let us reason together." Eventually Deady and Boise accepted that corporations would be a reality and proposed a number of limitations on them particularly in the matter of stockholder liability. Waymire too opposed corporations and, in John McBride's opinion, succeeded "in hedging them with such restrictions and limitations that their power has been less liable to abuse than in any other state in the Union."[28]

Despite the differences among delegates who were members of the Clique, others saw them as the hardly disguised dictators of the proceedings. The *Statesman* reported a heated exchange "during which it was charged or intimated that there had been party caucusing on the part of the majority of the convention, and that the majority were disposed to 'gag' and 'cram measures down the throats' of the minority." Delazon Smith dismissed the allegations as "false as hell."[29] Dryer and others regularly returned to the "caucus" theme.

As the convention moved to a close, Delazon Smith took the opportunity to deliver a long speech, ten pages in the *Proceedings*, summing up the work of the convention and its product and looking forward to what statehood would mean:

> We may ask and will receive liberal appropriations for the improvement of our navigable rivers and our harbors, and shall thus build upon this coast the interests of republicanism, of Christianity, of law and of education. Midway between the ancient nations of Asia and the modern nations of Europe, perfecting republican institutions here in this land, we can hold up this government to the gaze of the world and become, like the brazen serpent in the wilderness, an emblem of hope and political redemption to Asia, to China, and to those who inhabit the islands of the Pacific ocean. And, having done our whole duty, we may leave our children in the possession of a glorious boon, surrounded with the institutions of freedom, religion and law; and as a state and a people they will stand, like the Angel of the Resurrection, clad in robes of spotless white pointing the world to Freedom and bidding it hope in God.[30]

Apologizing for taking the delegates' time, Dryer took the floor to explain his stand: "I shall vote against this constitution, sir, for I supposed when we came here that we were to adopt a constitution not for a party but under which we could exercise all the rights that are granted by the constitution of the United States. That no man was to be proscribed or crushed for opinion's sake; that he should entertain his own views, and have a fair, at least a liberal, opportunity to express those views." Reflecting his longstanding opposition to the viva voce law, Dryer pointed to the convention's failure to deal with the question which he contended should have been submitted to the voters along with the slavery and exclusion provisions.[31]

The motion to adopt the constitution finally came on September 18. Thirty-five delegates, including the members of the Clique, voted in its favor. Ten, including Dryer, voted against adoption while other opponents, including Jesse Applegate, absented themselves from the proceedings.[32] Despite their opposition, eight of those who had voted against it, including Dryer, signed the constitution. The next step in the process was the submission of the draft constitution to the electorate. In addition to accepting or rejecting the constitution, the voters would decide between an article supporting slavery and another prohibiting it as well as one allowing African American immigration and another forbidding it. Depending on the outcome of the vote, the appropriate articles would be included in the constitution.

Prior to adjournment, Deady as president of the convention addressed the delegates.

> Gentlemen: I congratulate you upon the conclusion of your labors; you have labored more arduously, in session and out of session, than any deliberative body it has been my fortune to be acquainted with, and I trust the result will meet the approval of your constituents. . . . For myself, although objecting to some of the provisions of the constitution, considering with reference to probabilities of getting a better one, I approve it, and will support it at the polls. Before concluding, let me thank you for the kindness and courtesy you have shown me as presiding officer of this convention. The most appropriate return I can make you is the wish that your constituents may approve your conduct and endorse your work.[33]

In his 1902 address to the Oregon Pioneer Association, John McBride took the opportunity to assess the constitutional convention. He included descriptions, perhaps softened by time, of Clique members Deady, Waymire, and Smith and their roles in the convention. Matthew Deady was "large in stature, of impressive manner and bearing, smooth in speech, courteous and affable in intercourse, though he had dignity and firmness as a presiding officer." Fred Waymire was a "Far West David Crockett" who had common sense but little education and was "the most influential among the farmers in the convention." A convincing speaker who had come "to fight high taxes, high salaries and corporations 'tooth and toe-nail,'" Waymire was "a wise and shrewd guardian of the public interest" and "could come nearer getting what he wanted done than any other man." Regarding Delazon Smith, McBride echoed the contemporary view of his exceptional speaking skills: "He had a splendid voice, was rather under medium height, of good presence, could say beautiful things with splendid effect, and while not often indulging in the dramatic style, had great powers of imitation, and his powers of sarcasm and jibe were like the bolts of Jove." In McBride's opinion, Smith's one rival as a speaker during the convention was Thomas Dryer, "a ready speaker full of wit and humor." McBride admitted that Dryer was not a particularly good editor but was "well adapted to the rough and tumble of the times, was useful to the public, and deserves to have his memory embalmed as one of the most useful of pioneers."

Overall, McBride judged the convention and its delegates very favorably: "Sincerity, intelligence, integrity, and directness were manifest in all that was said and done at the convention. The membership was clearly controlled by convictions, and an intelligent knowledge of what was needed at the time and would be adapted to the wants of the future. . . . Williams, Deady, Grover, Logan, Dryer and a dozen others were men who would have been distinguished in any community where ability and statesmanship are recognized."[34]

The constitutional convention proved to be a training ground for its delegates. In subsequent years, many played major roles in Oregon government and politics—local, state, and national—as mayors, governors, state legislators, congressmen, and senators, as well as prominent members of the judiciary. Of the Clique, Deady served as a federal district court judge and Boise as chief justice of the Oregon Supreme Court. Grover became both governor and US senator. Nesmith was a US senator, and, later, a member of Congress. Although briefly, Smith too was a US senator as was Harding. Chadwick was a state senator, Oregon secretary of state, and governor; and Waymire served in the Oregon House.[35]

Although the convention had ended, the Bush-Dryer exchanges over the proceedings continued. Bush decried the opposition's "slang-wang" that accused the Democrats of caucusing nightly to discipline its members and dictate their positions on the next day's issues. He maintained that the Democrats had caucused only once, to choose their nominees for the convention's officers. Further,

> the only "Salem clique" that now exists, or ever existed, consists of the regular, hard democratic organization and party. It extends all over the Territory—has members in every section, in Linn, Polk, Benton, Lane, Douglas, Umpqua, Jackson and the other counties as well as in Marion. It is an extensive and powerful clique—this democratic party is. Grumblers, carpers, softs, soreheads and falsifiers had better get off its track before they are run over and "mashed."[36]

Dryer was undeterred. With the referendum on the draft constitution scheduled for November 9, he launched a tirade against its passage in his editorials in each of the four October editions of the *Oregonian*. Warning his readers to "look before you leap," he maintained that "it would not benefit, but seriously injure a large majority of the people of Oregon to go into a state organization at this time, because our taxes would be double, and the expenses increased." Democratic newspapers would "advise their followers to vote for it, because it will help them to steal, rob and plunder more rapidly and surely than they can do under a territorial government." Most important, "The truth is, none but the *Salem Clique* had anything to do with drafting that instrument. It was prepared in advance at Salem, to subserve the interest and preserve the controlling power in the hands of that little band known as the 'Salem Inquisition.'"[37]

The prospect of the election elicited much debate. In the *Statesman*, all sides of the argument were represented. A supporter of slavery, J. Cooley, maintained that Oregon should remain a free state and thus be a credible defender of the institution in the South. James Bassett, in a long letter in the same issue, refuted most of Williams's earlier arguments opposing slavery and belittled the "judge's genius." Bush let his readers know of the reactions of newspapers outside the Territory. The *San Francisco Chronicle* predicted that Oregon would face the violent confrontation that Kansas had endured. The *New York News* and the *Sacramento Union* opined that slavery was impractical for Oregon, while the *San Francisco Herald* lauded the decision to put the issue to the voters.[38]

Opposition to the proposed constitution from the *Oregonian* and other newspapers brought Bush's response:

> We have hitherto said that there are provisions in the Constitution
> which we wish other than they are. This, however, is our individual
> judgment. We never saw and never expect to see a Constitution
> which would exactly meet *our* personal views in every particular.
> A Constitution is itself but a compromise. In its adoption by
> a convention, or its ratification by the people, a contrariety of
> sentiment is expected to exist—this is inevitable, but—as in regard
> to every other matter under our form of government—the minority
> must yield to the views of the majority.[39]

Clique members canvassed the Territory in support of passage. From his base in Polk County, Nesmith assured Deady, in southern and less-populated Douglas County where opposition was more pronounced, that the prospects for its adoption were encouraging.[40] Nesmith was proven correct. The constitution passed by a vote of 7,195 for and 3,215 against. Regarding the two separate measures, voters opposed slavery by a vote of 7,727 to 2,645 and opposed the admission of free Negroes by 8,640 to 1,081. Both the ban on slavery and the exclusion of Negroes from the state were thus included in the Constitution. The section banning African Americans from Oregon remained in the Constitution until the 1926 Ballot Measure 3, "Repeal of Free Negro and Mulatto Section of the Constitution," passed by a vote of 108,332 to 64,954.

The voters' decision to prohibit slavery did not change Deady's mind. He wrote Nesmith that he was "in favor of the [United States] Constitution," in its protection of slavery.[41] Despite his repeated rejection of the Kansas-Nebraska Act and "squatter sovereignty" as contrary to the Constitution

of the United States, Joseph Lane was sufficiently politic to write Bush for
publication in the *Statesman*:

> I am much pleased to learn that our Constitution has been ratified
> by the people, but am sorry to find that there are some still harping
> over the slavery question. It has been settled by a vote of the
> people, and with their decision all should be satisfied. Our motto
> was, in the late canvass, and in our platform, and it is the true
> principle of the Kansas Nebraska bill, "leave it to the people." They
> have decided against slavery, and certainly no good democrat will
> now attempt to disturb the peace and success of the democratic
> party, on this question, settled, and for all time, so far as Oregon is
> concerned.[42]

CHAPTER SEVEN

"I am a democrat as true as steel, have never flinched and never will."

—Joseph Lane

With the Constitution approved and despite the fact that statehood had not yet been granted, the Territory's leaders moved on to the next step: electing men to the offices of governor and representative to Congress as well as to what would become the state legislature. The campaigns began immediately, complicated for Democrats by the growing divisions within the party. From Washington, Lane's concerns about the split and its potential effect on his career had already caused him to send his trusted clerk, young Ethelbert Hibben, to monitor the situation. Previously, Hibben had occasionally provided news of Washington and of Lane's efforts on behalf of the Territory to both the *Statesman* and the *Weekly Times,* the Portland newspaper that, unlike the *Democratic Standard,* was generally supportive of the regular Democratic organization. Shortly after the 1857 election, Hibben became editor of the *Times.* Initially skeptical of his reliability, the *Statesman* became more favorable when he used the *Times* to attack the Softs, particularly Alonzo Leland of the *Standard.*

The *Statesman's* endorsement only led some of Lane's closest friends in the Territory to question Hibben's commitment to Lane. Lane's anxieties intensified. In an effort to secure control of the party, he made a surreptitious attempt to purchase the *Statesman* through another emissary to Oregon, James O'Meara, a longtime newspaperman in California. O'Meara's instructions were to buy the *Statesman* with money provided by Lane but with the understanding that Lane's connection would remain a secret. At first, Bush was amenable to the sale but then changed his mind, to O'Meara's dismay. The negotiations resumed but in the end Bush again refused his offer. O'Meara considered buying the *Times* but ended up buying the *Standard,* a clear indication that his sympathies were with the Softs. O'Meara warned Lane that the Clique, Nesmith in particular, was working against him. Despite his own subterfuges, Lane was horrified: "But it cannot be possible that Nesmith, Bush or Curry can feel unkind to me! . . . I cannot even for one moment give room to suspicion, much less to act on such suspicion." He added, however, that O'Meara's report was "further proof of your kind feelings toward me."[1]

The rebellious Democrats began efforts to put into place a party structure. From Portland, Joseph Drew wrote Deady in remote Douglas County of the "new movement of the softs and bolters" calling themselves the National Democrats and led by O'Meara whom Drew characterized "not unlike some other Californians who of late have visited the wilds of Oregon . . . of vast pretentions with little bottom." Like Bush, Drew saw Hibben as a strong supporter of the Salem organization and its platform: "His paper of Saturday last pitches in to little O'Meara in fine Hoosier style."[2] Years later, with the benefit of hindsight, George Williams attributed the split in the Democratic Party to resentment of the Clique with its power and its command of patronage. Further, because its members "were all free state men, it was thought by some that they were not as friendly to General Lane as they might be." Whatever role the slavery issue played in the party's discord, Williams attributed the Democrats' problems to an undeniable reality, "there were more aspirants for office than there were offices to fill."[3]

In anticipation of statehood, the question of who would represent Oregon in the US Senate took center stage. In those days before the passage of the Seventeenth Amendment to the US Constitution, senators were elected by the state legislature rather than by the voters in a general election. Lane assumed his right to the post and, from Washington, began his efforts to win it. Although Deady had pledged his support, information that came from his contacts in Oregon made Lane doubt his commitment. Lane wrote his son-in-law, Lafayette Mosher, a letter skeptical of Deady's intentions. Mosher shared the letter with Deady expecting some reassurance but the letter only aroused Deady's displeasure. He sent Lane an angry response maintaining that such reports came from "men who live outside the Dem organization here, men in whom the Dem masses here have no confidence and never trust. Their prime object is and has been to incite internal discord in the local organization (which they call the Clique) and thereby break it down and elevate themselves in its stead." To accomplish that goal, they spread rumors of Deady's intention to challenge him.

To prevent such a rupture, Deady continued, he had declined to be a candidate and "it now depends upon you, whether these political anarchists and plotters shall keep the party in a ferment here by keeping up an apparent conflict between us for the Senate when, so far as I am concerned at least, none exists." Since he had made position clear, Deady felt he had a right to an immediate response from Lane "calculated to satisfy myself and our mutual friends that no misunderstanding exists between us." Lane, however, made it clear that he considered Deady's letter an insult to his commitment to the Democratic Party and its precepts: "Sir, if I prize anything highly and above price, it is the jewel of consistency as a democrat. From democratic principles, from the Democratic party organization I have never swerved for a single moment." The continued dominance of the party in Oregon was "of more importance to the advancement of her best interests, than my election to the US Senate."[4]

Meanwhile, Bush's concern about the Democratic convention and the success of Democrats in the coming election was not altogether altruistic. In the 1858 election, for the first time, the voters rather than the territorial legislature would decide who would be the official government printer. Bush wanted the post, an aspiration that was certainly evident to any observer. Deady, however, took offense: "Dr. Drew writes me that you are a candidate for the office of Public Printer. I hope you will be, but I suppose when you are you will let me *know in person*. I don't see any necessity of employing a 'go between' yet." Bush placated Deady then went on to request his help in the southern counties. He made it clear that the public printer post was his goal, adding that Benjamin Harding had nominated him for the assembly at the Marion County convention but he had declined.[5] From Roseburg, James Pyle tried to discourage Bush from pursuing the office while allowing that his victory would address "the everlasting clamor which has been raised and the notorious lies which have dinned in our ears about Yourself and the Salem 'Clique.'" But he feared that Bush might be defeated, adding, "I believe also that personally and pecuniarily you would be better off without the office and do not believe as many do that it is the public printing that keeps up the *Statesman*."[6] Bush was not persuaded by Pyle's arguments.

The atmosphere that prevailed in the approaching campaign was fore-shadowed by a meeting of the Softs in Portland on January 31. Attendees supported James Kelly for Congress and James O'Meara for public printer. Joseph Drew reported to Deady that each nominee spoke of the "duplic-ity, mendacity, treachery and arrogance assumed by the Salem *clique* to govern, control and direct the democracy of Oregon."[7] The deepening divi-sion in the Democratic Party manifested itself in separate conventions, the Hards meeting on March 16 in Salem and the Softs, with their new label "National Democrats," meeting on April 8 in Eugene. The Clique's concerns about party allegiance led Bush to write an editorial entitled "Good Faith in Politics," to remind those who would be attending the Salem convention of their obligations:

> Good faith and common honesty between man and man, as well as
> the well known rules and common usages of the party, dictate that
> they should abide the results openly and fairly arrived at. . . . We
> believe that a man's presence in a political meeting or convention
> is as good as his bond to secure good faith on his part in support
> of the nominations fairly made by such meeting or convention, in
> which he participates. . . . If he does not wish to abide the results
> of a nominating meeting or convention, no one wishes to see him
> assume the responsibility of taking part in such proceedings.[8]

When the convention met in Salem, the Hard delegates proclaimed their support for President James Buchanan and the platform of the 1857 Democratic National Convention in Cincinnati. The Salem convention endorsed "popular sovereignty" and the Dred Scott decision, a curious combination since the one was a contradiction of the other. Settling on a candidate for governor took a number of ballots. The eventual choice demonstrated the erosion of the Clique's power. John Whiteaker was the nominee, despite his conviction that Oregon should enter the Union as a slave state. In a *Statesman* opinion piece the previous October he had argued that, if Oregon became a free state, the country would submit to the abolitionists, which would eventually result in the "equality of the races."[9] The convention chose Lafayette Grover as their candidate for Congress and Bush as their candidate for public printer. Matthew Deady was nominated for the position of justice of the Oregon Supreme Court, but the delegates also passed a resolution endorsing his appointment by the president to the US District Court. Another resolution commended Lane for his service as delegate to Congress.

In a misguided attempt to calm the troubled waters, in February Lane had written a long letter to Hibben who published it in the *Times* on March 27, after the Salem convention had adjourned. Lane called on the wings of the Democratic Party to reconcile: "Should the germs of discord now existing in the democratic party in Oregon be speedily eradicated or suppressed, all will be well—should they be fostered and cultivated, it is easy to foresee what bitter fruits they will bring forth." The letter was so even-handed in its treatment of the two factions of the party and complimentary of the *Standard* that the Hards were outraged. Nesmith, having gotten wind of Lane's conspiracy with O'Meara to buy the *Statesman,* blasted the letter as "a senseless unmeaning mess of trash." Bush was equally vehement: "Don't be deceived, General, into the idea that these 'Nationals' will support you, if they had the Legislature. They will not do it. You have not a friend among them. . . . They have no more chance of carrying the Legislature than I have of being translated to Heaven. They are contemptibly weak." Even Lane's son Nat and his son-in-law Lafayette Mosher cautioned him against the Nationals and themselves remained with the Hards.[10] Lane's letter may have encouraged the National Democrats when they met in Eugene on April 8 to choose their own slate for office. They selected E. M. Barnum, a Salem attorney, for governor; James Kelly for Congress; and O'Meara for public printer. The Nationals too passed a resolution complimentary of Lane.

As yet unaware of the indignation his letter had caused, Lane adamantly defended himself to Bush: "I could part with my wife and all my children as easy as I could do anything to weaken the democratic party or disturb its organization, and I assure you that I shall do neither the one or the other." He went on to promote his candidacy:

> I am anxious to be one of the first senators, and I believe that I
> could be useful to the people of Oregon and also to the whole
> country. . . . I could not, would not, seek or desire a seat in the
> Senate at the expense of the party—I must be permitted however
> to say, that I have not a particle of doubt about the feeling of the
> Democrats of Oregon in regard to my self, nine out of every ten
> of them go for me for the Senate, and the fears of many are that

some unfair means is to be or will be resorted to for the purpose of defeating me.[11]

In between the two Democratic conventions, the Republicans met in Salem on April 2. After three ballots, they nominated John McBride over Thomas Dryer to run for Congress. The *Statesman* reveled in Dryer's loss while, in the *Oregonian*, Dryer abandoned the Republicans and called for the resurgence of the Whig party in the Territory.[12] In his anger and without any credibility, Dryer attributed his loss at the convention to the influence of German immigrants. His animosity toward immigrants was nothing new as reflected in his several editorials supporting the Know Nothings. The previous year he had cautioned his readers: "Let the people of Oregon look well to these gassy, swaggering, drinking, gambling, newly arrived immigrants, who sport a revolver hanging to their belts, and a knife handle sticking out between their vests and coats, as they will bear watching."[13]

In Dryer's mind, it was German Jewish immigrants who were chiefly responsible for his defeat. How he arrived at that conclusion is unclear. According to the Portland historian Carl Abbott, there were only 135 Jews in the city in 1860 and far fewer in the rest of the Territory. Whether in 1858 they could have had enough influence to turn the Republican convention against Dryer seems more than unlikely.[14] Negative opinions of Jewish immigrants among Oregonians were by no means unusual. After an 1852 visit to San Francisco, Bush had himself commented on the number of "that peculiar people who are yet looking for the advent of the Saviour." They owned small stores "which they cram with a mediocre article of pantaloons and coats, and where they stand ensconced the livelong day, waiting for a customer, and satisfied to argue and show their wares for an hour at a time, if there be a chance of making a nominal profit." Despite his derision, he went on to defend Jewish immigrants: "In justice to them we should say that they are among the quietest portion of our populace. How seldom is a Jew reported as drunk and disorderly? How seldom do they make themselves conspicuous in any way before the public, and yet through how many ramifications of trade do their dealings not run—with what class of society are they not brought in contact?"[15]

Dryer sarcastically dismissed the reaction to his diatribes, "Haas Bros. and Mayer and Co., two Jew firms in this city, have discontinued the *Oregonian*. Whether we shall be able to survive the shock or sustain ourselves

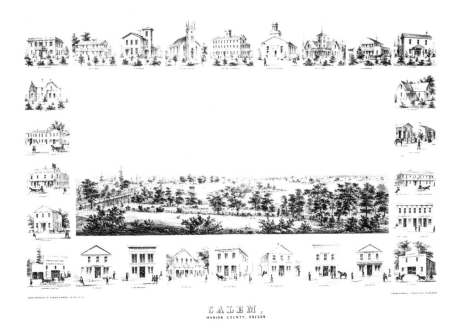

An 1858 lithograph of Salem. (Courtesy Oregon Historical Society, bb015021)

after this great loss of patronage, is a matter of deep and anxious solicitude with them, no doubt." He suggested that their neighbors would lend them their papers but warned that the same neighbors should watch to be sure their copies of the newspaper were not stolen from their doorsteps. When the *Statesman* called him "an irresponsible libeler" whose "object was to proscribe men on account of their birthplace and their religion," Dryer backed off a bit but with defiance:

> The Salem inquisitorial organs are trying hard to make us say
> something against the *German* or *foreign* population in relation to
> the late election. What we have said and what we meant to say, was
> in relation to the Jews, and we meant all we have said in its fullest
> and broadest extent, and we intend to say more in relation to this
> or any other sect, whenever they combine *as a sect* to control the
> political rights of the ballot box in this country. We have nothing
> to take back in all we have said, neither shall we be intimidated or
> driven from our purposes by misrepresentation or threats.[16]

Oregon's political atmosphere was increasingly contentious. Within the Clique itself, relations were not altogether harmonious. Bush's concerns about his election for public printer led to considerable tension between him and Deady. Before the Democratic convention, Deady had cautioned Bush that "if nominated for judge of course I do not expect to take any public part in the canvass." Instead he suggested that Bush have Smith and Nesmith campaign for him. Convinced that defeat in the southern counties would cost Bush the election, Drew wrote Deady that "Bush is very desirous that you should take the stump for him in your District. You can help him more than any one else. I am willing to do all I can, but you know that is but little, as I am as objectionable as he is said to be." Bush pressed Deady repeatedly: "If I can't coax, I'll try to skeere you. . . . If you don't go south, I'll 'spot you,' and I'll transmit the 'spot' to my posterity against the Deady race forever."[17] In Umpqua County, Chadwick, on the other hand, was more than willing to help out. Assuring Bush that he would campaign in nine or ten precincts, he added that Bush's prospects were improving, "Your abused name has suffered so much that already it has turned into sympathy—and a reaction is taking place." Delazon Smith reported his own efforts and their effect on the editors of the Territory's other newspapers: "The thorough work I am doing upon the stump arouses the ire of such men as Avery, Hall, Leland, O'Meara and company, and causes them to denounce and slander me." However, he was convinced that "the Democracy will gloriously triumph and abundantly honor and vindicate me."[18] Opposition newspapers attacked not only Smith but other members of the Clique, eliciting a strong defense from Bush:

> Men whose characters are respected by their neighbors in the communities in which they reside, are held up as the embodiment of everything accursed and hateful. The Hon. Delazon Smith, whom the yeomanry of Linn Country have always endorsed by majorities of from four to five hundred, is represented as a man perfectly destitute of principle and honor. Judges (George) Williams, (Matthew) Deady, and (Reuben) Boise are all assailed as *"trailing the ermine in the dust,"* yet no man who is acquainted with either of these gentlemen can point to a single instance of dereliction of public duty, and in private life their characters are known and admitted to be beyond reproach.[19]

Bush reminded his fellow Democrats of the significance of the coming election and their responsibilities:

> On Monday it is to be determined whether Oregon will take her place in the phalanx of democratic States, under the proud banner of the Constitution and the Union, or whether it will fall into line with sectionalism, fanaticism, and faction. This is the issue, and this is the question. At such a time, at an hour like this, will any *Democrat* be found *carping, complaining, fault-finding,* and *whining* about irrelevant, or if relevant unimportant questions? At such a time as this, will not *every true* democrat accord to his principles, his party and its standard bearers, an unhesitating, unconditional, enthusiastic and united support? He who does not has no right conception of what it is to be a democrat, *and practically is not one.*[20]

From Washington, Lane protested any suggestion that he was complicit in the rebellion against the regular Democrats:

> Dear Sir . . . I am the last man on the face of the earth who would indorse bolters or disorganizers. . . . You know there is not a man on the face of the earth who has stood by the Democratic party its organization its principles or its nominees more faithfully than myself. . . . I have never in my life encouraged dissension, discord, or trouble in the democratic ranks. . . . I am a democrat as true as steel, have never flinched nor never will.[21]

Despite the split in the party, the regular Democratic ticket—Whiteaker, Grover, Deady, and Bush—triumphed. Dryer was quick to point out that it was a narrow victory: "What a glorious cause these Salem democrats have for rejoicing over their fortunate escape from irretrievable rout, ruin and disgrace. . . . Hip, hip, huzza! For the invincible, unconquered, unwashed adamantines, who have escaped by the skin of their teeth, after an awful fright."[22]

While the ballots were still being counted, Deady wrote Bush, "I think you are elected. I hope so at least, for if not from the tone of your threatening letter I shall expect a fight when first we meet. I think that letter is indictable under the statute against threats."²³ Bush had not forgiven him: "I don't like your refusal to make a few speeches in Jackson and Josephine counties, and you can't satisfy me that you did your duty towards me or the democratic party in the matter. . . . The excuse that you were a judge or a candidate for one, is not satisfactory to me, at any rate. It is d——d nonsense." In a rather strange digression but one that is a reflection of the time, he added, whether as a joke or a warning:

> Drew says he has a letter written by Pat [Malone] from Sacramento last summer, in which he says he fell in with a dandy negro in going up to Sacramento, who inquired about you, and said he knew you well in Ohio and that he used to sleep and room with you. Pat says he told him that you were a pro-slavery man now, and the darky expressed great surprise and repeated that he used to sleep with you in Ohio. I do not relate this for the purpose of peddling Pat's stories but to put you on your guard against him. . . . Of course I don't pretend to credit Pat's story unless the nigger was a wench.²⁴

Despite internal differences, the Clique turned to more important issues. Although Oregonians had approved a state constitution and elected men to state offices, Oregon had in fact not yet become a state. Bills authorizing the people of the Oregon Territory to convene a constitutional convention had been introduced in the 1854, 1855, and 1857 congressional sessions but had failed to pass. Among a variety of arguments, opponents of statehood maintained that Oregon did not have a sufficient population to become a state. Such arguments, however, masked the fact that the real issue was slavery, an institution that Oregonians had rejected from the establishment of the provisional government in 1843 through the passage of the constitution. The prospect of another free state frightened southern advocates of slavery who feared that Oregon's admission would set a prec- edent affecting the entire West. Representative John Millson of Virginia pointed to the danger that representatives of new free states would com- bine with others in Congress to amend the US Constitution against the slavery interests of the South. On the other hand, Oregon's constitutional exclusion of African Americans was generally supported by southern sena- tors and other Democrats including Stephen Douglas, who noted that it was Illinois policy as well. Republicans were split on the matter.²⁵

While Oregon was dealing with the aftermath of the June elections, word came that the US Senate had at last passed the act granting statehood to Oregon by a vote of thirty-five to seventeen. Support came from northern Democrats and eleven of the seventeen Republicans. Even a very small majority of southern Democrats approved.[26] But, by the time the Senate bill reached the House of Representatives in July, the political landscape had changed. Because Democrats had triumphed in Oregon's June elections and in light of the provisions in Oregon's constitution that excluded African Americans and severely limited the rights of Chinese immigrants, Republicans were wary of granting statehood and made an effort to block the bill from coming to the floor. Democrats, on the other hand, perceived an opportunity to build on their majorities in the Senate and House. To the disappointment of Oregonians, consideration of the bill was deferred until the new congressional session began in December. Lane wrote Bush to assure him of his disappointment at the delay: "I regret the failure of this Bill very much, but it was not in my power to procure its passage."[27]

Despite the postponement, the newly elected Oregon legislature met on July 5 to, as Dryer put it, elect "two of the *unwashed* who may have been SELECTED by the Salem Inquisition to go on to Washington and aid Buchanan in propping up his crumbling administration."[28] After discussions and caucuses, the legislature chose Joseph Lane and Delazon Smith, both proponents of slavery, by acclamation. Instead of the usual six-year terms, both men were given shorter terms to ensure that Oregon's future senatorial elections would follow the national schedule. The new "Senators," along with "Representative" Lafayette Grover, left for Washington, Smith assuring his wife: "I do not allow myself to drink any thing stronger than tea and coffee; and I do not intend to. I am resolved to go to Washington and back, by the Grace of God, and drink no ardent spirits."[29]

The choice of Lane and Smith for the Senate was a clear indication of the erosion of the Clique's power over the Democratic Party. In the *Statesman,* Bush printed a report from a Washington correspondent whom he called "Metropolis," which accused Lane of delaying statehood until he could be assured of the Senate seat and the compensation that would come with it. He wrote a long letter to Lane dismissing his protestations of loyalty to the party and his questioning of Bush's own loyalty:

I'll tell you what I never did. I have not at every election failed to vote the Democratic ticket in Oregon. I was never claimed by the opposition, to belong to them, and my position towards parties was never so equivocal that the Democratic party was forced to declare that I was with it, while the Opposition party as stoutly affirmed that I was with *it*. The opposition never charged that I privately, to members of it, denounced the democratic platform, or any portion of it. And my especial friends were never found running upon or voting the opposition Ticket, and averring that they did it *as* friends of mine and by my sanction.[30]

The letter ended private communication between the two men for nearly two decades. Bush continued publishing articles blaming Lane for the delay of statehood. From Washington, Smith assured Bush of his own loyalty while regretting "the unhappy and most unfortunate state of feeling between yourself and Gen. Lane." Lane, he wrote, would welcome "a reconciliation on any terms that are honorable." Anticipating Bush's reaction to his letter, Smith added,

> Now, my dear sir, do not respond to what has gone before by saying that Lane has 'honeyfuggled and soft-scaped Smith' etc., etc. The *truth* is simply this: —if I had possessed a disposition to break and quarrel with Gen. Lane, it would have been, and would still be, *madness* to have done so, and had I entertained such a thought I should have promptly abandoned it on arriving here. The *truth* is that Gen. Lane is a faithful and zealous representative of the people of Oregon, and an earnest and constant advocate of their rights and interests.

Bush's dismissive response triggered another letter from Smith:

> You say "I firmly believe we did not go in at the last session because he did not know that he was Senator." I *know* that you are mistaken! And you will excuse me when I say that I must act upon my *knowledge* rather than your *belief*! But, my dear sir, whilst you demand of me that I shall act upon *your* judgment and *your* convictions—even pertaining to a state of things existing here

in Washington and of which I *must* be cognizant—you refuse to heed the most earnest, honest and friendly suggestions from me in regard to these very things![31]

Bush was not impressed by Smith's protests and regularly referred to him in both the *Statesman* and in his correspondence as "Delusion Smith."

Smith also defended himself and Lane to Nesmith who was convinced Lane had tried to get him removed from his position as superintendent of Indian Affairs over his reaction to Lane's "conciliation" letter. "The Gen. has never intimated to me any desire or thought of having you removed: on the contrary I have frequently heard him extol you personally and officially." Smith suspected that Bush now opposed statehood in order to further embarrass Lane and complained that Oregon newspapers were impeding the progress toward statehood: "It requires more labor here in Washington to counteract the influence of the Oregon press than it does to meet and vanquish all its other enemies. . . . The position, tone and influence of even the *Statesman* is with Dryer & O'Meara against the admission of Oregon." Still, he assured Nesmith, "You may bet high on the admission of Oregon early in the session. I have seen *every* member now in the city, and (you better believe) I have '*labored*' with them! Every body is for us." On the other hand, he wrote to his wife that there was more opposition than he had anticipated from the Republicans due to Oregon's exclusion of blacks and from Know Nothings because Oregon allowed aliens to vote. Despite such challenges, he boasted that he had managed to get the bill for statehood out of committee with a pass recommendation.[32]

In another letter to his wife, he reiterated his confidence that Oregon would be admitted despite opposition from "Know Nothings and Black Republicans." He went on to let her know that "I receive democratic newspapers from New York, Ohio and Iowa, containing long and very flattering notices of myself. I am every where kindly received, respected and honored." He was also optimistic about Oregon's future, expecting a large number of settlers to travel by land to the Territory in the spring: "With improved facilities, better roads, shorter routes, and horse or mule teams, the journey can be performed in about one half the time we consumed in 1852. We are having military posts established at proper points, and will also have the country east of the Cascade mountains, open for settlement in the spring."[33]

Lafayette Grover's arrival in Washington was delayed by an illness then known as "Panama fever," which he contracted on his journey across the Isthmus. Once there, he too defended Lane from Bush's accusations about his resistance to statehood: "In relation to the dispute raised between the Statesman and Gen. Lane as to his action last summer on our state question, there is absolutely nothing here to prove that the Gen was at all to blame for non-action." He added that many in Washington felt that Bush was "unduly unjust to have brought the matter up."[34]

In an earlier letter, Grover made an interesting and somewhat mysterious proposal to Bush: "Could not the Times be bought and sent to The Dalles? Then move the Statesman to Portland?" Something was in the air for Grover also mentioned the possibility of Bush receiving an appointment as the United States ambassador to Bolivia: "In case of our success here, I shall *push* for that foreign appointment in your behalf unless you say *hold*." Neither the move nor the appointment came up in other correspondence but talk of moving the *Statesman* must have been circulating in Oregon. George Williams, hardly Bush's confidant, while admitting that relocation of the newspaper to Portland would be advantageous financially, thought it would be a "political misfortune." He argued that "so far as the interests of the Democratic party are concerned it would be better for you to remain at Salem. You will undoubtedly have more influence in Marion, Linn & Polk to remain where you are than to come here."[35]

Reveling in the signs of division within the Democratic Party, Dryer intensified his attacks: "Democracy in Oregon means devotion to the personal interests of Asahel Bush. . . . It means that you must relish the egotism as well as the Toryism of D——y [Deady] and commend the recreancy of B——e [Boise] the Massachusetts Whig and laugh immoderately at the obscenity of 'Nes' [Nesmith] and down on your belly at their bidding where you must crawl, meekly looking up and eating any quantity of dirt that is set before you." Bush labored to maintain the Democratic Party while ramping up his criticism of Lane: "General Lane has, in Oregon always cultivated outside support, and kept hanging about the democratic organization as *his friends*—'Lane men'—a class of men who never voted for any other democrat. . . . All Gen. Lane's acts have unmistakably pointed to the building up of a *Lane party* here. . . . We believe that the successful formation of any mere personal party will sound the death knell of the democratic party. Man-worship and the support of principles and measures are incompatible."[36]

Meanwhile, in Washington, Lane was garnering considerable attention. Although the 1860 Democratic National Convention in Charleston, South Carolina, was more than a year away, speculation about the presidential nomination was on the rise. While well aware of Bush's animosity toward Lane, Grover wrote him of Lane's prospects. "There is some Presidential talk here in view of '60—Lane has some strength that way—more than you would believe." Smith was more adamant: Lane's "chances for the Charleston nomination are *better* that those of any other living man!"[37]

In January 1859, the House Committee on Territories at last reported out the statehood bill. The floor debate was contentious, with each side accusing the other of abandoning principle. When it finally came on February 12, the vote was close and reflected an ironic reversal of sides. The House approved Oregon's statehood by a vote of 114 to 103, with seventy-three of eighty-eight Republicans in opposition and forty-one of fifty-seven southern Democrats in support. The fifteen Republicans who voted for statehood were denounced by Horace Greeley in the *New York Tribune*. He predicted that Oregon's votes in the Electoral College would lead to the election of a proslavery president in 1860. President Buchanan signed the statehood legislation on February 14. The news of statehood did not reach Oregon until the arrival in Portland of the ship *Brother Jonathan* on March 15.[38]

While Bush's reaction to Oregon's statehood was for the most part a continuation of his attacks on Lane, Dryer saw it as the fulfillment of a Clique conspiracy:

The faces of our citizens too plainly exhibited the index of their souls—the evidence of mourning rather than rejoicing—when the news arrived of our admission. . . . No man can be found in this community, unless it be some office-hunting, non-tax-paying Dimocrats who think that Jo. Lane and Delazon Smith made the world and all things that are therein, and that when the earth is destroyed, all Dimocrats will be saved, and the world will become a perfect paradise in consequence of getting rid of the Whigs, Americans, Know-Nothings, Republicans and all who don't worship the Democratic calfs of Oregon. . . . The statehood project was conceived by a few political office-seekers, who urged it upon the people as a party measure, calculated to strengthen the party fetters and more closely rivet the shackles of slavery upon all those who could be wooed or won by the canting and hypocritical cry of 'Democracy' to a matrimonial alliance, in which the office-holders should become the tyrannical masters, and the masses of the people their slaves and serfs forever. . . . These party Lazarones, known as the Salem clique, to whom the Democracy of Oregon have ever been compelled to bow the knee and acknowledge supremacy, have induced the people to ask the admission of Oregon as a state.[39]

CHAPTER EIGHT

"As a statesman, Mr. Lincoln takes rank—nowhere."

—Asahel Bush, Oregon Statesman

Statehood at last in hand, sparring for office commenced. The endless maneuvers and speculation led Deady, who was selling a horse, to write Nesmith, "Following the order you have established, I will speak of the horse first and the Jackasses afterwards." As for himself, he was not interested in being a candidate against Smith for the Senate. Deady added in sardonic imitation of Lane's contrived reluctance about running for office: "However if my friends think 'the good of the country requires it' and I can be made useful when the time comes they may use my name."[1]

The US Senate was not Deady's objective. Deady was anxious to have President Buchanan appoint him as the first justice of Oregon's US District Court once Oregon achieved statehood. Since such an appointment required the approval of the Senate, it was customary for a president to ask for recommendations from a state's senators. Bush, well aware of Deady's ambitions, wrote him that, according to Lafayette Grover, Delazon Smith would oppose his appointment and that Grover was unsure of Lane's stand.[2] But Deady's support for the Lecompton Constitution and its protection of slavery in the Kansas Territory, a major focal point of the Buchanan administration, had greatly improved his previously tenuous relationship with Lane. Lane may also have seen a judicial appointment as a means for securing his Senate seat from any future challenge by Deady. He shared Deady's views on the Kansas question with the president and Buchanan made the appointment. Deady moved permanently from his landholding in Douglas County to Portland and would preside over the Court until his death in 1893.

Since Delazon Smith's term as senator would end with the adjournment of Congress and he had little or no chance of being chosen again by the legislature, there was considerable speculation about who would win the Senate seat. When Deady questioned him about whether Nesmith should run, Bush responded that he wanted him to be a candidate, "if he [could] be elected. His election would be a decided triumph and [Bush would] be glad to see it." If Nesmith could not be chosen at the convention, Bush wrote that he would "cheerfully go for Williams to beat Delazon."[3] His statement was further evidence of the estrangement between Bush and Smith, particularly since Williams had never been a Bush favorite.

In anticipation of the coming state Democratic convention, Lafayette Grover promoted his candidacy for Congress to Bush, "I am, I believe, what I was taken to be when elected, not devoted to the interests of any particular man, but making an effort at all times to devote myself truly to the interest of the state and people. If this will not do I am ready to retire. . . . If I should come back here I think I could do something for Oregon. Since being here this time, I have avoided all notoriety and sought to labor quietly for the measures in which we were interested. . . . I have, I think, the confidence of many leading members of the House who will come to the next Congress."[4]

The Oregon Democrats met on April 20, 1859, to choose their candidates for office. The convention, however, demonstrated the division in the party and the strength of the Lane faction. Its candidate, Lansing Stout, who had recently moved to Oregon from California, narrowly defeated Grover for the nomination to Congress. The Republican *Argus* maintained that the choice of Stout demonstrated that "for the first time in the history of Oregon the issue was now fairly made between the Republicans as the friends of free laborers and the Jo Lane Democracy as the advocates of Negro-breeding, Negro-extension fanaticism."[5] Stout defeated the Portland Republican David Logan in the June election, confirming Lane's standing and the deterioration of the Clique wing of the Democratic Party. While the *Statesman* had supported Stout as required of a Democratic Party newspaper, Bush secretly hoped for Logan's victory as a swipe at Lane. Still he could not have been happy that, for the first time, the Republicans won in Marion County.[6]

An important underpinning of the Clique's strength was lost when Lane successfully prevailed on President Buchanan to let Democrats in

Oregon know that future presidential appointments would depend on the party's support for him. Bush responded with self-righteous anger. If, in earlier years, "it had been proposed to democrats to place a large number of lucrative public offices, and the disbursement of a large amount of public money, at the disposal of a single individual—no matter whom—to be used in rewarding personal services, and purchasing personal fealty, the proposition would have been treated with scorn and derision." In a second editorial, Bush reminded his readers that "it was once supposed that, under our democratic form of government, public offices were instituted only for the public use and convenience; and that public officers were selected with reference to faithfulness and capacity as servants of the people." Now, however, "by means of the power and influence placed in his hands by the democratic voters of Oregon, Gen. Lane has succeeded in transforming all the federal patronage, the salaries of federal officers, and all the federal money disbursed within the State, into a stupendous corruption fund, by means of which he hopes to control the democratic organization and keep himself in the United States Senate."[7]

Most members of the Clique were hoping that Lane's popularity was waning. Nesmith optimistically wrote Deady, who remained a Lane supporter, that "the sentiment of opposition to Joseph is daily becoming stronger; and however much you may regret it . . . his career of humbugging, dishonesty, and deception, is rapidly drawing to a close."[8] Nesmith was proven wrong. The state Democratic convention confirmed Lane's stature when it convened on November 16. Despite the resistance of the Hards, Lane's men controlled the proceedings. They chose Lane, Deady, and Stout as Oregon's delegates to the national convention and instructed them to vote for Lane for the presidential nomination.

The magnitude of the Lane/Clique quarrels raised apprehensions about the future of the Democratic Party, even on the Soft side. William Farrar, President Franklin Pierce's appointee as district attorney for Multnomah County, wrote Nesmith, "I would be glad if we could once more be united, and in place of slaughtering our own friends that our weapons were turned against the common enemy." He had expected Nesmith to use his influence to bring the party together, but Nesmith had failed to make the necessary effort. If the divisions in the party were not overcome, Farrar was sure the situation would lead to "the triumph of the Black Republican party."[9]

While criticizing Lane's "especial fawners and advocates," his former agent James O'Meara too urged Nesmith to take action: "With you, we would not be called upon to swallow a bitter dose, and with it a share of our own vomit, for while you have been a chief advisor and member of the so-called Clique, your public position (officially) has never devolved upon you the accumulation of rancor which the others have caused and acquired." While O'Meara was confident of Nesmith's loyalty to the party, he distrusted "the fealty under great pressure of so reckless and indiscreetly ambitious a man as Williams under command of his wife; nor as malleable and impressive a softling as Chesterfield Grover." In his judgment, Nesmith was "rough and blunt and manly, with plenty of rude obstinacy to assure us of sincerity in what you say, and to ensure as against probability of weakening under heavy opposition." O'Meara was sure that Bush would support Nesmith, with O'Meara stating, "After all, he is worth all the rest put together, as a backer. You and Bush can *coerce* Williams and *mould* Grover. Harding has little grip outside of Marion, and can either be controlled or disregarded."[10]

The local divisions in the Democratic Party were mirrored on the national level. There, however, the issue was not so much intra-party rivalries but rather the question of slavery. For Bush, the possibility of a civil war was real. Convinced of the Republicans' culpability in provoking southern hostility, he predicted that slavery would be "the principal, and perhaps the only issue in the Presidential campaign of 1860." He warned that the election would decide "whether the government of our great country shall be abandoned to the misrule of sectional fanatics, or shall continue to be administered for all sections alike, irrespective of geographical distinctions and intolerant prejudice."[11]

Bush cautioned the Democrats who would meet in Charleston to nominate their candidate for the presidency: "If that convention settles upon any other policy than that of the non-intervention of the federal authorities, let its president have the power to appoint an extraordinary committee, whose duty it shall be to write the story of the defeat of the democratic party." At the same time, Bush made his own solution to the dilemma quite clear:

What can be done to stay the destroying tide of blind fanaticism
and insure beyond peradventure the perpetuity of our national

institutions? Who can and will lead the hosts of Democracy to certain triumph in the approaching strife? Who but the gallant Democratic statesman and leader of the Northwest—the champion of popular sovereignty—the uncompromising advocate of the rights of all the states and the foe to sectionalism in any guise and in every quarter—*Stephen A. Douglas!*[12]

Deady rejected Bush's candidate. A visit to Washington reinforced his view of Lane's prospects for the approaching Democratic convention and the election that would follow. Allowing that Washington was "a great place for Flunkeyism and etiquette," he let Nesmith know that "Lane's room is full from morning till night with accomplished knee-benders who look upon him as a sure card for the Presidency. He has a kind and acceptable word for them all and they go away thinking him the greatest man in the nation."[13]

Although the Hard Democratic state convention had chosen Deady as one of its delegates to the national convention, Deady for whatever reason chose not to attend. Lansing Stout and Isaac Stevens, the former governor of the Washington Territory, were Oregon's only delegates. The convention met in Charleston, South Carolina, on April 23 and, through fifty-seven ballots, could not agree on a nominee. Douglas's support for popular sovereignty made him unacceptable to the southern delegates, who withdrew from the convention on April 30 rather than allow his nomination. After some hesitation, the Oregon delegates joined the exodus. Lane briefed Deady on the situation: Douglas supporters were "busy and noisy" since the convention had broken up and would accept no one but Douglas. "One thing, however, is certain, that is Douglas cannot nor will not be nominated, for if he should be the south will bring out a candidate and run him with the certainty of giving him the entire south."[14] As Lane anticipated, when faced with the prospect of Douglas's nomination by the northern faction of the Democratic Party, the bolters took the initiative. They gathered in Baltimore and nominated the current vice president and strong advocate of slavery, John C. Breckinridge of Kentucky, for president. Joseph Lane was chosen as his running mate. Because of his ties to Lane, Isaac Stevens was named the manager of the Breckinridge/Lane campaign.

After weeks of negotiations and maneuvers, northern Democrats reconvened in Baltimore with a sufficient number of delegates to nominate

Douglas for the presidency. In an effort to ameliorate the South, they named the senator from Georgia, Herschel V. Johnson, their vice presidential nominee. When word of the Douglas nomination reached Oregon, opinions were divided. Joseph Drew wrote Bush of his own enthusiasm for Douglas but reported a conversation with Deady who bet that Douglas could never get more than eighty votes out of the electoral college's 303. He added, "Deady seldom speaks well of an anti-Lane man, while he is the constant apologist of the Lane bummers of every hue and often their eulogist."[15]

Bush had no doubt as to who was responsible for the splintering of the party:

> The hand of President Buchanan is visible in every part of this
> revolt. His petulant and personal spleen toward Senator Douglas
> has been the ruling motive of his whole administration. Time
> and again it has been published that he has become reconciled to
> Douglas, but each time it has turned out that the decadent old man
> was only taking breath and seeking a new opportunity to destroy
> the rising statesman by the power of the government.[16]

There was some truth to Bush's allegation. Buchanan, with his southern sympathies, had done all he could to keep Douglas from getting the nomination.

While the drama within the Democratic Party played out, the Republican National Convention met in Chicago. In part because the date of the convention had been moved up from June 13 to May 16, only two of Oregon's five delegates, Joel Burlingame and Franklin Johnson, were able to attend. In accordance with the rules of the convention, the three absent delegates chose alternates from among the delegates of other states. Each of those delegates would then have a second vote in the proceedings. Oregon's alternate delegates were the influential New York publisher Horace Greeley; a member of Congress from Massachusetts and ardent abolitionist, Eli Thayer; and another abolitionist, Henry Buckingham, who published the Kansas newspaper, the *Republican Valley Empire.* All were instructed to support Edward Bates of Missouri for the nomination, which they did in the first and second ballots. Greeley's main objective in the convention was to prevent the nomination of his fellow New Yorker

Senator William Seward. Aside from their personal animosity, Greeley was convinced that Seward could not win the presidency because of his passionate opposition to the nativist doctrines of the Know Nothings, his attacks on slavery and the South, and his association with the corrupt New York City "boss," Thurlow Weed.

When the convention convened, Abraham Lincoln of Illinois emerged as a prospective nominee. Lincoln's campaign for the Senate against Stephen Douglas, while unsuccessful, had nevertheless earned him national recognition. His candidacy was also helped by the fact that the convention met in his home state. In the first two ballots, the contest was clearly between Seward and Lincoln. The favorite of the Oregon delegation, Edward Bates, was far behind. On the third ballot, Greeley was able to convince his fellow alternates, Thayer and Buckingham, as well as the Oregon delegates Burlingame and Johnson to support Abraham Lincoln, which turned the tide and gave Lincoln the nomination.[17]

Bush was harsh in his evaluation of the Republican nominee:

> As a statesman, Mr. Lincoln takes rank—nowhere. He has neither ability to manage intricate affairs of state, nor experience. Four sessions in the Illinois legislature, the captaincy of a company of volunteers in the Black Hawk war, the usual career of a legal practitioner, with occasional intervals of stumpspeaking in political campaigns, and one term in Congress, sum up the public life of this aspirant to the Presidency. He is undoubtedly a pretty good stump orator, a thrifty lawyer, and a passable legislator; but his party certainly looked upon the success of their peculiar principles as very doubtful, when they discarded all their old leaders, and took up Abraham Lincoln as their standard-bearer. Of all the candidates who were before the Convention, there is not one who is not his superior in ability, though he may surpass some of them in political tact.[18]

The 1860 election was further complicated by yet another presidential candidacy when old-line Whigs formed the Constitutional Union party. In an apparent effort to achieve balance on their ticket, they nominated the slave owner John Bell of Tennessee and Edward Everett of Massachusetts on a platform that avoided any mention of slavery.[19]

Many Democrats anticipated catastrophe as a result of the splintering of the party. Bush took a different stance:

Amid the disaster and gloom which now seem to envelop the democratic party of Oregon, we can perceive many cheering rays of hope and comfort. Strengthened and purified by adversity, and purged from the corrupt and debasing elements which unprincipled selfishness and heartless ambition have foisted upon it, the democracy, reformed and reorganized, will go into the next contest with new vigor and with the confidence of success which is assured by conscious power, and honesty of principle and purpose.

He denounced Lane as "the tail of a treasonable ticket" and castigated opposition Democrats who preferred "Lincoln and disunion to Douglas and the Union."[20] Despite his admonition, most of the Democratic newspapers in the state, including those in Albany, Eugene, Corvallis, Jacksonville, and Roseburg, as well as the Portland *Daily News*, endorsed the Breckinridge/Lane ticket.[21] Still, Bush expected Oregonians to come through and "administer a withering rebuke to the false delegates who misrepresented Oregon, in the National Democratic Convention, and at the bidding of Lane joined the seceding traitors. Oregon is democratic to the core; and though our organization has been usurped and our councils betrayed by treachery and fraud, most nobly will we redeem our State, by giving her electoral vote to the candidate of the Union democracy—Stephen A. Douglas."[22]

In Oregon, the summer of 1860 featured battles over the approaching legislative election. The campaign was particularly contentious because the new legislature would elect the next senators. A sharp exchange ensued between Deady and Nesmith when Deady accused Nesmith of supporting Republicans in his effort to elect candidates who would vote against Lane and Smith for the Senate. Nesmith responded angrily that, while it was true that one of the candidates was a Republican, he was one who opposed any intervention by the Congress on the slavery issue. Nesmith said that Lane and Smith had, "after inflicting all the injury upon me that they could, tried to justify their conduct by lying about [Nesmith] last year from every stump in the state." Smith had even threatened revenge if Nesmith campaigned against him in Linn County. Nesmith defiantly pursued his campaign in the county and "to my surprise the poltroon refused to give fight when it was offered, but cringed, cried and begged for quarter."[23]

Deady responded: "[This was] the first letter that I ever received from you during an uninterrupted correspondence of ten years that breathes a spirit of hostility and unkindness. . . . Considering our different relations to public men and public questions you may have had noisier friends and more mercenary advocates but I think none more sincere or disinterested." He went on to defend himself:

> I have never supposed that your object in supporting the opposition ticket in Linn was primarily to give aid to the Republicans, but that your first object was to beat Lane and Smith. To do this you labored for the defeat of the Dem ticket in Linn and to elect the opposition ticket. . . . The *consequence* of your action was to give them (the Repub.) aid. I do not state this to find fault with you. Your position was a difficult one and as I think almost necessarily drove you in that direction. I regret that it is so, but being so, do not consider it a cause of a quarrel with you.[24]

Nesmith was apologetic. His letter had attempted "some sort of vindication of my acts." He admitted he had written "in a bad humor" and under pressure. Indeed he could not remember what he had written. He asked Deady to visit him and bring his letter with him. Nesmith did not comment on the final two sentences of Deady's letter, predicting that Jackson and Douglas Counties would support Breckinridge and Lane and adding: "I expect to vote for them."[25]

When the Oregon Legislature met in September, Bush taxed it with its responsibilities: "Within the next six years the floor of the Senate will be a battlefield of liberty more memorable than any that ever smoked with mere human gore. There the genius of popular government must vindicate herself against ambitious treason, or blushingly confess that liberty, anarchy, bloodshed and despotism is the inevitable form of human progression. It behooves us to elect two Senators who, in any event, and at all hazards, will sternly treat any step toward disunion as high treason." A legislator's support of a Lane candidacy would make him complicit in the destruction of the Union.[26]

Democrats dominated the Oregon House but were split between the Douglas faction with eighteen members and the Breckinridge faction with seventeen, giving the thirteen Republican representatives the balance of power. When the legislature met, several Breckinridge supporters walked out, leaving the legislature without a quorum. After Governor Whiteaker called a special session, it took eighteen ballots and prolonged negotiations for the Douglas Democrats and the Republicans to reach a compromise. Nesmith was chosen by two votes over Deady to gain the first seat. The second seat went to the Republican Edward Dickinson Baker. Although he had only recently arrived in Oregon from California, Baker was known to be a close friend, if a sometime rival, of Abraham Lincoln in Illinois where Lincoln had won the seat in Congress that Baker had previously held. Baker favored popular sovereignty, which Lincoln did not, but it was expected that their friendship would benefit Oregon should Lincoln be elected.[27]

The possibility of Baker's selection had surfaced before the legislative session. From San Francisco, the Democrat Charles E. Pickett weighed in with Nesmith saying he could not believe that "you will so damage your future prospects and injure the interests of Oregon as to make terms with that newly imported gassbag, Col. Baker. . . . I know you too well to believe you can affiliate in any particular with the narrow-minded, prejudiced, bigoted, blue bellied crew, who will then necessarily become your confreres." As to the presidential election, Pickett predicted that Breckinridge would carry California "by a considerable majority over all the other tickets combined. The Douglasites will mostly have disappeared by the ides of November."[28]

The Oregon Legislature's choice of Nesmith and Baker was an embarrassment to Lane, who feared the election of strong antislavery senators would be seen as a rejection of him and would jeopardize the chances of the Breckinridge-Lane ticket in the presidential elections. Still the majority of Oregon's Democratic papers continued to support him. Bush, on the other hand, resumed his attacks.[29]

On November 6, the voters disappointed the hopes of both the Douglas and the Breckinridge factions. Benjamin Harding was in San Francisco during the election and reported on the mood there when he visited the polls. "Men of all parties seemed to be at work earnestly for their particular candidates, but I saw very little of intoxication and no quarreling or bloody noses." The Republicans were in "high glee," the Douglas men "in good spirits," and the "Breckinridgers very much depressed." He added, "It is now 10 o'clock and it is considered certain that Douglas or Lincoln has carried the state." Actually, Lincoln had.[30]

While many in the West and elsewhere blamed the Breckinridge/ Lane candidacy for Douglas's defeat, in fact, Lincoln's victory cannot be attributed to the split in the Democratic Party. Oregon, California, and New Jersey were the only northern states to give Lincoln a plurality rather than a majority of the votes cast. In Oregon, he won with 5,344 votes to Breckinridge's 5,074 and Douglas's 4,131. Perhaps as a result of Lane's lingering popularity, Oregon was the only northern state to give Breckinridge a larger vote than Douglas. The limits of Bush's influence may be seen in the fact that only in Marion and Polk counties did voters support Douglas over Lincoln or Breckinridge.[31]

Bush ascribed his candidate's loss to the damage done to the Democratic Party by the well-documented corruption of the Buchanan administration and the president's support for slavery. In the face of defeat, he maintained that the election would strengthen the Democratic Party by relieving it of dissidents: "The democratic party has been purified and consolidated, and its great principles have become better understood by the events of the last year. We are now happily rid of all the rubbish that has drifted to us during the years of our success." The "rubbish" would find their home in the other parties: "All who are venal enough to forego their principles for the sake of office, have found a purchaser in the present administration; and all who are too deeply tinctured with anti-slavery to co-operate with a thoroughly national party, or who have a weakness for a rising sun, have gone over to Lincoln."[32]

As a result of the election, the Clique and the Democratic Party in Oregon lost much of the patronage Democratic presidents had provided, a significant component of their influence. Republicans, on the other hand, benefited. Deady reported, "Everything is going along here in the same old way. Every ship that goes out takes an assorted lot of Republicans, as you say, going to Old Abe to ask their daily bread."[33] Having sold the *Oregonian* to Thomas Pittock, Thomas Dryer was one of those who profited from the president's largess. In appreciation of his vote for Lincoln when he represented Oregon in the Electoral College, he was appointed the United States Commissioner to the Sandwich Islands, as Hawaii was then known. Remembering Dryer's declaration during the constitutional convention of his intention to vote for the exclusion of Hawaiian natives, or Kanakas, from Oregon, Bush could not resist a comment: "The Kanakas will probably eat Dryer just as they did Captain Cook." A year later, he printed a portion of an article that had appeared in the *Yreka Union*, "It is reported that T. J. Dryer, US Commissioner to the govt. of Hawaii is so constantly drunk as to render him unfit to discharge the duties of his office."[34]

From all sides, speculation began as to the consequences of Lincoln's victory. Joseph Drew wrote Bush, "What are we going to do? I believe the South will bluster and threaten a great deal, but *do nothing*, and I am afraid the Repubs. will weaken and comprise and conciliate the cotton states."[35] In contrast to Drew, most Oregon observers expected the southern states to secede from the Union. Bush taxed Lincoln with the responsibility of dealing with the anticipated rebellion:

> We think its prominence and importance will depend very much upon the spirit with which it is met by President Lincoln. . . . If he undertakes to compound the matter by buying the disunionists up with promises and conciliation, he puts rebellion at a premium and pays villainy a reward for its crimes. If he adopts a timid, temporizing policy, for the sake of screening himself and saving his party, we may expect to hear the tramp of hostile regiments in the Federal city; but if he has the courage to employ all the powers of the government whenever any overt act of treason shall be committed, there is reason to hope the serpent will be crushed before it is hatched.[36]

His stand reflected the reaction of his fellow Douglas Democrats to the prospect of the secession of the southern states but some saw his pronouncement as a refutation of his decade-long support for states' rights in accordance with Democratic doctrine. His friend Butler P. Anderson, the public printer of the Washington Territory, wrote: "From the tone of the *Statesman* since Lincoln's election I feel you have taken a chute in which I as an old supporter and friend cannot follow you. It seems to me now that you advocate doctrines against which the Democratic Party has fought since its organization. . . . You now believe that the government of the United States is a centralized consolidated government—not with 'delegated' powers, but sovereign and supreme in its authority."[37]

After the election, Joseph Lane publicly dismissed the possibility of southern secession. As the *New York Times* reported, "Gen. Lane, who ridiculed the idea of secession or disunion, had a long interview with the Sec'y of War. . . . The General claims that a suspicion of secession is an imputation upon the intelligence of the southern States." Privately, however, Lane wrote Deady, "Tomorrow Congress will assemble for the last time that a national Congress will ever assemble under the constitution as it now is. And it is by no means certain that such amendments can be made as will justify the south in remaining in the Union. I don't believe there is any chance of a satisfactory settlement of the trouble or difficulty, consequently look upon the Union as broken up."[38]

Lane had no doubt that the South would be victorious. The southern states would "go out of the union into one of their own; forming a great, homogeneous and glorious southern confederacy." Lane placed the responsibility for the coming civil war squarely on Lincoln's shoulders. In a letter to his son, he wrote, "Lincoln does not understand the principles or framework of our Government and the consequence will be war, fierce and bloody. The fact is he is no account. He is a miserable creature, and will be a mere tool in the hands of a miserable corrupt sectional party that will destroy and break the country."[39]

With the prospect of the dissolution of the Union, the notion of a Pacific Republic independent of the United States again emerged. The concept was not a new one. Thomas Jefferson considered a Pacific Republic, settled by American citizens, as the best way to address the remoteness of the western territories. Sam Houston at one point proposed a republic consisting of Texas, California, Oregon, and some Mexican provinces. Horace Greeley thought an independent republic encompassing the Oregon and California territories would have the advantage of saving the federal government substantial expenditures.[40] Deady considered the establishment of a Pacific Republic likely if the Union collapsed into separate parts. But he anticipated that such a republic would be of little consequence.[41] As conceived in 1860, the republic would be an ally of the seceding South and a proponent of slavery. Bush accused Lane of favoring such an arrangement and rejected it out of hand:

What a ridiculous figure would the Pacific Republic cut among nations. With a population of little more than half a million scarcely able to protect ourselves from the inroads of the Indians upon our borders, hardly rich enough to sustain the expenses of our economical state governments, and dependent upon the bounty of the general government for military protection, mail facilities, and for the salaries of a large number of our public functionaries, what would be our fate were we to cast ourselves loose from the protection and assistance which we receive from it? . . . With Mexico upon one side, British Columbia on the other, a defenseless sea-coast in front, and a horde of hostile savages and marauding Mormons in the rear, and unable to protect ourselves on any side, we could only preserve our existence by forming an alliance with some powerful government which could afford us protection at the price of our liberty.[42]

Lane did not openly espouse a Pacific Republic but looked forward to a southern confederation of fifteen states that would "command the respect and confidence of all the nations of Europe." What would become of the northern states he could not anticipate. He had no doubt as to who was at fault: "Let the blame and responsibility rest upon that sectional fanatical party who have destroyed the best form of govt. ever created by the wisdom of man." Shortly after the election, a friend recorded in his diary that Lane "thought disunion inevitable, and said when the hour came that if his services could be useful, he would offer them unhesitatingly to the South." Overestimating his own influence, Lane was convinced that Oregon voters would support the South. The *Statesman* reprinted a letter he had written to a Georgia newspaper: "I am glad the people of Oregon have determined to leave a union that refuses you equality and protection."[43]

Lane's assumptions regarding the sentiments of his fellow Oregonians proved mistaken. When he returned to Oregon, only a very few old friends welcomed him while other Oregonians hung him in effigy. To avoid the towns where he was regarded as a traitor, he took a circuitous route to his home in Douglas County. Deady was sympathetic to Lane and critical of George Curry, who owed his years as the Territory's governor to Lane but had avoided Lane on his arrival: "I would have thought more of C— if he had shown him some respect and attention." Nesmith concurred with Deady's judgment but was not surprised by Curry's behavior, stating "The little fellow will some day die of his self importance and the family will have a Hell of a time in ascertaining the cause of the disease."[44]

As anticipated, Lincoln's election precipitated the secession of seven southern states: South Carolina, Mississippi, Florida, Alabama, Georgia, Louisiana, and Texas. After his inauguration, hostilities began on April 12 when secessionist forces fired on Fort Sumter, a US Army installation in Charleston, South Carolina. Soon Virginia, Arkansas, North Carolina, and Tennessee joined the rebellion. The Confederated States of America was formed and the Civil War began.

Despite his espousal of slavery and his vote for Breckinridge/Lane, Deady vehemently supported the Union. When people defended the right to secession as protected by the Constitution, he rejected their reasoning and attributed it to a serious misunderstanding of the premises on which the country was founded. In his eyes, Thomas Jefferson was to blame: "Jefferson overthrew the Federal govt. as well as the Federal party with his resolutions of '98, and today we are reaping the consequences. He has been the model for every disturber of the public peace ever since, and his resolutions and Declaration of Independence contain enough of revolution, nullification, secession and anarchy to set the four corners of the world by the ears."[45] Deady was referring to Jefferson's "Kentucky Resolution" in which he asserted that the states were sovereign and that the Constitution was only a "compact." Therefore, the states had the right to reject actions by the federal government that violated their sovereignty. Then serving as vice president, Jefferson traveled to Kentucky and convinced the majority in the state legislature to approve the resolution. As Deady noted, the Kentucky Resolution was the basis for the "states' rights" argument that was used to justify the secession of the southern states that led to the Civil War.[46]

Nesmith responded with his own appraisal:

I look upon 'peaceable separation' as impossible. There are too many conflicting interests, and too extensive a border for the maintenance of peaceable relations between two great Republics based upon the antagonistic ideas of slavery and freedom. If two confederacies are to be formed upon such a basis, they will by the very nature of things both degenerate into military Despotisms. . . . Both sections are now in a condition where nothing but blood-letting will satisfy them. The days of war will soon produce a havoc which will bring them to their senses, however little it may do to restoring 'good feeling' between the North and the South.[47]

Bush attached enormous significance to the war: "It is to determine whether or not free institutions can stand the shock of formidable rebellion and insurrection. If they fail now, they fail forever, and the world goes back a thousand years. Under the war just bursting upon the nation rests the hope of mankind, and the treason which has inaugurated it constitutes the blackest crime against human liberty and human kind that history records or tradition perpetuates."[48]

CHAPTER NINE

"Would as soon vote for Jeff Davis as an abolitionist."

—William S. Ladd

The Oregon historian and newspaperman Leslie Scott asserted that the influence of Asahel Bush, along with that of James Nesmith, "was more potent than that of any other man in holding Oregon to the Union." He added that Bush "had remarkable breadth of vision and gift of foresight; was endowed with outstanding courage; used his influence for the obvious advantage of Oregon in national affairs."[1] As a US Senator, Nesmith strongly supported the Union and the federal actions that were essential to its preservation. Through the Civil War, he served on the Senate's Committee for Military Affairs. Because of his experience in Oregon's American Indian Wars, he was occasionally called upon by Union generals for advice on military strategies.

Whether or not it was due to Bush and Nesmith, Oregon was on the Union side of the divide. The majority of those Oregonians whose sympathies had been with the South and the institution of slavery came over to the Union after the secession of the southern states. A great many including, surprisingly enough given his father's espousal of slavery, Delazon Smith's son Volney, went east to join the Union army. A few others, including Lane's son John who was a graduate of the military academy at West Point, maintained their prewar loyalties and joined the Confederate army. But even among those who supported the Union, opposition to the abolitionist movement remained strong. The influential Portland banker William Ladd was convinced that "we have too many *abolitionists* for leaders in our army." Ladd also reflected those Oregonians and other Americans who felt that there was a strong possibility of French and British intervention in the war, although he did not predict which side either would support.[2]

Members of the Clique whose allegiance might have been questioned upheld the Union. From San Francisco, Orville Pratt, in his usual histrionic fashion, wrote Nesmith that he would sacrifice his life and his fortune on its behalf. "I say this in no feeling other than to animate you as a Senator with the feeling that I am with you in all your efforts to save the government in this its terrible hour of need. I beg you then to forget and forgive all such old political enemies as you may now find struggling, in common with yourself, to perpetuate the institutions you and I have so much cause to cherish."[3]

His support for slavery and his very public support for the Breckinridge/Lane ticket in 1860 made many doubt Matthew Deady's loyalty to the Union. Jesse Applegate advised him to take a public stand, "Your position and former political associations give you much prominence if not responsibility in this matter. The Government party charge you with sympathizing and perhaps advising the course of the opposition press. The opposition press *claim* you as one of their party. As I know from yourself that this is not your true position, I earnestly advise you to take immediate steps to place yourself right before the people."[4]

Before long, talk of removing Deady from his position as Justice of the US District Court surfaced, particularly in Portland where William Farrar promoted the idea. Applegate defended Deady, even writing Edward Bates, the attorney general in Lincoln's cabinet, on his behalf.[5] When Deady questioned Nesmith's commitment to him, Nesmith responded testily: "I never intimated to Farrar or any other individual that I would cooperate either directly or indirectly in an effort to legislate you out of office. On the contrary I did tell him that I was opposed to any interference with the Judiciary." In time, Nesmith mellowed. After Deady's report that he had voted for the Union ticket in the 1862 elections, Nesmith wrote that he was "glad to hear that you supported it, if for no other reason than to quiet the gabbling of those who have pretended to doubt your loyalty. For my own part, I never required any such proof of your fidelity to the government."[6]

Because of Oregon's distance from the battlefields, the Civil War had a limited impact. Before the war, the Oregon Military District had been something of a training ground for the leadership of the Union Army. Generals Philip Sheridan and William T. Sherman, who became important commanders, were stationed in Oregon when the war began. Others, including Generals Ulysses S. Grant, George B. McClellan, and John

C. Fremont, had previously served there.[7] With the outbreak of the war, federal forces were recalled, leaving Oregonians, especially in the eastern and southern parts of the state, vulnerable to Native American attacks. In response to the hazard, the federal government recruited volunteers from California, and Oregon raised its own companies of troops.

One of those California volunteers, Royal Bensell, kept a journal that provides some insight into the atmosphere in Oregon during the Civil War. He found his duties at Fort Yamhill extremely monotonous. Life did not get any better when he was on leave because Salem was "muddy and dull." And, when he went to church there, he "didn't see a handsome face in the house." Among civilians there was an occasional "exhibition of temper" when someone encountered a southern sympathizer but, from his observation, the people were generally indifferent to the war.[8]

Reports that the Union armies were meeting with little success on the battlefields led to fears of an insurrection in Oregon, particularly in the southern counties. Along with the fears came rumors that Joseph Lane would command such an insurrection.[9] Reflecting his own concerns as well as those of Boise and Harding, Bush wrote Nesmith urging Lane's arrest: "We are of the opinion that if there is an outbreak here he must head it. He is the only man that they have got to do it. It would help the security of matters in Oregon amazingly to arrest him. Don't fail to have it done at once, if not done already." Three days later, he added, "If you have old Lane arrested, *don't let him be discharged.*" Deady thought their alarm ridiculous: "Lane is upon his 'much-loved farm' and is never heard from or of, except when the operators in the Statesman office, stir him up occasionally for the benefit of the party. Bush is not disposed to let him die, and evidently thinks, that in a small way, he may be made useful as a Bugaboo in politics."[10] Despite Bush's efforts, Lane was not arrested.

The anxieties of Oregonians were raised by reports of a clandestine organization, the Knights of the Golden Circle, dedicated to the South's cause and committed to the destruction of the Union. Reportedly 2,500 men, including Lafayette Lane, had joined one or the other of the ten lodges the group established in Oregon. In great secrecy, they trained and purchased guns and ammunition in a plot to seize the Union Army's fort at Vancouver. Their efforts came to nothing but their potential frightened many.[11] Also feared was the influence of the "secessionist" newspapers. In 1862, five Oregon newspapers were "suppressed," that is, deprived of the federal postal subsidy and banned from the mails. Included in the suppression were the *Albany Democrat,* the *Jacksonville Gazette,* the *Portland Advertiser,* the *Corvallis Union,* and the *Eugene Democratic Herald,* all newspapers that had supported the Breckenridge/Lane ticket. Bush did not come to the defense of freedom of the press: "The *Democrat* and *Gazette* have been excluded from the mails. They were the mildest of the lot. The *Union* and *Advertiser* are much ranker. I am sorry any went until all did—the others blow about it so." As late as November, 1864, apprehensions had not been quieted. Deady wrote Nesmith of a Salem meeting "to suppress *insurrection.*" While he was not sure how serious the threat was he suspected there was some truth in a rumor that "arms have been shipped here from Cal, and distributed through the interior of the State."[12]

The war had its effect on Oregon political life. In 1862, the first challenge for the newly elected legislature was the selection of a successor to Senator Edward Baker. When the southern states declared their intention to secede, Baker had annoyed his fellow Republicans in Washington by counseling patience and mollification. After Fort Sumter, however, he abandoned his hope for compromise and enlisted in the Union army although he did not surrender his Senate seat. A colonel and then a major general in command of a Pennsylvania regiment, he was killed on October 21, 1861, in the Battle of Balls Bluff in Virginia. Governor Whiteaker, who ostensibly supported the Union but remained a proponent of slavery, appointed the prominent Portlander Benjamin Stark to serve in the Senate until the legislature could make its choice.

Outrage followed. The secretary of the Oregon Senate, Lucien Heath, forwarded to Nesmith in Washington a letter written by Reuben Boise warning that Stark "is known to us from his often repeated sentiments, to be opposed to the vigorous prosecution of the war against insurgent and revolted States; and in favor of recognition of the so-called Confederate States, and also in favor of establishing on this coast a separate Government, and, therefore, an enemy of the United States to whose councils he is appointed." Stark, Boise added, "does not represent the true interests or sentiments of the people of Oregon, a large majority of whom are loyal, ready and willing to support and maintain the Government to the last extremity in putting down the present rebellion, and bringing to justice the wicked and reckless men who have wantonly undertaken the overthrow of the best Government that ever blessed mankind."[13]

Whiteaker did not back down, and when Nesmith made no particular effort to convince the Senate to refuse to seat Stark and then voted to seat him, Bush warned, "There is a good deal of complaint among your friends because you support Stark's claim to a seat. . . . The universal wish, so far as I know, of Union men is that Stark shall not get the seat. I expected you would vote for him for I knew he would talk at you till you would say yes, to get rid of him."[14] Stark held the senate seat until the legislature could choose a successor.

With the 1862 elections approaching, Bush was committed to fashioning a Union Party ticket that would have the support of both the Douglas Democrats and the Republicans. William Farrar was not optimistic. In a letter to Nesmith, he maintained that the Republicans did not want to ally themselves with the Douglas Democrats and that many Douglas Democrats preferred to make common cause with the Breckinridge Democrats. Farrar warned that "there is really a stronger secession sentiment and element in Oregon than in any other state yet adhering to the Union."[15]

Nesmith also heard from William S. Ladd who was critical of Bush for his derogatory comments about the Methodist editor and publisher, and possible choice for the Senate, Thomas Pearne. In Ladd's opinion, Bush's actions could cause a split in the Union party that would result in the party's losing the election. He hoped that Nesmith could make "any suggestions" to Bush that might end his insults. Ladd was particularly opposed to the possibility that the Union party might nominate the Republican John McBride for Congress: "McBride is considered by many as a rank abolitionist[;] if so [I] can not support him, would as soon vote for Jeff Davis as an abolitionist."[16]

When the Union party's nominees for state and county offices became public, Bush explained matters in a letter to Nesmith: "The repubs. have acted with a selfishness and meanness in the nominations, where they could control them, worthy of the little handful of abolition leaders who head that faction. About one third of the republicans are conservative and *honorable* men. The balance are downright abolitionists and as dishonest as they are fanatical." He regretted the concessions he had had to make "but there was no other way now to keep the state out of the hands of the secessionists." Bush was no more friendly to those in the national Republican party who were determined "to see no end to this war until there is also an end of slavery." He allowed, thankfully, that President Lincoln was not an abolitionist but expected that the hardships of the war would ultimately end slavery. The southern states "should have considered this before they decided on rebellion."[17]

In another report from Salem, Benjamin Harding sent Nesmith his own guess as to the outcome of the elections for the legislature. While he had no doubt that Union men would prevail, "the Repubs expect—and the Douglas Democrats fear—that they will have a majority of one to three in the House and one or two in the Senate" and would therefore choose the next senator. He expected "little or nothing from them that will be moderate or practical," while the Breckinridge Democrats were "still worse." Harding had an understandable interest in the makeup of the coming legislature because its members would choose Baker's successor. Prevailing opinion saw the contest as between him and Asahel Bush. Bush was not particularly aggressive about his candidacy but Deady could not resist teasing: "McCracken says you must be a candidate for the Senate, when you degenerate into such politeness as 'please.'"[18]

After all the speculation, the Union ticket triumphed in 1862. Voters replaced Governor Whiteaker with the Republican Addison Gibbs. Despite the charges that he supported the abolition of slavery, they also chose the Republican John McBride over the Democratic nominee Judge Aaron Wait for Oregon's sole seat in Congress. Matthew Deady, certainly not an abolitionist, voted for McBride instead of Wait, a vote that was quite public because of viva voce. Accused of being a traitor to the Democratic Party, Deady explained: "The Methodist church has always had control of the Oregon delegation in Congress. From Thurston down to the admission of the State, Lane, Grover, Stout, and the Senators have been tools of that church, and it dictated their conduct on any matter in which it took interest." Deady had become impatient with the church's control and voted for McBride "who has no religion at all, and I don't think can be used by any church or sect." After his term in the House, McBride sought appointment to a judgeship. Deady again supported him, writing Nesmith that McBride would "make a better judge than any man who has been appointed to the bench of the neighboring territories since you and I were in that business. On some of the minor morals he is not up to the Old Puritan Standard but that is more contrariness and dislike of the Methodists than any innate tendency to lewdness."[19]

When the legislature met in September 1862, the members demonstrated their commitment to the Union by passing a resolution condemning the actions of the South as "unjustifiable, inexcusable, and wicked" and calling for unquestioned support for the government's efforts to "subdue the present revolt against the best and wisest government ever devised by man."[20] Next they addressed the question of Baker's replacement in the Senate. While Deady expected Bush to triumph, Bush was not optimistic. "I have little, if any, expectation of being chosen. A majority of the Democrats in the legislature would prefer me, I think, but the republicans will pretty certainly prefer Ben Harding to me and his chance of election is now best of anybody's. . . . I think Ben would be willing enough to have me selected, but of course would prefer himself and as the repubs will prefer him, and my few friends and all the democrats willing enough to support him, I reason that he will get it."[21]

The legislature confirmed Bush's expectation. Their choice was not surprising considering their familiarity with Harding, who had served in the legislature for a number of terms both during the days of the Territory and after statehood and had been chosen Speaker of the Oregon House of Representatives for the 1860 session. Bush's only office had been that of public printer. Informed of the outcome, Nesmith wrote Deady, "I would have preferred Bush but am perfectly satisfied with a result which I feared at one time would make me the colleague of the 'Holy Cobbler,'" referring to Thomas Pearne. Deady responded that "Ben had the inside from the start." He went on to forecast the demise of the Union party. "Bush is breaking ground against his Republican brethren and the time is not far distant when he and they will quit the *entente cordiale*—it only exists in name now." In an earlier letter, Deady reported another political development. Harding had made it clear that he would not seek reelection when his Senate term ended in 1865. Reuben Boise wanted to succeed him and Harding had pledged his support.[22] The Clique may have collapsed but its members had not lost their political ambitions or their associations.

Bush took his defeat in stride and turned to other concerns. Late in 1862, the prospect of the emancipation of the slaves arose. Bush opposed it as a radical idea and distinguished between supporting the Union and supporting emancipation, declaring himself for the Union and the Union only. Writing in the third person, he reiterated his commitment, saying that he was "in favor of *maintaining the Government at every hazard and to the last extremity.* He wouldn't destroy the Government either to enslave or liberate niggers; he believes it to be a Government of white men, and if the liberties of that race can be preserved, he regards it of comparatively little consequence what fate betides the nigger." After Lincoln's Emancipation Proclamation on January 1, 1863, Bush continued to question whether it was a wise move, emphasizing that the focus should be on winning the war.[23]

While relations among members of the Clique were certainly not as close after 1860 as they had been previously, two private episodes indicate that substantial intimacy remained. When Deady wrote expressing his sympathy at Nesmith's loss of his young daughter, Nellie, to diphtheria, Nesmith shared a remembrance. "She was a remarkably quiet and observing child, and for the short time that she had attended school gave great promise of being a fine scholar. She bore her distressing illness without a murmur, and had her faculties perfectly to the last, not half a minute before she died, and with her last breath she said to her mother 'Ma, it will kill me.'"[24]

When Bush's wife Eugenia was afflicted with tuberculosis in 1863, she was treated by Dr. Rodney Glisan from Portland. As her condition worsened, Bush prevailed upon Deady to ask Glisan about her prospects for recovery. Deady spoke to the doctor and wrote Bush: "He was not disposed to be very communicative, told me that he had expressed his opinion to you unreservedly, and left it to you to determine how far Mrs. Bush should know, but thought best that she should not. However in the course of the conversation, I came to the conclusion that he thought the chances were against her recovery. . . It is a sad conclusion for you, but I suppose you prefer to know the worst."[25]

Bush responded, "For a few days I have feared the worst, but I *cannot* give up hope. She *must* recover." Eugenia Zieber Bush died on September 11, 1863, at the age of 30. Nesmith wrote Deady, "I regret to hear of Mrs. Bush's death. She was a kind, amiable woman and one of our best friends."[26] The deaths of Nesmith's daughter and Bush's wife were only two of several family tragedies in a time of infectious diseases and primitive medical care. When Boise lost his wife, apparently in childbirth, Deady wrote, "I have seldom heard of a death that has shocked me more. It seems that we are reaching that point in the race of life, when we may expect our old set to be dropping off and falling down occasionally."[27]

At the end of November, Deady wrote that Bush had been in Portland for a week: "He is in good health, and extracts about as much of his kind of fun out of the world as ever. He is *pyson* on the Republicans. In his element, the Opposition." Bush had left his children with their grandparents and was headed to San Francisco, planning to spend the winter there. Because of the memories it evoked, Salem was painful for him. In fact, he would have liked to move to San Francisco, but said, "I see no way for me to take care of my children here."[28]

As both Deady and Nesmith knew, Bush had for some time been look-ing for a buyer for the *Statesman*. Shortly after his wife's death, he sold the paper to a group of men including, ironically, George Williams. It was soon combined with the *Argus* which had moved to Salem. The *Argus* editor, D. W. Craig, assumed the editorial responsibilities.[29] Benjamin Harding responded to news of the sale: "I regret very much that the paper can no longer be controlled by you. In times like the present it is impossible to tell how long we could agree in political matters and therefore if I expected to continue in politics—and I do not—my regrets arise from no political con-siderations." Rather he predicted that "we shall have no paper in Oregon that will so fearlessly expose the corruption, fanaticism, and ignorance of aspirants and place men, as the Statesman has done, or exercise so whole-some an influence over the people of Oregon." As to the possibility that Bush might leave Oregon, "I am certain there is no man in Oregon that I could miss as much as yourself. I do not know how it is with you, but I would have our personal relations continue as they have been. . . .Wherever you are you will have my kindest wishes, and in afflictions—from which I hope you may be spared—my warmest sympathies."[30]

Throughout his time in the US Senate, Nesmith regularly reported to his friends and former colleagues on events and sentiment in Washington while they kept him informed about happenings and opinions in the state. Their interchanges provide a vivid account of an era when so much of the attention of contemporaries, as well as of later historians, was focused on the battlefields of the Civil War. Of particular interest is the correspondence between Deady and Nesmith. Along with its detailed reports, their letters also suggest that their friendship, as time passed, was the closest among the Clique. Deady offered encouragement: "I am glad to see and hear that as a man and a Senator you are generally spoken well of. I think the people of Oregon are pretty well satisfied with you so far, and are inclined to feel proud of you as one to the manor born, a fair specimen of *home brewed*." He felt free to advise, "Vote as you think right, and if ever you are in doubt about what is right, vote with the *minority*."[31]

When he considered it necessary, Deady did not hesitate to bring up rather sensitive matters. In an 1864 exchange, he relayed a remark he had heard about Nesmith's gambling. While neither his original letter nor Nesmith's response has been preserved, Nesmith apparently assured him that he no longer played cards. Deady answered that he was glad to hear that, "You know that I always regarded gaming as your only danger, and that I have often expressed a desire to have you turn your back on it." Around the same time, Deady let Nesmith know that someone, unidentified, had suggested that "the Senator," also unidentified, was somehow involved with a woman who worked in the Treasury department. While his letter again is not in the file, Nesmith appears to have denied that there was any truth to the allegation. Deady responded, "I am glad to hear what you say about the supposed lady in the Treasury Dept. Nothing was ever said about it here, but I thought it nothing more than an act of friendship to suggest the matter to you." Deady said he had defended Nesmith "at the cost of some good will to myself. I make no boast of this thing. It was nothing more than was due from one friend to another." The next sentence, however, reveals some tension in the relationship: "But it hurts me a little to read from you that you are satisfied with what I say *publicly* (underscored in yours) which means if it means anything that I say otherwise privately. . . ."[32]

Deady was not above pressuring Nesmith for an increase in his salary as a member of the federal judiciary, although he did so humorously. "As to the increase of my salary, if you put your hand to that, I want it distinctly understood that it is not to influence your portrait in the future chronicles of Oregon. To use the hackneyed head of the old Statesman, 'No favor sways us, no fear shall awe.'"[33] Nor did Deady refrain from passing along gossip. He reported that Pratt's daughter Lucy, having stolen $5000 from her father, had eloped to Australia with her music teacher, Signor Abecco, a married man with children. Pratt had gone after them and brought Lucy, who was pregnant, back to San Francisco: "It is a horrible affair. I can but pity the Judge. He is cursed in his children and was unfortunate in the selection of a mother for them."[34]

While he continued to support Salem as the state capital, Deady promoted Portland as the commercial center of Oregon and asked Nesmith to see that various federal offices would be located there. Deady warned him that he was perceived as opposed to Portland while his potential opponent in the next senatorial race, Thomas Pearne, was seen as a Portland supporter. He also decried any efforts to elevate California over Oregon. "Oregon is the greater state of the two now. San Francisco is the city of the whole coast, and now is principally dependent upon the Oregon trade for her business. The rest of the state with the exception of a few agricultural counties has the dry rot."[35]

The Deady/Nesmith correspondence provides substantial insight into Deady's political outlook. When a letter Lincoln had written chastising Radical Republicans in Missouri became public, Deady complimented the president, "He is the only man in eminent position in the US that could write letters, without recoil. His make capital for himself every time, without apparently intending to." Whatever his support for the president, Deady opposed the military strategy of the Union forces: "Our policy should have been, and should be now, to husband our resources, with a view of *wearing out the enemy*, but instead of that, we have lavished them pell mell, in the hope of *crushing them out* by main strength and awkwardness and I might add extravagance."[36]

With the 1864 elections approaching, Deady disavowed any political loyalties and attributed his political decisions to pragmatism. "I belong to no political party, and take no part in the deliberations of any. I voted the Union ticket, and probably will again, because it is better to attempt to control the people for their good than to butt your brains out trying to oppose what is inevitable." When he learned that Grover, Nesmith, and Bush were supporting General George McClellan, the Democratic nominee for the presidency, he rejected their decision: "The people have tried changing their President once in 4 years, ever since Jackson's time, and got tired of it. Each change was supposed to be an improvement, but after a trial found to be worse. For the 40,000 thieves who have grown rich off this war, and are now satisfied to be half way honest, and keep other folks from stealing. A change of administration would only substitute 40,000 other thieves, hungry and rapacious." While he voted for Lincoln, Deady was critical of his policies, maintaining that the war would rage on because of the "manifest tendency of the Administration to avow abolitionism and emancipation of the slaves of the South."[37]

The Civil War ended with the surrender of the commander of the Confederate army, Robert E. Lee, to the commander of the Union army, Ulysses S. Grant, at Appomattox on April 9, 1865. Six days later, Abraham Lincoln was assassinated. Over the years, the war remained a matter of controversy among the old compatriots. In 1889, Deady argued with Bush about what to call the Civil War. Deady rejected that term, as well as "war between the states," preferring "the war of the Rebellion." He maintained that "the conflict was a Rebellion by a part of the Union (Nation) against the government of the whole. Otherwise the war was one merely of conquest on the part of the north without any legal or logical justification whatever." No doubt to Bush's dismay, he placed the blame for the war on Stephen Douglas: "He will [be] known in history, as a restless unscrupulous demagogue who to further his vulgar ambition tuckered with the slavery question, until he precipitated a war between the sections, which but for him might never have occurred."[38]

"A liberal policy toward the conquered states is the one, in our judgment, most worthy of the nation."

—Asahel Bush

Speculation of a resurgence of the Salem Clique arose with the end of the Civil War. In 1865, Joseph Gaston, a Portland businessman and at the time Oregon's leading promoter of railroad transportation, sent Nesmith a clipping from the *Oregonian*, which he described as a newspaper "now being run by the 'forty thieves' for the benefit of Portland 'Jews and shit asses.'" Along with other newspapers, including O'Meara's *States Rights Democrat* and the *Jacksonville Oregon Reporter,* the *Oregonian* reported on a revival of the Clique. Bush, Harding, and Nesmith planned to "debauch" and then control the Democratic Party.[1] Even as late as 1878, in a letter to the *Sacramento Record Union,* the Oregon Republican Samuel Asahel Clarke reported that "the 'Salem clique' seems to be reviving, and the graybeards who bear the names of the young and original members seem galvanized again into spasmodic existence."[2]

While some historians have perceived such revivals, in fact they came to nothing. Still, the "graybeards" of the late and largely unlamented Clique played significant roles in postwar Oregon. After his substantial career in the state legislature and his brief service in the US Senate, Benjamin Harding retired to his farm in Marion County. He remained a voice in local and state politics and later served as a judge in the circuit court. Asahel Bush became a very successful banker and a prominent shareholder in a number of companies. He was also, at one point, Oregon's representative on the Democratic National Committee. Lafayette Grover and James Nesmith pursued both commercial and political endeavors. Nesmith completed his term as Senator and later served one term in Congress. Grover was governor of Oregon then stepped down when he was elected to the US Senate. When Grover resigned to take the Senate seat, Stephen Chadwick, then secretary of state, succeeded him as governor. Matthew Deady continued as a judge of the US District Court. Reuben Boise served on the Oregon Supreme Court. In 1865, when Boise talked of resigning, Deady wrote Nesmith, "I don't think he will. . . . You know what Jefferson said of officeholders, Judges and Senators included I suppose, 'they seldom die and *never resign*."[3] Deady was proven correct. Boise did not resign but continued on the court serving as chief justice for two terms. In 1870 he won reelection by only eighteen votes of seventeen thousand cast. When his opponent Benjamin F. Bonham indicated that he would challenge the outcome, Boise stepped down as chief justice. He subsequently served two terms as associate justice and later returned to the circuit court.[4]

Through the postwar period, much of the old camaraderie continued. The veterans sought counsel or assistance from one another although their occasionally conflicting stands on contemporary issues sometimes strained their relationships. The most pressing concern in 1866 was the question of how to put the Union back together. President Andrew Johnson proposed a course of action that gave the southern states a good deal of freedom in the matter. As a result, several of their legislatures immediately passed codes that restricted the rights of blacks, whether or not they were former slaves, as to their occupations, housing, education, and voting rights. When Radical Republicans attacked the president for allowing the codes, some Democrats, including James Nesmith, came to Johnson's defense.

Oregon's other senator, George Williams, adamantly opposed Johnson, but many Oregonians applauded Nesmith for his stand. William Ladd's son, John Wesley Ladd, congratulated him for his support for "the principles of sound government and common sense." He added "I believe with you 'that this is a white man's government' and however beautiful in theory and imagination an equality of races is, *it won't work practicably*." The former congressman and ally of Joseph Lane, Lansing Stout, wrote Nesmith, "No man at all acquainted with the history of our country for the last five years can reasonably conclude that secession will ever again be attempted, and no one can be opposed to such measures as will restore friendship but he who has something besides the preservation of the Union at heart."[5] Bush weighed in on the controversy in a letter to the *Statesman*, "Surely there is a love of country which shall not combine with too great a veneration of the Negro. . . . A liberal policy toward the conquered states is the one, in our judgment, most worthy of the Nation and best calculated to harmonize the clashing antagonisms of a broken Union and soothe the virulence of a discomfited people; and for that, no excess of radical majorities shall drive us to the confessional."[6]

On the Johnson matter, Deady agreed with Nesmith but pointed to a difference between himself and the Senator: "Your political opinions and conduct, like those of many of the best men that ever lived, are influenced in a great measure, by your *personal relations and predilections.* On the other hand mine are mainly controlled by what are sometimes sneeringly called abstractions or the ideal." He made one distinction clear, "I have probably more sympathy for the southern people than you have, because while I know they were legally in the wrong, I am equally well satisfied that in all the moral causes which led to the rebellion and the consequent civil war, they were as much sinned against as sinning."[7]

Concurrent with the postwar controversies was the approaching senatorial election. Nesmith certainly wanted to remain in the post but his prospects were not encouraging. Deady expected that the legislature would reject him precisely because of his support for Johnson: "I believe you have more friends in the Union party than the other, but the Union party of this state, particularly the brains and conscience of it, is thoroughly on the side of Congress and against Andy, and I do not think any personal considerations (and all these are in your favor) will induce them to support any one for the Senate that does not agree with them on this issue and all questions included in it." Deady encouraged him to withdraw his name from consideration and instead return to the army where he could assume the rank of brigadier general. "Your qualifications for a seat in a deliberative assembly are fair, and would be better if your early training had been equal to your native ability. But as an executive or administrative officer you have few equals and less superiors." In addition, since Nesmith had several daughters, "The position will aid you to marry them advantageously, and although some people may sneer at this suggestion, yet I think a *father* can appreciate it." Deady recognized the possibility that Johnson would offer Nesmith the post of secretary of the interior but thought the army a better idea.[8]

As Deady had predicted, the legislature did not choose Nesmith for a second term in the Senate. Johnson nominated him for ambassador to

Austria but, because of the controversy surrounding his support for the president, the Senate refused to confirm him. Rather than pursue Deady's recommendation of a career in the army, he returned to private life in Oregon while remaining an influential leader of the Democratic Party. Deady was well aware that Nesmith continued to have an interest in public office. When Ulysses S. Grant was elected president, Deady remarked, "I hear that your old friend Grant has been elected Pres. And I trust and hope that you will find occasion and inclination to renew your friendly relations with him."[9] In 1873, after the death of his cousin, Congressman J. G. Wilson, Nesmith was chosen to finish out his term. Deady again assumed his role as Nesmith's advisor, but with a measure of restraint: "I hope these few friendly remarks will not breed a quarrel with you, but that they will be received in the spirit in which they are written."[10]

While Nesmith served in Congress, President Ulysses S. Grant appointed his attorney general, George Williams of Oregon, to the post of chief justice of the Supreme Court. Reawakening their animosity during the Reconstruction era, Nesmith did all he could to prevent Williams's confirmation. When the Judiciary committee declined to recommend Williams's appointment to the full Senate, Williams withdrew, blaming Nesmith for his loss. From Oregon, Lafayette Grover congratulated Nesmith for his efforts: "We are all glad to get rid of Williams in this State as a politician but don't think he is fit for the place occupied by Marshall, Taney and Chase."[11]

During Nesmith's brief time in the House of Representatives, Massachusetts Senator Charles Sumner, the victim of the 1857 caning, died. Sumner had been a prominent leader of the antislavery movement and of the Radical Republican opposition to Andrew Johnson's policies. The Massachusetts congressional delegation requested that Nesmith deliver Sumner's eulogy before Congress. Their choice seemed a strange one but, despite their radically different political views, Sumner and Nesmith had been close friends when they served together in the Senate. The Massachusetts delegation's choice also demonstrates the regard in which Nesmith was held by his former colleagues.[12] He did not run for another term in the House and was succeeded by Joseph Lane's son, Lafayette. Nesmith returned to his business endeavors. When, however, he felt he could be of service, he was quick to come forward. In July of 1878, new hostilities broke out between settlers and Native Americans. In response, Nesmith posted a broadside in Salem: "The Lives of our People in Eastern Oregon are in great peril, at the hands of the savage hordes of that region. It is within our power to render them important assistance and protection if we act at once, and we ought to do it. . . . I call upon any man who can raise a rifle, forty rounds of ammunition and a blanket, to rendezvous with me at Salem to-night, and start to the scene of hostilities to-morrow."[13]

In many ways, Matthew Deady was the most prominent of the "grey-beards" after the war. Besides his judiciary duties and his primary contribution to the codification of Oregon's civil and criminal laws, he continued the weekly column on Oregon affairs in the *San Francisco Bulletin,* an undertaking he had launched in 1863 to supplement his income. He was one of the founders of the Portland public library. He was a member of the Board of Regents of the University of Oregon, and his efforts on behalf of the university and its School of Law resulted in a campus building being named after him. Deady's reputation extended beyond the state. California Senator Leland Stanford appointed him as a regent of his university. Even in those times, however, some of Deady's views would have been regarded as unenlightened. Commenting on a pamphlet promoting eugenics, Deady wrote Nesmith:

It is a pity his plan of breeding humans could not be put into practice. I am sure it would improve the race, even if it led to the extinction of the present families. . . . I have often thought and said that the building and maintaining of costly asylums for the education and then propagation of the blind deaf and dumb was a misapplication of philanthropy and benevolence. In the same way these orphan asylums in the large cities which good people support and carry on are mostly nurseries where the fruit of crime and the offspring of vice, ignorance and brutality are nurtured and reared to be turned loose and prey upon society. But it is easier to find fault with these things than to correct them.[14]

Deady had not abandoned his sympathetic attitude toward slavery: "I am inclined still to think that the relations between capital and labor before the war, at the south, were quite as good as those at the north today."[15] On another issue, however, he took a more moderate stance. Chinese immigration remained highly controversial during the 1870s. Members of the former Clique differed fiercely on the matter. In a change of heart from his attitude during the constitutional convention, Deady fought for the protection of the Chinese immigrants who were being attacked by mobs. Lafayette Grover was on the opposite side of that argument. While he welcomed immigration in his inaugural address to the Legislature in 1871, Governor Grover made an exception where the Chinese were concerned. In his eyes, the Chinese immigrant disdained American values and was "uninfluenced by our examples and observances; our Courts, even, can administer no oath which will bind his conscience. He is a Pagan in his religion, and an absolutist in his ideas of government. He comes with no family, but his associations are with harlots of his own race." Europeans and Americans would not come to Oregon if it meant competing with a Chinese labor force. "Which will we have—the wealth, the intellect, the virtues, the accumulations and the association of our kinsmen, or the vices of the Pagan, and the absorbing and leeching process of his work among us?"[16]

After the Civil War, Lafayette Grover had turned his attention to his various business endeavors, enjoying considerable success. By 1870, however, his political aspirations resurfaced. He made a concerted effort to rebuild the Democratic Party and succeeded to the point that "the party gospel at that time [was] entirely subject to his interpretation of the text" according to the later governor, Theodore Geer. Geer added that "in those days Lafayette Grover was a power in the land, and he understood how to wield it in a way that would best serve his personal ambitions." Grover won the governorship, defeating the Republican candidate Joel Palmer, another name from the territorial era.[17]

Through his campaign and after he took office, Grover took a strong stand against government subsidies to railroads and against protective tariffs. H. H. Haight, the governor of California, praised his efforts, condemning any Democrat who would support such measures that "interfere with natural liberty, deny to citizens the unrestricted right to dispose of the fruits of their own industry, & levy contributions upon the tax paying & laboring community for the aggrandisement of incorporated capital." He concluded that "Your stand against this species of legalized extortion will encourage the friends of political reform in other states and entitles you to their thanks."[18]

Grover was able to impose his own convictions on Oregon, not always to a positive end. In 1869, Congress passed and sent to the states for ratification the Fifteenth Amendment to the Constitution, guaranteeing the right to vote regardless of "race, color or previous condition of servitude." In his inaugural address, Grover adamantly opposed the amendment as an attack on the right of the states to determine suffrage. He cited George Washington's warning in his Farewell Address against amendments "which impair the energy of the system, and thus undermine what can not be directly overthrown."[19] Oregon's legislature was one of seven state legislatures to reject the amendment and did not ratify it until 1959.

The controversial 1876 presidential contest between the Republican Rutherford B. Hayes and the Democratic Samuel J. Tilden brought Grover to national attention. Tilden won the popular vote but the prospective vote in the Electoral College was very close. Grover tried to aid Tilden's efforts by disqualifying one of Oregon's Republican electors, maintaining that the elector was ineligible because he was a US Post Office, and therefore a government, employee. The governor replaced him with a Democrat. Although Hayes won the presidency in the end, Grover's action won him praise from Democrats and Tilden supporters around the country: "Your late *legal, just, brave* and *noble deed* in the matter of Presidential Electors has brought you Honor to the eyes & hearts of all true American Patriots. It was a grand coup d'etat based on both Law & Equity that may yet be the means of saving our Great Republic from drifting into a Military Despotism."[20]

Others were not so pleased. Public resolutions circulated in Ashland, Portland, and Salem denouncing Grover. Whether or not related to the Tilden question, the factory of his Willamette Woolen Manufacturing Company, the company he had founded in 1857, was destroyed by fire. Grover was burned in effigy in Portland and in Jefferson City, Missouri, where he was labeled 'the Benedict Arnold of Oregon, bought by Tilden's gold.' The charge of corruption was not substantiated by a subsequent congressional inquiry.[21] In 1878, Grover left the governorship when he was elected to the US Senate. He did not run for a second term, instead returning to his business pursuits. Although initially very successful, his ventures ultimately failed, leaving him in near poverty and forgotten by the time of his death in 1911.

Through the years, Deady records a number of encounters with Bush in his correspondence and his diary. In an 1866 letter to Nesmith, he described Bush as looking "pretty well, but time is writing some wrinkles on his brow and dropping the white frost of age upon his once handsome locks." After sharing with Bush a letter from Nesmith, Deady reported their joint observation that "since you became a Senator, you might have improved in poker, but that you had gone back in pen writing. Don't take this as a censure, but as it was meant—a joke with some foundation in fact."[22]

As had been true at the time of his wife's death, Bush considered Deady something of a confidant. Deady, with particular relish, recorded in his diary the details of Bush's failed 1871 romance with Sallie Stratton. Bush planned to marry her but rumors circulated of her affair with a man in Eugene. After Nesmith learned of Stratton's infidelities, he reported them to Bush. Bush confronted her and she ended their relationship. Deady wrote of a conversation with Stratton, "It appears she would not marry him, but cannot bear to have him forget her. A good deal of human nature about that—particularly *fe*male human nature." In an 1874 entry, Deady observed that Bush "ought to have remarried and been hen-pecked."[23]

Deady is complimentary of Bush's home and of his daughters, although he did allow that Estelle, "a smart bright person," was "a trifle queer." Still he could take offense. When they happened to meet one day in Salem, Bush invited Deady to join him for dinner with Orville Pratt who was visiting from San Francisco. Deady declined: "I thought if he wanted me at his house he ought to have invited me before I left home. For many reasons, I have made up my mind never to visit his house except upon a direct and pressing invitation and then it will depend on circumstances."[24]

Despite his substantial success as a banker, Asahel Bush retained an interest in public office. When talk of a seat in the Senate came up in 1878, James Nesmith and Benjamin Harding were very supportive of Bush's prospects. Even Deady favored him, "As one of the old set, I would like to see him succeed. He is the only one among the candidates (Dem) who is able, pecuniarily, to go to Washington and live there as he ought to do without being in the paw of some private interest." Still he could not resist a humorous observation: "He is running pretty industriously for the Senate. The experience will at least improve his manners."[25] In the end, facing defeat, Bush removed himself from consideration. In an unexpected and unexplainable turn of events, Bush accepted Governor W. W. Thayer's appointment as superintendent of the Oregon penitentiary and served in that capacity from 1878 until 1882, declining compensation in the first two years and significantly cutting the cost of maintaining the penitentiary.

Thayer's appointment might have been prompted by the fact that he was Bush's grandson.

In some contrast to the occasional discord in his relationship with Bush, Deady was very solicitous of the aging Joseph Lane, congratulating him on his seventy-eighth birthday and following up with an invitation: "Mrs. Deady and I want you to come and dine with us at our boarding house, Mrs. Hills, on tomorrow evening or some other evening this week that will suit you better, at half past 5 o'clock."[26] After Jesse Applegate wrote him recommending Lane for the Oregon Senate, noting that Lane accepted "the results of the war as settling the questions embodied in the amendments to the Constitution finally and forever, and thinks the preservation of the Union the greatest good to all sections," Deady encouraged Lane to run in 1880. Lane was very appreciative, writing in his last days, "Before I pass off I desire to renew to you the assurance of my esteem and of my great confidence in your honesty, integrity and ability." Deady responded immediately, "My dear friend, your brief word of farewell of this date was received this evening. I thank you a thousand times for the kind remembrance and will cherish it as the legacy of a good man gone to his rest and reward."[27]

Lane's last years also saw a reconciliation with Bush. His former advocate, and then adversary, provided financial support for Lane's campaign for the Oregon Senate and sympathy after his devastating defeat. Lane responded with a very affectionate letter asking for a photograph of Bush, adding, "I have not long to stay."[28] Lane died on April 19, 1881. Bush was a pallbearer at his funeral.

Clearly, time had moderated Bush's opinions. In his memoir, Theodore Geer, Oregon's governor from 1899 to 1903, wrote of an encounter on a Salem street. At the time editor of the *Statesman*, Geer had reprinted a Bush editorial critical of Lane from fifty years before. Bush chastised him, concerned about the effect the piece would have on Lane's family, "Lane was a pretty good man, after all, and we were living in exciting times and many things were said that it would have been just as well to have left unuttered." Geer added that, before Lane's death, he and Bush "renewed their earlier friendship and often laughed at the bitterness which characterized the contests in which they had engaged."[29]

Geer described Asahel Bush as "a very cultured gentleman of the old school. He still wears the tall standing collar of the old-time gentlemen of ante-bellum days, and has worn precisely the same style of hat for forty years without change,—always new and becoming, totally unlike that ever worn by any other man, since no other man has been able to discover where it is obtained." He went on to write that Bush's name would "remain among the first on a remarkable list of brave and ambitious men who managed the public affairs of Oregon during the formative period of its existence, in the decade immediately preceding the Civil War." Bush's reputation extended beyond Oregon. According to Geer, he was among those on President Grover Cleveland's short list for appointment as secretary of the Treasury.[30]

In his 1889 *History of the Pacific Northwest*, Elwood Evans wrote that he had never known "a handsomer, quicker witted man, with a keener or truer scent for a fellow mortal's foibles" than the Bush he became acquainted with in 1850. He added, "When his race is run, few persons, if any, will be more missed or longer remembered."[31]

Another contemporary was of a different opinion. T. W. Davenport, writing in 1908, referred to a sarcastic *Statesman* editorial critical of James McBride on the occasion of his appointment to a diplomatic post by President Abraham Lincoln: "That the editor who perpetrated this heartless assault upon even a Black Republican, is still living after a lapse of nearly half a century, goes to prove that he carries the mark of Cain."[32]

Epilogue

A detailed study of the Salem Clique suggests that many of those who have written about Oregon in the 1850s may have given too much credence to Thomas Dryer's editorials in the *Portland Oregonian*. Using such adjectives as "Jesuitical" and "Inquisitorial," Dryer repeatedly charged the "Salem Clique," as he named it, with corruption, fraud, and coercion. At one point, he accused the Clique of planning to establish a "Pacific Republic" independent of the United States. At another, he claimed they were conspiring with Brigham Young to turn the Oregon Territory into a polygamous Mormon republic. Again and again, he maintained that the Clique was committed to bringing African American slavery to Oregon.

Since that time, down to ours, many historians have concluded that the Clique was a single-minded coterie of able but vicious men. Under the direction of Asahel Bush, a man as powerful as any of the eastern political bosses, they imposed their joint command on a submissive population. Any opposition was met with harsh retribution.

In fact, the Clique was made up of ambitious young men who were at once friends and rivals. They supported one another's aspirations except when those aspirations conflicted with their own, which they often did. Their correspondence indicates that they were frequently in disagreement regarding the important issues of the day, including slavery and the possibility of its introduction into the Oregon Territory. Certainly they did not readily submit to the orders of their "boss." Nor was the Salem Clique's command of the Democratic Party as absolute as it is usually portrayed. As the decade progressed, challenges to its dominance emerged from within the party, challenges that proved to be far more significant than any from opposition political parties.

If historians have perhaps exaggerated the supremacy and the unanimity of the Salem Clique, the fact remains that it played a significant role in Oregon's politics and government through the 1850s and beyond. Its influence was felt both locally and nationally. Would Oregon have achieved statehood as early as 1859 without the Clique's efforts? Would Oregon's constitution have taken its shape and won the voters' approval without the Clique's presence in the convention? Indeed, would Oregon have remained committed to the Union had the Clique supported the Confederacy? In many ways, the impact of the Clique is felt even today.

Notes

CHAPTER 1

1. Clark, *Eden Seekers*, 244.
2. Hull, "The Movement in Oregon," 181.
3. Davenport, "The Slavery Question in Oregon," 228.
4. Owens, "Pattern and Structure in Western Territorial Politics," 373ff.
5. Etulain, *Beyond the Missouri*, 122.
6. Ibid.
7. Heider and Dietz, *Legislative Perspectives*, 7; Gibson, *Farming the Frontier*, 127ff; Schoenberg, *A History of the Catholic Church*, 26ff.
8. Unruh, *The Plains Across*, 36.
9. Etulain, *Beyond the Missouri*, 123.
10. Snyder, *Early Portland*, 4ff.
11. Wyeth's Journal, February 3, 1833. Cited by Frederick V. Holman, *Dr. John McLoughlin*, 46. In 1957, the Oregon Legislature honored McLoughlin with legislation declaring him to be the "Father of Oregon." Marschner, *Oregon 1859*, 20.
12. Beneficiaries of McLoughlin's generosity included later Clique member James Nesmith to whom McLoughlin lent cows on the occasion of Nesmith's marriage. Evans, *History of the Pacific Northwest*, 492.
13. Stoel, "Oregon's First Federal Courts," 3ff.
14. Johnson, *Founding the Far West*, 51.
15. November 20, 1842. Cited by Shippee, "The Federal Relations of Oregon—VII," 357.
16. Carey, *General History of Oregon*, 325.
17. Jetté and Zacharias, "The State of Oregon," 1000.
18. Berwanger, *The Frontier Against Slavery*, 83, 13n.
19. Johnson, *Founding the Far West*, 43.
20. Bartlett, *John C. Calhoun*, 331ff.
21. Carey, *General History of Oregon*, 456.
22. Quoted by Turnbull, *History*, 26ff.
23. Turnbull, *History of Oregon*, 41ff.
24. Knuth and Gates, "Oregon Territory in 1849–1850," 7.
25. Bartlett, *John C. Calhoun*, 360.
26. Cited in T. T. Geer, *Fifty Years in Oregon*, 42.
27. Jesse Applegate, Mi 176 Bancroft, Reel 7, p. 3, OHS. The contributions of Senators Linn and Benton were recognized when the first Oregon counties were named.
28. Lee, "Slavery and the Oregon Territorial Issue," 114.
29. *Oregon Spectator*, January 25, 1849. See Knuth and Gates, "Oregon Territory in 1849–1850."
30. Shippee, "The Federal Relations," 352–53. Polk also recorded his own opinion of Taylor: "a well meaning old man" but "uneducated, exceedingly ignorant of public affairs and, I should judge, of very ordinary capacity."
31. Mss 2202, Oregon Historical Society Research Library, hereafter OHS.
32. Johnson, "Politics, Personalities, and Policies," 49.
33. Robertson, "The Genesis of Political Authority in Oregon," 52.
34. James Hendrickson, *Joe Lane of Oregon*, 9.

35 Knuth and Gates, "Oregon Territory in 1849–1850," 7.
36 Lovejoy to Lane, May, 18, 1850. Mss 1146, OHS.
37 Grover, *Public Life*, 96; Bancroft, *Bancroft's Works*, 115.
38 Hazelett, "To the World!!," 196ff.
39 Ibid., 24n.
40 Cited by Bancroft, *Bancroft's Works*, 137, 72n.
41 "Diary of Samuel Royal Thurston," OHQ, XV, September 1914. Samuel Thurston, "Oregon, Its Climate, Soil, Productions, etc." *Stryker's American Register* (July 4, 1850): 222, cited by Johnson, *Founding the Far West*, 47.
42 Holman, *Dr. John McLoughlin*, 132–33.
43 Thurston to several Linn County supporters, July 28, 1850. Mss 581, OHS.
44 "The History of the Origin of the *Oregon Statesman*," 5.
45 Thurston to Bush, August 11, 1850. Mss 581, OHS.
46 Bush to family, December 20, 1850, Bush House Archives. While the salutation of the letter is "Dear Friends," Bush signed it "Your affectionate son and brother." He also instructed: "Tell Ma that I have got on my flannel both *undershirt* and *drawers*."
47 Cited by Carey, *General History of Oregon*, 650.
48 Quoted in William Robbins, "Oregon Donation Land Law," Oregon History Project, Oregon Historical Society.
49 Thurston to Bush, November 10, 1850. Bush House Archives.
50 Thurston to Bush, November 30, 1850. Mss 581, OHS.
51 Thurston to Bush, August 11, 1850. Mss 581, OHS.
52 Bush to Thurston, December 23, 1850. Bush House Archives.
53 Notson, *Making the Day Begin*, 3.

CHAPTER 2

1 Thurston to Bush, August 11, 1850. Mss 581, OHS.
2 Thurston to Bush, September 3, 1850. Bush House Archives.
3 December 20, 1850. Bush House Archives.
4 Nesmith interview, June 13, 1878, Bancroft, OHS.
5 Lafayette Grover's statement to Bancroft, Bancroft Library, July 13, 1878, 84, 85.
6 Williams, "Political History of Oregon," 25.
7 Bush to "Friends," December 20, 1850. Bush House Archives.
8 December 28, 1850. Cited in Sidney Teiser, "Reuben P. Boise, Last Associate Justice of the Oregon Territory Supreme Court," *Oregon Historical Quarterly* 66, no. 1 (Mar. 1965), 7n1.
9 Belknap, "George Law Curry."
10 *Oregonian*, April 30, 1873.
11 Williams, "Political History," 28.
12 *Oregonian*, March 13, 1852.
13 Chadwick to Bush, Mss 581, File 12, April 24, 1852.
14 Deady to Bush, June 16 and July 2, 1851. Bush House Archives.
15 Bush to Deady, July 17 and 18, 1851. Mss 48, OHS.
16 Deady to Nesmith, October 3, 1852. Mss 577, OHS.
17 Boise to Bush, February 13, 1855. Mss 581, OHS.
18 Deady to Bush, June 16, 1851. Bush House Archives.
19 Samuel Bowles, SB 73, p. 90. OHS.
20 Bush to Deady, November 2, 1856. Mss 48, OHS.
21 Deady to Bush, January 19, 1853. Mss 581, OHS.
22 Deady to Nesmith, February 23, 1851. Mss 577, OHS.
23 Bush to Thurston, February 23, 1851. Bush House Archives.
24 Thurston to Bush, January 27 and February 9, 1851. Mss. 581, OHS.
25 *Oregon Statesman*, March 28, 1851

26 Deady to Bush, February 23, 1851. Mss 581, OHS.

27 Bush to Deady, April 8, 1851. Mss 48, OHS.

28 Deady to Bush, May 23, 1851. Bush House Archives.

29 Boise to Bush, March 28, 1851. Bush House Archives.

30 *Oregon Statesman,* April 4, 1851.

31 Boise to Bush, April 11, 1851. Bush House Archives.

32 Lyman, *History of Oregon* IV: 289, quoted in Turnbull, *History of Oregon*, 82.

33 Davenport, "The Slavery Question," 250.

34 Jetté and Zacharias, "The State of Oregon," 1006.

35 Nesmith to Deady, September 17, 1851. Mss 48, OHS; Deady to Nesmith, September 21, 1851. Mss 577, OHS.

36 *Oregon Statesman,* April 4, 1851

37 Applegate to Bush, November 8, 1851. Bush House Archives.

38 Bancroft, *Bancroft's Works*, 135

39 Deady to Nesmith, February 23 and 25, 1851. Mss 577, OHS. *Oregon Statesman,* April 18, 1851.

40 Delazon Smith to Bush, May 23, 1853. Bush House Archives.

41 Lafayette Grover's statement to Bancroft, Bancroft Library, July 13, 1878, 83; Williams, "Political History," 27.

42 Bush to Deady, April 17, 1851. Mss 48, OHS. *Oregonian,* April 26, 1851.

43 Deady to Bush, May 4, 1851. Bush House Archives.

44 Boise to Bush, undated, Bush House Archives. Deady to Bush, May 4, 1851. Mss 581, OHS. Harding to Bush, May 7, 1851. Mss 581, OHS.

45 Harding to Bush, May 7, 1851. Mss 581, OHS. Deady to William M. King, May 5, 1851. Mss 1142, OHS.

46 Hendrickson, *Joe Lane of Oregon,* 29.

47 Deady to Bush, April 17, 1851. Bush House Archives; Deady to William King, May 5, 1851. Mss 1142, OHS.

48 Bush to Deady, May 21, 1851. Mss 48, OHS. Bush to Deady, June, dated only "Sunday morning," 1851. Mss 48, OHS.

49 Jett and Zacharias, "The State of Oregon,"1008.

50 Nicholas Lemann, "Paper Tigers," *The New Yorker,* April 13, 2009, 72. Jeffrey L. Pasley, "*The Tyranny of Printers*," 3.

51 *Oregon Statesman,* March 28, 1851.

52 Bush to Deady, undated. Mss 48, OHS.

53 *Oregon Statesman,* June 13 and 27, 1851.

54 *Oregon Statesman,* April 11, 1851.

55 Woodward, *The Rise and Early History*, 57, 88.

56 Geer, *Fifty Years in Oregon*, 81; Davenport, "The Slavery Question," 244.

57 *Oregon Statesman*, June 27, 1851.

58 *Oregonian,* August 9, 1851; *Oregon Statesman,* August 19, 1851.

59 Johnson, *Founding the Far West,* 56.

60 Boise to Bush, April 9, 1851, Bush House Archives; *Oregon Statesman,* August 5, 1851.

61 Bush to Deady, August 19, 1851, Bush House; Johnson, *Founding the Far West,* 53.

62 Deady to Bush October 20, 1851. Mss 581, OHS. Pratt to Robert Kinney, November 28, 1851. Mss 426, OHS.

63 Deady to Lane, December 4, 1851. Mss 1146, OHS.

64 James McBride to Lane, January 15, 1852. Mss 1146, OHS. Pratt to Lane, February 4, 1852. Mss 1046, OHS. McBride was the father of the earlier-cited John McBride.

65 *Oregonian,* March 13, 1852.

66 Gaines to Lane, January 2, 1852. Mss 1146, OHS. Pratt to Lane, June 4, 1852. Mss 1146, OHS.

67 Sidney Teiser, "Reuben P. Boise," 12, 31n, 17.

68 Harding to Bush, October 23, 1851. Mss 581, OHS. Harding to Deady, October 1, 1852. Mss 48, OHS.

69 Carey, *General History of Oregon,*
    482, 517.

CHAPTER 3

1   Lane to Bush, December 22, 1851.
    Mss 581, OHS. *Oregon Statesman,*
    February, 24, 1852.
2   Nesmith to Deady, February 6, 1852.
    Mss 48, OHS.
3   Johnson, *Founding the Far West,* 56.
4   Davenport, *The Slavery Question,*
    244.
5   Turnbull, *History of Oregon,* 85.
6   *Oregon Statesman,* January 27, 1852.
7   *Oregonian,* January 31, 1852.
8   Cited by George Belknap in the 1968
    publication of "Treason" by the Yale
    University Press, 13.
9   Deady to Nesmith, February 8, 1852.
    Mss 577; Bush to Deady, August 5,
    1852. Mss 48, OHS.
10 Bush to Deady, no date. Mss 48,
    OHS.
11 *Oregonian,* February 6, 1852; *Oregon
    Statesman,* February 10, 1852;
    Oregonian, March 13, 1852.
12 Deady to Bush, August 9, 1852. Mss
    581, OHS.
13 Curry to Lane, March 10, 1852. Mss
    700, OHS.
14 Deady to Boise, May 28, 1852.
    Willamette University Archives.
15 Bush to Deady, April 10 and 15,
    1852. Mss 48, OHS.
16 Wait to Lane, June 22, 1852. Mss
    1146, OHS.
17 George Curry to Lane, June 26, 1852.
    Mss 700, OHS.
18 Chadwick to Bush, April 24, 1852.
    Mss 581, OHS.
19 Lovejoy to Lane, October 30, 1852.
    Mss 1146, OHS.
20 Nesmith to Lane, October 30, 1852.
    Mss 1146, OHS.
21 *Oregonian,* December 25, 1852.
22 Boise to Bush, January, 1853, Bush
    House Archives. The exact date of
    the letter is not indicated.
23 Lane to Bush, September 19, 1851.
    Mss 581, OHS; *Oregon Statesman,*
    December 23, 1851.

24 Lane to Deady, October 20 and
    December 1, 1852. Mss 48, OHS.
25 Lane to Deady, February 19, 1852.
    Mss 48, OHS; Lane to Bush,
    February 19, 1852. Mss 581, OHS;
    Deady to Lane, July 16, 1852. Mss
    1146, OHS.
26 T'Vault to Lane, May 22, 1852. Mss
    1146 OHS; Lane to Nesmith, August
    17, 1852. Mss 577, OHS; Nat Lane to
    Lane, October 1, 1852. Mss 1146,
    OHS.
27 Lane to Bush, October 19, 1852. Mss
    581, OHS; Lane to Deady, October
    20, 1852. Mss 48, OHS.
28 Nesmith to Deady, November 19,
    1852. Mss 48, OHS.
29 Curry to Lane, November 24, 1852.
    Mss 700, OHS. For reasons that are
    not clear, Curry's letters are in his
    file rather than in the file of the
    recipient as is generally the case.
30 Sidney Teiser, "First Associate Justice
    of Oregon Territory: O. C. Pratt,"
    Oregon Historical Quarterly 3, no.
    49 (March 1948): 185.
31 Lane to Deady, December 1, 1852.
    Mss 48, OHS; Lane to Bush,
    December 2, 1852. Mss 581, OHS.
32 Curry to Lane, November 24, 1852.
    Mss 700, OHS; Bush to Lane,
    December 27, 1852. Mss 1146, OHS.
33 Bush to Lane, December 27, 1852.
    Mss 1146. OHS.
34 Bush to Lane, December 29, 1852.
    Deady to Lane, December 28, 1852.
    Mss 1146, OHS.
35 Lane to Nesmith, January 2, 1853.
    Mss 577, OHS; Nesmith to Deady,
    February 25, 1853. Mss 48, OHS.
36 Michael Simmons to Lane, January
    12, 1853. Mss 1149, OHS.
37 Deady to Bush, February 10, 1853.
    Mss 581, OHS; Bush to Deady, April
    4, 1853. Mss 48, OHS.
38 *Oregon Statesman,* February 21,
    1853; Smith to Bush, March 15,
    1853. Mss 581, OHS.
39 Knuth, "Oregon Know Nothing
    Pamphlet," 47.
40 Smith to Bush, May 23, 1853. Mss
    581, OHS.

41 Bush to Deady, May 20, 1853. Mss 48, OHS. Hendrickson, *Joe Lane of Oregon*, 73.

42 Lane to Nesmith, August 1, 1853. Mss 577, OHS.

43 *Oregon Statesman*, July 4, 1853.

44 *Oregon Statesman*, July 26, 1853.

45 Nesmith to Deady, October 21, 1853, Mss 577. Nesmith to Lane, October 21, 1853. Mss 1146, OHS.

46 Harding to Lane, October 25, 1853. Mss 1146. Nesmith to Deady, January 1, 1854. Mss 48, OHS.

47 Waterman to Lane, December 11, 1853. Mss 1169, OHS.

48 Deady to Nesmith, May 10, 1854. Mss 577, OHS.

49 Olney to Lane, n.d. Mss 1146. Davis to Lane, December 6, 1853. Mss 1146, OHS.

50 Deady to Nesmith, December 20, 1853. Mss 577, OHS.

51 Deady to Bush, November 27, 1853. Bush House Archives.

52 Lane to Nesmith, December 13, 1853. Mss 577, OHS.

53 Nesmith to Lane, May 20, 1854. Mss 1146, OHS Deady to Lane, August 18, 1854. Mss 1146, OHS.

54 Hendrickson, *Joe Lane of Oregon*, 90.

55 Lane to Nesmith, January 18, 1854. Mss 577, OHS.

56 Lane to Bush, October 1, 1853. Bush House Archives.

57 Lane to Bush, August 12, 1854. Mss 581, OHS.

CHAPTER 4

1 Waymire to Lane, April 4, 1854. Mss 1146, OHS.

2 Pratt to Lane, February 15 and 16 and March 29, 1854. Mss 1146, OHS.

3 Pratt to Lane, June 15, 1854. Mss 1146, OHS.

4 Waterman to Lane, January 4, 1854. Mss 1146, OHS.

5 Carey, *General History of Oregon*, 25, 40n.

6 *Oregon Statesman*, April 11, 1851.

7 Nesmith to Deady, January 8, 1854. Mss 48, OHS.

8 Governor George L. Curry's Legislative Message, December 10, 1856. Oregon State Archives, Oregon Provisional and Territorial Records, 1856, Calendar No. 8001.

9 Knuth, "Oregon Know Nothing Pamphlet," 41.

10 "Constitution of the Grand Wigwam of the Territory of Oregon," Oregon Historical Society Library. The document indicates that it was printed at the *Spectator* office in 1854. The Know Nothing constitution was later reprinted by the *Oregonian* press.

11 *Oregon Statesman*, August 2, 1851, and March 30, 1852.

12 Woodward, *The Rise and Early History*, 9; Hendricksen, *Joe Lane*, 94; Knuth, "Oregon Know Nothing Pamphlet," 49.

13 Deady to Nesmith, August 21, 1854. Mss 577, OHS.

14 Curry to Deady, August 25, 1854. Mss 700, OHS.

15 Palmer to Lane, March 6, 1854, and August 7, 1854. Mss 1146, OHS.

16 Pratt to Lane, September 6 and 24, 1854. Mss 1146, OHS.

17 Nesmith to Lane, September 24, 1854. Mss 1146, OHS.

18 Nat Lane to Lane, September 28, 1854. Mss 1146, OHS. At the end of his letter, Nat added a bit of family news: "We have a little Boy born I think since my last he is now four months old."

19 Deady to Bush, September 30 and October 23, 1854. Mss 581, OHS.

20 Nesmith to Lane, September 24, 1854. Mss 1146, OHS.

21 *Oregonian*, August 26, 1854. Nat Lane to Lane, September 28, 1854. Mss 1146, OHS.

22 Curry to Lane, September 18, 1854. Mss 700, OHS.

23 Bush to Lane, Salem, October 7, 1854. Mss 1146, OHS. Palmer to Lane, October 18, 1854. Mss 1146, OHS.

24   Nesmith to Lane, October 20, 1854. Mss 1146, OHS. Waymire to Lane, November 4, 1854. Mss 1146, OHS.

25   Deady to Bush, Bush House, October 15, 1854. Palmer to Lane, December 30, 1854. Mss 1146, OHS. Lane to Bush, December 17, 1854. Mss 581, OHS.

26   Pratt to Lane, December 9, 1854. Mss 1146, OHS. Lane to Nesmith, December 26, 1854. Mss 577, OHS

27   *Oregon Statesman*, October 10, November 21 and 28, and December 12, 1854; Woodward, *The Rise and Early History*, 67, 1n.

28   Nesmith to Lane, November 29, 1854. Mss 1146, OHS.

29   Schouler, *Constitutional Studies State and Federal*, 97, 236.

30   Heider and Dietz, *Legislative Perspectives*, 16. *Oregon Statesman*, December 12, 1854. When the state constitution was written in 1857, viva voce was included. Efforts to remove it did not succeed until 1872.

31   *Oregonian*, May 5, 1855.

32   Nesmith to Lane, January 1, 1855. Mss 1146, OHS. Palmer to Lane, January 14, 1855. Mss 1146, OHS. Nesmith to Deady, April 2, 1855. Mss 48, OHS.

33   Bush to Deady, January 21, 1855. Mss 48, OHS.

34   *Oregon Statesman*, January 30, 1855.

35   Bush to Lane, March 3, 1855. Mss 1146, OHS. Smith to Bush, March 18, 1855. Mss 581, OHS.

36   Deady to Bush, March 7, 1855. Mss 581, OHS.

37   Bush to Deady, March 29, 1855. Mss 48, OHS. Smith to Bush, March 1, 1855. Mss 581, OHS. Boise to Bush, February 13, 1855. Bush House.

38   Lane to Nesmith, April 14, 1855. Mss577, OHS.

39   Deady to Bush April 29, 1855. Bush House. Deady to Bush, May 7, 1855. Mss 581, OHS.

40   Deady to Nesmith, April 18, 1855. Mss 577, OHS.

41   Deady to Bush, April 24, 1855. Mss 581, OHS. Deady to Nesmith, April 29, 1855. Mss 577, OHS.

42   Drew to Bush, May 7, 1855. Mss 581, OHS.

43   Deady to Bush, May 7, 1855. Mss 581, OHS. Deady to Nesmith, undated. Mss 577, OHS. The identities of "Joshua broak" and "Single bow" are unclear. Deady wrote Nesmith that he had assured Bush that he had only used the term "scribbling chick" for Bush because he could not think of anything else that would rhyme with "Clique." July 23, 1856. Mss 577, OHS.

44   Williams, "Political History," 9. Deady to Nesmith, July 14, 1855. Mss 577, OHS.

45   Bush to Nesmith, September 9, 1855. Mss 577, OHS. Drew to Bush, September 19, 1855. Mss 581, OHS. Bush to Deady, September 30, 1855. Mss 48, OHS. *Oregon Statesman*, November 3 and December 1, 1855, also in a number of other issues.

46   *Oregon Statesman*, July 14, 1855. .

47   Deady to Bush, October 30, 1855, Bush House. Deady to Bush, January 21, 1856. Mss 581, OHS. Also Delazon Smith to his wife, January 7, 1856. Coll 26, OHS.

48   Terence O'Donnell, *An Arrow in the Earth: General Joel Palmer and the Indians of Oregon* (Portland: Oregon Historical Society Press, 1991), 131.

49   Palmer to Lane, March 30, 1854. Mss 1146, OHS. *Oregon Statesman*, May 28, 1853. O'Donnell, 163ff.

50   Office of Indian Affairs, August 3, 1853.

51   Deady to Bush, October 30, 1855. Mss 581, OHS.

52   *Oregon Statesman*, October 13, 1855; *Oregonian*, October 20, 1855.

53   Legislative Message, 1857. Oregon State Archives, Oregon Provisional and Territorial Records, 1857, Calendar No. 9376.

54   *Oregonian*, June 12, 1858.

55   *Oregon Statesman*, November 23, 1858.

CHAPTER 5

1   Thurston to Bush, September 3, 1850. Mss 581, OHS.
2   *Oregon Statesman,* April 11, 1851.
3   *Oregonian,* July 28, 1851. *Oregon Statesman,* December 9, 1851.
4   Harding to Lane, February 13, 1852. Mss 1146, OHS. Lane to Bush, March 21, 1852. Mss 581, OHS.
5   *Oregon Statesman,* November 8, 1851.
6   *Oregon Statesman,* February 21, 1854. Grover to Deady, March 13, 1854. Mss 48, OHS. Davis to Lane, March 29, 1854. Mss 1146, OHS.
7   Pratt to Lane, June 16, 1854. Mss 1146, OHS.
8   *Oregonian,* August 5, 1854.
9   *Oregon Statesman,* August 15, 1854. Carey, "The Creation of Oregon," 292
10 Carey, "The Creation of Oregon," 295. Turnbull, *History of Oregon,* 97.
11 *Oregon Statesman,* August 11, 1855.
12 *Democratic Standard,* July, 1855. *Oregonian,* July 28, 1855. *Oregon Statesman,* September 8, 1855.
13 *Oregon Statesman,* August 11, 1855.
14 Boise to Bush, August 28, 1855, Bush House.
15 *Oregon Statesman,* March 25, 1856.
16 Jetté and Zacharias, p.1013.
17 Bush to Deady, November 2, 1856. Mss 48, OHS. Deady to Bush, November 17, 1856. Mss 581, OHS.
18 Deady to Bush, December 14, 1856 and April 21, 1857. Mss 581, OHS.
19 Deady to Bush, February 9, 1857. Mss 581, OHS. *Oregon Statesman,* October 20, 1857. The identity of "Intrusts" is not clear.
20 Thurston to Bush, November 30, 1850, Mss 581, OHS.
21 *Oregon Statesman,* January 27, 1852.
22 Elizabeth McLagan, *A Peculiar Paradise: a History of Blacks in Oregon, 1788–1940* (Portland, Ore.: The Georgian Press, 1980), 36. R. Gregory Nokes, *Breaking Chains: Slavery on Trial in the Oregon Territory* (Corvallis: Oregon State

University Press, 2013), 75ff. Berwanger, *The Frontier Against Slavery,* 82.
23 *Oregon Statesman,* June 13 and August 5, 1851, and November 14, 1854.
24 Grover to Rhoades, July17, 1854. Mss 1069, OHS.
25 *Oregon Statesman,* August 22, 1854.
26 Carey, "The Creation of Oregon," 304; Berwanger, *The Frontier Against Slavery,* 85–86.
27 Lane to Bush, May 30, 1856 and July 18, 1856. Mss 581, OHS. Lane to Bush, December 17, 1856, Bush House.
28 James M. McPherson, *Battle Cry of Freedom: The Civil War Era* (New York: Oxford University Press, 1988), 311.
29 *Oregonian,* June 27, 1857.
30 Deady to Bush, February 9, 1857. Mss 581, OHS. Delazon Smith to his wife, January 7, 1856. Coll26, OHS.
31 *Oregonian,* November 1, and 8, 1856. Deady to Bush, December 14, 1856. Mss 581, OHS.
32 Franz M. Schneider, "The Black Laws of Oregon." Thesis, Santa Clara University, 1970, p. 31.
33 *Oregon Statesman,* January 20, 1857.
34 *Oregon Statesman,* January 13, 20, March 31, 1857.
35 *Oregon Statesman,* January 13, 1857.
36 *Oregon Statesman,* March 11, 1857.
37 *Oregonian,* March 7,1857.
38 Williams, "Political History," 13. John C. Fremont was the Republican candidate for President in the fall 1856 election.
39 *Oregon Argus,* February 21, 1857, cited by Berwanger, *The Frontier Against Slavery,* 85. Originally based in Oregon City, the *Oregon Argus* moved to Albany when it became the organ of the Republican Party.
40 *Oregonian,* March 21, 1857.
41 *Oregon Statesman,* January 20, 1857.
42 *Oregon Statesman,* March 31, 1857, January 13, 20, March 31, 1857.
43 *Oregon Statesman,* April 14, 1857.

44 *Oregon Statesman,* April 21, 1857.
45 *Oregon Statesman,* June 9, 1857.
46 *Oregonian,* May 23, 1857.
47 *Oregonian,* May 23 and June 20, 1857.
48 McPherson, *Battle Cry,* 149ff. Hendrickson, *Joe Lane of Oregon,* 131.
49 Lane to Grover, June 18, 1856. Mss 1069, OHS.
50 Deady to Nesmith, May 27, 1856; September 16, 1856. Mss 577, OHS.
51 Deady to Nesmith, April 25, 1856. Mss 577, OHS.
52 Lane to Bush, December 17, 1856; March 4, 1857. Mss 581, OHS.
53 Nesmith to Deady, July 7, 1857. Mss 48, OHS
54 Lane to Bush, March 4, 1857. Mss 581, OHS.
55 Hendrickson, *Joe Lane of Oregon,* 157. *Oregonian,* February 14, March 7, April 4, 1857.
56 *Oregon Statesman,* June 30, 1857.

CHAPTER 6

1 Johnson, *Founding the Far West,* 41; Jetté and Zacharias, "The State of Oregon," 1014.
2 John McBride, Address to the Oregon Historical Society, December 20, 1902. Included in Carey, ed., *The Oregon Constitution and Proceedings,* 491. Hereafter *Proceedings.*
3 Johansen, "A Tentative Appraisal of Territorial Government," 497; Deady to Benjamin Simpson, July 29, 1857. Mss 48, OHS.
4 *Oregonian,* July 4, 18, and 25. Dryer had not abandoned his allegations of a secret alliance between the Democratic Party and the Mormon Church.
5 *Oregon Statesman,* July 28, 1857, reprinted in *Oregon Historical Quarterly* 9, no. 3 (Sep. 1908), 254–73.
6 *Oregon Statesman,* July 28, 1857, reprinted in *Oregon Historical*

Quarterly 9, no. 3 (Sep. 1908), 254–73; James M. Pyle to Deady, August 4, 1857. Mss 48, OHS.
7 Deady to Bush, August 14, 1857. Mss 581, OHS.
8 *Oregonian,* July 25, 1857. Williams, "Political History," 16. McLagan, 45.
9 *Sacramento Daily Union,* August 27, 1857. Cited by Johnson, *Founding the Far West,* 66.
10 *Oregonian,* October 10, 1857.
11 *Oregonian,* July 18, 1857.
12 *Proceedings,* 65ff.
13 *Proceedings,* Oregonian report, 81, 94, 95.
14 *Proceedings,* Oregonian report, 101, 103. As the convention progressed, the Indiana constitution served as a model for the Oregon constitution.
15 *Proceedings,* Oregon Statesman report, 105; Grover, "Notable Things in a Public Life in Oregon," 54. Mss 1069, OHS.
16 *Proceedings,* Oregon Statesman report, 296ff.
17 *Proceedings,* Oregon Statesman report, 296ff.
18 *Proceedings,* 79–85.
19 *Proceedings,* Oregon Statesman report, 88.
20 *Proceedings,* Oregonian report, 361-62. "Kanakas" was the contemporary designation for native Hawaiians.
21 *Proceedings,* Oregonian report, 405.
22 *Proceedings,* Oregonian report, 308ff, 402.
23 *Proceedings,* Oregon Statesman report, 368-9.
24 *Oregon Statesman,* September 29, 1857. Bush later changed his opinion. At an annual school meeting in 1867, he strongly supported public schools and the taxes necessary to fund them. Robert Carlton Clark, *History of the Willamette Valley Oregon.* (Chicago: The S. J. Clarke Publishing Company, 1927), 588.
25 *Proceedings,* Oregonian report, 317ff.

26 *Oregon Statesman,* September 29, 1857.

27 *Proceedings, Oregonian* report, 233, 250.

28 *Proceedings, Oregon Statesman* report, 265, 269; McBride's 1902 speech to the Oregon Historical Society, *Proceedings,* 488.

29 *Proceedings, Oregon Statesman* report, 199.

30 *Proceedings, Oregon Statesman* report, 387–397.

31 *Proceedings, Oregonian* report, 381–384.

32 *Proceedings, Oregonian* report, 381.

33 *Proceedings, Oregonian* report, 398.

34 McBride's speech in *Proceedings,* 486ff.

35 Harrison Rittenhouse Kincaid, *Political and Official History and Register of Oregon,* 1899. Kincaid was Oregon's secretary of state and had been directed by the Legislature to compile a listing of those who held public office through the periods of Oregon's territorial and state governments.

36 *Oregon Statesman,* September 29, 1857.

37 *Oregonian,* October 3, 10, 17, 24, 1857.

38 *Oregon Statesman,* August 25, September 29, October 16, and November 11, 1857.

39 *Oregon Statesman,* October 16, 1857.

40 Nesmith to Deady, October 24, 1857. Mss 48, OHS.

41 Deady to Nesmith, November 14, 1857. Mss 577, OHS.

42 Lane to Bush, January 3, 1858, Bush House. *Oregon Statesman,* February 16, 1858.

CHAPTER 7

1 January 3, 1858, Hendrickson, *Joe Lane of Oregon,* 154ff.

2 Joseph Drew to Deady, January 31, 1858. Mss 48, OHS.

3 Williams, "Political," 19.

4 Lane to Deady, April 17,1858. Mss 48, OHS.

5 Deady to Bush, January 27, 1858. Mss 581, OHS. Bush to Deady, February 12 and 16, 1858. Mss 48, OHS.

6 James M. Pyle to Bush, March 9, 1858. Mss 581, OHS.

7 Drew to Deady, January 31, 1858. Mss 48, OHS.

8 *Oregon Statesman,* March 9, 1858.

9 *Oregon Statesman,* October 27, 1857.

10 Nesmith to Lane, August 6, 1858, Lane papers, cited by Hendrickson, "The Rupture of the Democratic Party in Oregon, 1858," *Pacific Northwest Quarterly* (April 1967), 69. Bush to Lane, April 4, 1858. Lane Papers, cited by Hendrickson, "Rupture," 71. Nat Lane and Lafayette Mosher; Ibid., 70.

11 Lane to Bush, April 2, 1858. Mss 581, OHS.

12 *Oregon Statesman,* April 6, 1858. *Oregonian,* April 10 and 24, 1858.

13 *Oregonian,* October 3, 1857.

14 Carl Abbott, *Portland in Three Centuries: The Place and the People* (Corvallis: Oregon State University Press, 2011), 43.

15 *Oregon Statesman,* January 27, 1852.

16 *Oregonian,* June 19, 1858. *Oregon Statesman,* June 22, 1858. *Oregonian,* June 26, 1858.

17 Deady to Bush, March 7, 1858. Mss 581, OHS. Joseph Drew to Deady, May 11, 1858. Mss 48, OHS. Bush to Deady, May 12 and 18, 1858. Mss 48, OHS.

18 Stephen F. Chadwick to Bush, May 19, 1858. Mss 581, OHS. Delazon Smith to Bush, May 16, 1858. Mss 581, OHS.

19 *Oregon Statesman,* May 25, 1858. Although he was a Democrat at the time, historians have not considered Williams a member of the Clique and he, in his later writings, certainly did not consider himself one.

20 *Oregon Statesman,* June 1, 1858.

21 Lane to Bush, June 2, 1858. Mss 581, OHS.
22 *Oregonian,* June 19, 1858.
23 Deady to Bush, June 11, 1858. Mss 581, OHS.
24 Bush to Deady, July 1, 1858. Mss 48, OHS.
25 Simms, "The Controversy," 358, 361, 362.
26 Jetté and Zacharias, "The State of Oregon," 1019.
27 Lane to Bush, June 18, 1858. Bush House Archives.
28 *Oregonian,* Monday, July 5, 1858. The "crumbling" of the Buchanan administration reflected the rupture that the slavery question created in the Democratic Party.
29 Smith to his wife, September 20, 1858. Coll 26, OHS.
30 *Oregon Statesman,* August 3, 1858; Bush to Lane, August 16, 1858. Lane Papers, Indiana University. Cited by Hendrickson, "Rupture," 72.
31 Smith to Bush, November 30, 1858. Coll 26, OHS; Smith to Bush, February 2, 1859. Mss 581, OHS.
32 Smith to Nesmith, November 30, 1858. Mss 577, OHS; Smith to his wife, December 17, 1858. Coll 26, OHS.
33 Smith to his wife, January 16, 1859. Coll 26, OHS. He concluded with a long passage reminding his wife how well off she was: "How many of your sex *have not* all these blessings! Learn, my good wife, to look upon the *bright side of the picture!*"
34 Grover to Bush, February 17, 1859. Mss 581, OHS.
35 Grover to Bush, January 18, 1859; Williams to Bush, February 5, 1859. Mss 581, OHS.
36 *Oregonian,* December 18, 1858. *Oregon Statesman,* February 2, 1859.
37 Grover to Bush, January 18, 1859. Smith to Bush, February 2, 1858. Mss 581, OHS.
38 Jetté and Zacharias, "The State of Oregon," 1020.
39 *Oregonian,* March 19, 1859.

CHAPTER 8
1 Deady to Nesmith, April 13, 1859. Mss 577, OHS.
2 Bush to Deady, April 2, 1859. Mss 48, OHS.
3 Ibid.
4 Grover to Bush, March 5, 1859. Mss 581, OHS.
5 *Argus,* April 30, 1859, cited by Woodward, "The Rise and Early History," 155.
6 Johannsen, *Frontier Politics,* 80.
7 *Oregon Statesman,* October 11 and 18, 1859.
8 Nesmith to Deady, October 7, 1859. Mss 48, OHS.
9 Farrar to Nesmith, November 18, 1859. Mss 577, OHS.
10 O'Meara to Nesmith, February 13, 1860. Mss 577, OHS.
11 *Oregon Statesman,* July 5, 1859.
12 *Oregon Statesman,* December 20, 1859.
13 Deady to Nesmith, January 4, 1860. Mss 577, OHS.
14 Lane to Deady, May 13, 1860. Mss 48, OHS.
15 Drew to Bush, May 21, 1860. Mss 581, OHS.
16 *Oregon Statesman,* May 29, 1860.
17 Leslie M. Scott, "Oregon's Nomination of Lincoln," *Oregon Historical Quarterly* 17, no. 3. September, 1916.
18 *Oregon Statesman,* June 26, 1860.
19 McPherson, *Battle Cry of Freedom,* 221.
20 *Oregon Statesman,* June 5 and July 24, 1860.
21 Johannsen, "Spectators of Disunion," 134.
22 *Oregon Statesman,* July 31, 1860.
23 Nesmith to Deady, July 15, 1860. Mss 48, OHS. Deady's June 29 letter that provoked Nesmith's response is not in the file at the Oregon Historical Society.
24 Deady to Nesmith, August 4, 1860. Mss 577, OHS.

25 Nesmith to Deady, August 18, 1860. Mss 48, OHS.

26 *Oregon Statesman,* September 11, 1860.

27 Etulain, *Lincoln and Oregon Country Politics,* 76.

28 Charles E. Pickett to Nesmith, August 25, 1860. Mss 577, OHS.

29 Johannsen, "Spectators of Disunion," 122. *Oregon Statesman,* September 9 and 11, 1860.

30 Harding to Bush, November 7, 1860. Mss 581, OHS.

31 Woodward, *The Rise and Early History,* 188. McPherson, *Battle Cry of Freedom,* 232.

32 *Oregon Statesman,* November 12, 1860.

33 Deady to Nesmith, January 20, 1861.

34 *Oregon Statesman,* May 6, 1861; *Oregon Statesman,* March 31, 1862.

35 Joseph W. Drew to Bush, November 20, 1860.

36 *Oregon Statesman,* November 26, 1860.

37 Anderson to Bush, February 10, 1861. Mss 581, OHS.

38 November 9, 1860, cited by Heider and Dietz, *Legislative Perspectives,* 29. Lane to Deady, November 12, 1860. Mss 48, OHS.

39 Lane to Deady, January 27, 1861. Mss 48, OHS; Lane to Lafayette Lane, March 5, 1861, Lane Papers, Indiana University, cited by Hendrickson, *Joe Lane of Oregon,* 248.

40 Ellison, "Designs for a Pacific Republic," 319, 327.

41 Deady to Nesmith, February 28, 1861.

42 *Oregon Statesman,* December 10, 1860.

43 Lane to Deady, January 27, 1861. Mss 48, OHS; Hendrickson, *Joe Lane of Oregon,* 238; *Oregon Statesman,* February 25, 1861.

44 Deady to Nesmith, May 16, 1861. Mss 577, OHS. Nesmith to Deady, June 24, 1861. Mss 48, OHS.

45 Deady to Nesmith, May 16, 1861. Mss 577, OSU.

46 Joseph J. Ellis, *Founding Brothers,* 200.

47 Nesmith to Deady, June 24, 1861.

48 *Oregon Statesman,* July 17, 1861.

CHAPTER 9

1 *Oregon Statesman,* March 28, 1931. Scott's declaration might have been colored by the fact that he was writing for the eightieth anniversary edition of the *Oregon Statesman.*

2 William S. Ladd to Nesmith, February 13, 1862. Mss 577, OHS. Ladd later became Bush's partner in the establishment of Salem's Ladd and Bush bank.

3 O. C. Pratt to Nesmith, December 20, 1861. Mss 577, OHS.

4 Applegate to Deady, October 27, 1861. Mss 48, OHS.

5 Applegate to Edward Bates, December 30, 1861. Mss 233, OHS.

6 Nesmith to Deady, December 30, 1961, and September 20, 1862. Mss 48, OHS.

7 Platt, "Oregon and Its Share," 104, 105.

8 Bensell, *All Quiet on the Yamhill.* His negative impressions did not keep Bensell from settling in Oregon after he was discharged from the army. He involved himself in the state's political life, representing Benton County in the legislature and serving as a justice of the peace and later as mayor of Newport.

9 LaLande, "'Dixie' of the Pacific Northwest."

10 Bush to Nesmith, February 6 and 9, 1862. Mss 577, OHS; Deady to Nesmith, August 19, 1862. Mss 577, OHS.

11 Carey, *General History of Oregon,* 633–34.

12 Bush to Nesmith, March 18, 1862. Mss 577, OHS. Deady to Nesmith, November 16, 1864. Mss 577, OHS.

13 Lucien Heath to Nesmith, December 6, 1861. Mss 577, OHS.

14 Bush to Nesmith, March 7, 1862. Mss 577, OHS.

15 Farrar to Nesmith, January 7, 1862. Mss 577, OHS.

16 William S. Ladd to Nesmith March 6 and May 14, 1862. Mss 577, OHS.

17 Bush to Nesmith, April 29, 1862. Mss 577, OHS.

18 Harding to Nesmith, May 16, 1862. Mss 577, OHS. Deady to Bush, August 7, 1862. Mss 581, OHS.

19 Deady to Nesmith, June 4, 1862. Mss 577, OHS. Quoted by John McBride in his address to the Oregon Historical Society, December 20, 1902. See Carey, *Proceedings,* 483. "Campbellite" refers to members of the Disciples of Christ Church. Deady to Nesmith, November 11, 1865. Mss 577, OHS.

20 Carey, *General History,* 650.

21 Bush to Nesmith, August 13, 1862. Mss 577, OHS.

22 Nesmith to Deady, October 1, 1862. Mss 48, OHS; Deady to Nesmith, November 22 and October 22, 1862. Mss 577, OHS.

23 *Oregon Statesman,* December 12, 1862, March 9, 1863.

24 Nesmith to Deady, October 20, 1862. Mss 48, OHS.

25 Deady to Bush, July 27, 1863. Bush House.

26 Bush to Deady, July 29, 1863. Mss 48, OHS; Nesmith to Deady, November 16, 1863.

27 Deady to Nesmith, December 24, 1865. Mss 577, OHS.

28 Deady to Nesmith, November 30, 1863. Mss 577, OHS; Bush to Deady, December, 1863. Mss 48, OHS.

29 Turnbull, *History of Oregon,* 133.

30 Harding, to Bush, November 1, 1863. Mss 581, OHS.

31 Deady to Nesmith, May 16, 1861. Mss 577, OHS.

32 Deady to Nesmith, August 21 and October 24, 1864. Mss 577, OHS.

33 Deady to Nesmith, January 12, 1862. Also February 1 and September 20, 1865. Mss 577, OHS.

34 Deady to Nesmith, December 30, 1864. Mss 577, OHS.

35 Deady to Nesmith, April 22 and October 28, 1864. Mss 577, OHS.

36 Deady to Nesmith, November 30, 1863, and June 20, 1864. Mss 57, OHS.

37 Deady to Nesmith, August 21, October 24, and December 30, 1864.

38 Deady to Bush, April 21, 1889. Mss 581, OHS.

CHAPTER 10

1 Gaston to Nesmith, October 26, 1865. Mss 577, OHS.

2 Letters of Samuel Asahel Clarke to the *Sacramento Record Union,* November 12, 1878. Samuel Bowles 226B, OHS.

3 Deady to Nesmith, December 24, 1865. Mss 577, OHS.

4 Sidney Teiser, "Boise," 22ff.

5 John Wesley Ladd to Nesmith, January 1, 1866. Mss 577, OHS. Stout to Nesmith, March 4, 1866. Mss 577, OHS.

6 *Oregon Statesman,* November 5, 1866.

7 Deady to Nesmith, October 30, 1866. Mss 577, OHS.

8 Deady to Nesmith, July 18, 1866. Mss 577, OHS.

9 Deady to Nesmith, November 27, 1868. Mss 577, OHS.

10 Deady to Nesmith, February 20, 1874. Mss 577, OHS.

11 Grover to Nesmith, December 3, 1873. Mss 577, OHS.

12 "Biographical Sketch of Honorable J. W. Nesmith," *Constitution and Questions from the Register of the Oregon Pioneer Association,* 35.

13 Mss 1514, Military Collection, Box 3, Folder 3. Oregon Historical Society.

14 Deady to Nesmith August 2, 1877. Mss 577, OHS.

15 Ibid.

16 Grover Inaugural Address, 1871. Oregon State Archives.

17 Geer, *Fifty Years in Oregon,* 91–92.

18 Haight to Grover, November 14, 1870. Mss 1069, OHS.

19 Heider and Dietz, *Legislative Perspectives*, 43.

20 Louis Hough to Grover, December 16, 1876. Mss 1069, OHS.

21 Harold Dippre, "Corruption and the Disputed Election Vote of Oregon in the 1876 Election," *Oregon Historical Quarterly* 67, no. 1 (Mar. 1966).

22 Deady to Nesmith, May 1, 1866.

23 Clark, *Pharisee*, 18ff, 157.

24 Ibid., 260, 447.

25 Ibid., 260, 263.

26 Deady to Lane, December 29, 1879, and January 13, 1880. Mss 1146, OHS.

27 Applegate to Deady, June 7, 1878. Mss 233, OHS. Lane to Deady, March 30, 1881. Mss 48, OHS. Deady to Lane, March 30, 1881. Mss 1146, OHS.

28 Lane to Bush. November 19, 1880.

29 Geer, *Fifty Years*, 82–83.

30 Ibid., 84.

31 Evans, *History of the Pacific Northwest*, 236–37.

32 Davenport, "The Slavery Question," 250.

Bibliography

PRIMARY SOURCES

Mss 48, Matthew Deady Papers, Oregon Historical Society Research Library.

Mss 233, Jesse Applegate Papers, Oregon Historical Society Research Library.

Mss 581, Asahel Bush Papers, Oregon Historical Society Research Library.

Mss 700, George Curry Papers, Oregon Historical Society Research Library.

Mss 1069, Lafayette Grover Papers, Oregon Historical Society Research Library.

Mss 1142, William M. King Papers, Oregon Historical Society Research Library.

Mss 1146, Joseph Lane Papers, Oregon Historical Society Research Library.

Mss 1514 Military Collection, Oregon Historical Society Research Library

Coll 26, Delazon Smith Papers, Oregon Historical Society Research Library.

Reuben Boise Collection, Willamette University Library

Asahel Bush Collection, Bush House Archives.

Ben Maxwell collection, Salem Public Library.

Hugh Morrow collection, Salem Public Library.

George Curry, Governor's Legislative Message, 1857. Oregon State Archives, Oregon Provisional and Territorial Records, 1857, Calendar No. 9376.

NEWSPAPERS

Oregon Statesman
Oregonian
Oregon Spectator

BOOKS

Abbott, Carl. *Portland in Three Centuries,* Corvallis: Oregon State University Press, 2011.

Bancroft, Hubert Howe. *Bancroft's Works,* vol. 30, *Oregon II, 1848–1888.* San Francisco: The History Company, 1888.

Bartlett, Irving H., *John C. Calhoun.* New York: W. W. Norton, 1993.

Bensell, Royal A., *All Quiet on the Yamhill: The Civil War in Oregon.* Edited by Gunter Barth. Eugene: University of Oregon Press, 1959.

Berwanger, Eugene. *The Frontier Against Slavery: Western Anti-Negro Prejudice and the Slavery Extension Controversy.* Urbana: University of Illinois Press, 1967.

Bowles, Samuel. *Across the Continent: A Summer's Journey to the Rocky Mountains, the Mormons, and the Pacific States with Speaker Colfax.* Springfield, MA: Samuel Bowles and Co., 1869.

Carey, Charles. *General History of Oregon.* Portland: Binfords & Mort, 1971.

———, ed. *History of the Oregon Constitution and Proceedings and Debates of the Constitutional Convention of 1857.* Salem, OR: State Printing Department, 1926.

Carey, Robert. *History of Oregon,* vol. 2. Chicago: Pioneer Historical Publishing Company, 1922

Clark, Malcolm, Jr. *Eden Seekers: The Settlement of Oregon, 1818–1862.* Boston: Houghton Mifflin, 1981.

———, ed. *Pharisee Among Philistines: The Diary of Judge Matthew P. Deady, 1871–1892.* Portland: Oregon Historical Society Press, 1975.

Clark, Robert Carlton. *History of the Willamette Valley Oregon.* Chicago: The S. J. Clarke Publishing Company, 1927.

Corning, Howard McKinley. *Willamette Landings.* Portland: Oregon Historical Society, 1973.

Dodds, Gordon B. *Oregon: A Bicentennial History.* New York: Norton, 1977.

———. *The American Northwest.* Arlington Heights, IL: Forum Press, 1986.

Ellis, Joseph J. *Founding Brothers: The Revolutionary Generation.* New York: Alfred A. Knopf, 2001.

Etulain, Richard W. *Lincoln and Oregon Country Politics in the Civil War Era.* Corvallis: Oregon State University Press, 2013.

———. *Beyond the Missouri: The Story of the American West.* Albuquerque: University of New Mexico Press, 2006.

Evans, Elwood. *History of the Pacific Northwest: Washington and Oregon.* Portland: North Pacific History Company, 1889.

Gaston, Joseph. *The Centennial History of Oregon.* Chicago: The S. J. Clarke Company, 1912.

Geer, T. T. *Fifty Years in Oregon.* New York: The Neale Publishing Company, 1912.

Gibson, James R. *Farming the Frontier: The Agricultural Opening of the Oregon Country, 1786–1846.* Seattle: University of Washington Press, 1985.

Heider, Douglas, and David Dietz. *Legislative Perspectives: A 150-Year History of the Oregon Legislatures from 1843 to 1993.* Portland: Oregon Historical Society Press, 1995.

Hendrickson, James E. *Joe Lane of Oregon: Machine Politics and the Sectional Crisis, 1849–1861.* New Haven: Yale University Press, 1967.

Hines, H. K. *An Illustrated History of the State of Oregon.* Chicago: The Lewis Publishing Company, 1893.

History of the Willamette Valley, Chicago: S. J. Clarke Publishing Co., 1927

Holman, Frederick V. *Dr. John McLoughlin: The Father of Oregon.* Cleveland: The Arthur H. Clark Company, 1907.

Hussey, John. *Champoeg: Place of Transition, A Disputed History.* Portland: Oregon Historical Society Press, 1967.

Jetté, Melinda Marie, and Tim Zacharias. "The State of Oregon." In *The United States: The Story of Statehood for the Fifty United States,* vol. 3: Oklahoma to Wyoming. Edited by Benjamin F. Shearer. Westport, CT: Greenwood Press, 2004.

Johannsen, Robert W. *Frontier Politics and the Sectional Conflict: The Pacific Northwest on the Eve of the Civil War.* Seattle: University of Washington Press, 1955.

Johnson, David A. *Founding the Far West: California, Oregon and Nevada, 1840–1890.* Berkeley: University of California Press, 1992.

Kelly, M. Margaret Jean. *The Career of Joseph Lane, Frontier Politician.* Washington: Catholic University of America Press, 1942.

Kincaid, H. R. *Political and Official History and Register of Oregon,* 1899.

Lang, H. O., ed. *History of the Willamette Valley,* Portland: Himes and Lang, 1885.

Lansing, Jewel. *Portland: People, Politics and Power 1851–2001.* Corvallis: Oregon State University Press, 2003.

Lyman, Horace S. *History of Oregon: The Growth of an American State* (New York: The North Pacific Publishing Society, 1903), IV.

MacColl, E. Kimbark, and Harry H. Stein. *Merchants, Money and Power: The Portland Establishment 1843–1913.* Portland: The Georgian Press, 1988.

Marschner, Janice. *Oregon 1859: A Snapshot in Time.* Portland: Timber Press, 2008.

McLagan, Elizabeth. *A Peculiar Paradise: A History of Blacks in Oregon, 1788–1940.*

The Oregon Black History Project. Portland: The Georgian Press, 1980.

McPherson, James M. *Battle Cry of Freedom: The Civil War Era.* New York: Oxford University Press, 1988.

Nokes, R. Gregory. *Breaking Chains: Slavery on Trial in the Oregon Territory.* Corvallis: Oregon State University Press, 2013.

Notson, Robert. *Making the Day Begin: The Story of the* Oregonian. Portland: Oregon Publishing Company, 1976.

O'Donnell, Terence. *An Arrow in the Earth: General Joel Palmer and the Indians of Oregon.* Portland: Oregon Historical Society Press, 1991

Pasley, Jeffrey L. *The Tyranny of Printers: Newspaper Politics in the Early American Republic.* Richmond: University Press of Virginia, 2001.

Peterson del Mar, David. *Oregon's Promise: An Interpretative History.* Corvallis: Oregon State University Press, 2003.

Portrait and Biographical Record of the Willamette Valley Oregon. Chicago: Chapman Publishing Co., 1903.

Robbins, William. *Landscapes of Conflict.* Seattle: University of Washington Press, 2004.

Schneider, Franz M., "The Black Laws of Oregon." Thesis, Santa Clara University, 1970.

Schoenberg, Wilfred P. *A History of the Catholic Church in the Pacific Northwest; 1743–1983.* Washington, DC: The Pastoral Press, 1987.

Schouler, James. *Constitutional Studies: State and Federal.* New York: Dodd, Mead, 1897.

Snyder, Eugene E. *Early Portland: Stump-Town Triumphant.* Portland: Binfords & Mort., 1970.

Stoel, Caroline. "Oregon's First Federal Courts." In *The First Duty: A History of the U.S. District Court for Oregon,* ed. Carolyn Buan. Portland: Oregon Historical Society, 1993.

Turnbull, George. *History of Oregon Newspapers,* Portland: Binfords & Mort, 1939.

——. *Governors of Oregon.* Portland: Binfords & Mort, 1959.

Unruh, John D. *The Plains Across: The Overland Emigrants and the Trans-Mississippi West.* Urbana: University of Illinois Press, 1979.

Walls, Florence. "The Letters of Asahel Bush to Matthew P. Deady 1851–1863." BA thesis, Reed College, 1941 (OHS Library).

Woodward, Walter Carleton. *The Rise and Early History of Political Parties in Oregon, 1843–1868*. Portland: J. K. Gill, 1913.

JOURNALS

Belknap, "George Law Curry, Public Printer," *Pacific Northwest Quarterly* 47, no. 3. July 1956.

Bergquist, James M. "The Oregon Donation Act and the National Land Policy," *Oregon Historical Quarterly* 58, no. 1 (Mar. 1957).

Burton, Claudia. "The Oregon Constitution's Legislative History," *Willamette Law Review* 37, no. 2 (2001).

Carey, Charles. "The Creation of Oregon as a State," *Oregon Historical Quarterly* 26, no. 4 (Dec. 1925); 27, no. 2. (Mar. 1926).

Clark, Malcolm, Jr. "The Bigot Disclosed: 90 Years of Nativism," *Oregon Historical Quarterly* 75, no. 2 (June 1974).

Davenport, T. W. "The Slavery Question in Oregon," *Oregon Historical Quarterly* 9, no. 3, and 9, no. 4 (Sep. and Dec. 1908).

Dippre, Harold. "Corruption and the Disputed Election Vote of Oregon in the 1876 Election," *Oregon Historical Quarterly* 67, no. 3 (Sep. 1966).

Edwards, Thomas. "Six Oregon Leaders and the Far-Reaching Impact of America's Civil War," *Oregon Historical Quarterly* 100, no. 2 (spring 1999).

Ellison, Joseph. "Designs for a Pacific Republic, 1843–62." *Oregon Historical Quarterly* 31, no. 4 (Dec. 1930).

Fenton, William D., "Political History of Oregon from 1865–1876," *Oregon Historical Quarterly* 2, no. 2 (spring 1901).

Hazelett, Stafford. "To the World!! The Story Behind the Vitriol," *Oregon Historical Quarterly* 116, no. 2 (summer 2015): 196ff.

Hendrickson, James E. "The Rupture of the Democratic Party in Oregon, 1858." *Pacific Northwest Quarterly* 58 no. 2 (Apr. 1967).

Himes, George H., "History of the Press in Oregon," *Oregon Historical Quarterly* 3, no. 3 (Sep. 1902).

"The History of the Origin of the *Oregon Statesman*," *The Ladd & Bush Quarterly* 3, no. 1 (Jan. 1915).

Hull, Dorothy. "The Movement in Oregon for the Establishment of a Pacific Coast Republic," *Oregon Historical Quarterly* 17, no. 3 (Sep. 1916).

Johannsen, Robert. "The Kansas-Nebraska Act and the Pacific Northwest Frontier," *Pacific Historical Review,* May, 1953.

———. "Spectators of Disunion: The Pacific Northwest and the Civil War," *Pacific Northwest Quarterly* 44, no. 2 (July 1953).

Johansen, Dorothy. "Oregon's Role in American History: An Old Theme Recast." *Pacific Northwest Quarterly* 40, no. 2 (Apr. 1949).

———. "A Tentative Appraisal of Territorial Government in Oregon." *Pacific Historical Review* (Nov. 1949), 497.

Johnson, Donald A. "Politics, Personalities, and Policies of the Oregon Territorial Supreme Court 1849–1859," *Environmental Law* 4 (fall 1973).

Jones, Alfred C. "Salem editor, banker Bush did his best, left his legacy." *Salem Statesman Journal,* Apr. 1, 1991.

Judson, Lewis H. "Civil War Days in Salem." *Marion County History* 9, 1965–1966.

Knuth, Priscilla, "Oregon Know Nothing Pamphlet Illustrates Early Politics" *Oregon Historical Quarterly* 54, no. 2 (Mar. 1953)

Knuth, Priscilla, and Charles M. Gates, eds. "Oregon Territory in 1849–1850," *Pacific Northwest Quarterly* 40, no. 1 (Jan. 1949).

LaLande, Jeff. "'Dixie' of the Pacific Northwest: Southern Oregon's Civil War." *Oregon Historical Quarterly* 100, no. 1 (spring 1999).

Lee, Alton. "Slavery and the Oregon Territorial Issue," *Pacific Northwest Quarterly* 64, no. 3 (July 1973).

Lockley, Fred. "Some Documentary Records of Slavery in Oregon," *Oregon Historical Quarterly* 2, no. 2 (Mar. 1901).

Ludington, Flora Belle. "The Newspapers of Oregon," *Oregon Historical Quarterly,* 26, 3 (Sep. 1925).

Mahoney, Barbara. "Oregon Democracy: Asahel Bush, Slavery and the Statehood Debate." *Oregon Historical Quarterly* 110, no. 2 (summer 2009).

Maxwell, Ben. "Salem in 1859," *Marion County History* 5 (June 1959).

McBride, John. "The Oregon Constitutional Convention, 1857." In *Proceedings of the Oregon Historical Society,* Fourth Annual Meeting, December 20, 1902.

McLoughlin, John, "Letter of Dr. John McLoughlin to the *Oregon Statesman,*" June 8, 1852; *Oregon Historical Quarterly* 8, no. 2 (June, 1907).

"Mr. Asahel Bush," *Ladd & Bush Quarterly* 2, no. 2 (Apr. 1914).

Moore, Saundra. "Oregon's First Capitals," *Marion County History* 5 (June 1959).

Nash, Lee M. "Scott of the *Oregonian*: The Editor as Historian," *Oregon Historical Quarterly* 70, no. 3 (Sep. 1969).

Oliver, Egbert S., "Obed Dickinson and the 'Negro Question' in Salem," *Oregon Historical Quarterly* 92, no. 2 (spring 1991).

Owens, Kenneth N., "Pattern and Structure in Western Territorial Politics," *Western Historical Quarterly* 1, no. 4. (Oct. 1970).

Platt, Robert Treat. "Oregon and Its Share in the Civil War." *Oregon Historical Quarterly* 4, no. 2 (June 1903).

Prosch, Thomas. "Notes from a Government Document on Oregon Conditions in the Fifties." *Oregon Historical Quarterly* 8, no. 2. June, 1907.

———. "Oregon in 1863," *Oregon Historical Quarterly* 16, no. 1 (Mar. 1915).

Richard, K. Keith, "Unwelcome Settlers: Black and Mulatto Oregon Pioneers," *Oregon Historical Quarterly* 84, nos. 1 and 2 (Mar. and June 1983).

Robertson, J. R. "The Genesis of Political Authority in Oregon," *Oregon Historical Quarterly* 1, vo1. (Mar. 1900).

Scott, Leslie M. "The *Oregonian* in Oregon History." *Oregon Historical Quarterly* 29, no. 3 (Sep. 1928).

———. "Oregon's Nomination of Lincoln," *Oregon Historical Quarterly* 17, no. 3 (Sep. 1916).

Shippee, Lester Burrell. "The Federal Relations of Oregon—VII." *Oregon Historical Quarterly* 19, no. 2 (June 1918); 19, no. 3 (Sep. 1918); 19, no. 4 (Dec. 1918); 20, no. 1 (Mar. 1919); 20, no. 2 (June 1919); 20, no. 3 (Sep., 1919); 20, no. 4 (Dec. 1919).

Simms, Henry. "The Controversy over the Admission of the State of Oregon." *Mississippi Valley Historical Review,* 32, no. 3 (Dec. 1945).

Teiser, Sidney. "A Pioneer Judge in Oregon." *Oregon Historical Quarterly* 46, no. 2. (March 1945).

———. "First Associate Justice of Oregon Territory: O.C. Pratt." *Oregon Historical Quarterly,* 66, no. 1 (Mar. 1965).

———. "Reuben P. Boise, Last Associate Justice of the Oregon Territory Supreme Court." *Oregon Historical Quarterly* 67, no. 1 (Mar. 1965).

Thurston, Samuel R. "Diary of Samuel Royal Thurston." *Oregon Historical Quarterly* 15, no. 3 (Sep. 1914).

Williams, George W. "Political History of Oregon from 1853–1865." *Oregon Historical Quarterly* 2, no. 1 (Mar. 1901).

———. "Slavery in Oregon." *Oregon Historical Quarterly* 9, no. 3 (Sep. 1908).

Index

Note: Photographs, illustrations, and lithographs are indicated with an italic page number. Information from the Notes is indicated by an italic "n" and note number.